PRAISE FOR *UNFINISHED*

"I bought ten thousand copies of Rich Stearns's first book, *The Hole in Our Gospel*, because I wanted everyone in my church to read it. Rich's new book, *Unfinished*, just might challenge everything you thought you understood about your Christian faith. *Unfinished* is a call to finish the job Christ gave his church to do. If every Christian read this book and took it seriously, the world would never be the same again."

— Bill Hybels
Senior pastor, Willow Creek
Community Church; and chairman,
Willow Creek Association

"Just when I've gotten comfortable with my faith, here comes Rich Stearns, reminding me what matters and who God loves and why. Just when my world is the way I want it, Rich reminds me the world is not the way God wants it. Hungry families. Malnourished kids. Just when I dare think my work is done, Rich reminds me that we are just getting started. First in *The Hole in Our Gospel*, now in *Unfinished*, Rich gives me a kind, gracious kick. Thanks, Rich. (I think.)"

— Max Lucado
Pastor and best-selling author

"Okay, admit it: sometimes you wonder . . . don't you? Is this it? The life you're living. Is there more? From his journey in corporate and nonprofit leadership—in very good causes—Rich Stearns concludes there is, indeed, more. More purpose. More meaning. More life. In *Unfinished* you will discover how your life can be about more."

— Elisa Morgan
Author; speaker; publisher, FullFill;
and president emerita, MOPS
International

"Rich Stearns has done it again! In this winsome, engaging, and challenging book, he calls us back to some of the key issues of what it means to be followers of Christ in a world full of distractions and false gods. This is a book for everyone, about finding the place of our calling in God's global mission. It is a book about fulfillment, adventure, and a lifetime of transformation. It made me hungry for more of the life God has in store for us."

— Dr. Stephen Hayner
President, Columbia Theological
Seminary

"Your story can be a part of the Great Story. Rich Stearns knows the story and lives the story. *Unfinished* may call you to the greatest chapter of your life."

— John Ortberg
Senior pastor, Menlo Park Presbyterian
Church; and author, *Who Is This Man?*

"Insightful and inspirational work from one of the most important evangelical voices of our time. Rich Stearns reminds us about God's initiative in the world and [shows] that we are privileged to participate in God's unfolding story in the world. With powerful stories and practical solutions, *Unfinished* directs us out of our passivity toward an active and authentic faith."

— Soong-Chan Rah
Author, *The Next Evangelicalism*;
and Milton B. Engebretson Associate
Professor of Church Growth and
Evangelism, North Park Theological
Seminary

"*Unfinished* is the book I wish I had written after *Halftime*. Let me say why. Rich Stearns has lived out this dream like no one else I know, turning his faith into action—transforming his first-half life of corporate success to following a life aligned with God's purposes on behalf of the world's poorest people. If you are a faithful Christian who feels something is still missing in life, this is the book for you."

— Bob Buford
Founder, Leadership Network; and
author, *Halftime* and *Finishing Well*

"The kingdom is both already and not yet, the work of Christ both finished and to be completed. Stearns reminds readers of every Christian's responsibility to live on mission, in light of Jesus' example and call. Richard shows us by his life, the ministry he leads, and the passion of this book that there is much to be done and we are to be a part of God's grand plan."

— Ed Stetzer
President, LifeWay Research; and
author, *Subversive Kingdom*

"Rich has written another beautiful book. It's an invitation from a good friend to sit together by the fire and have an honest talk about life, passion, purpose, and Jesus. You can't read this book and not have the coals in your faith stirred as you consider once again just how purpose-filled a life following Jesus can be."

— Bob Goff
New York Times best-selling author,
Love Does; and founder, Restore
International

"*Unfinished* is a book that challenges Christians to more fully join Jesus in building a new world that he called the kingdom of God. Each one of us has an important role in this mission, as we find our purpose in God's purpose. I commend it to all who seek a deeper, world-changing discipleship."

— Jim Wallis
President and CEO, Sojourners

"The Christian life is an outliving of the in-living Christ, and when we are obedient to this, he gives us purpose, meaning, and significance. *Unfinished* is a book for the church now, a road map to return to the Truth."

— John Perkins
Cofounder, John & Vera Mae Perkins
Foundation and Christian Community
Development Association

"The greatest privilege for the follower of Jesus is to be summoned into the gospel work God is accomplishing in the world today. What *Unfinished* will do is summon you into this very kingdom work to join the many, many whose stories Rich has told so well. We are not called to heroics but simply to respond in ordinary ways to ordinary, needy people around us with the love God gives us for the ordinary. Suddenly, in doing the ordinary kingdom work, we discover we are part of a flash mob of other kingdom workers."

— Scot McKnight
Professor of New Testament, Northern
Seminary

"In *Unfinished* Rich Stearns reminds us eloquently that when Jesus preached his gospel—the gospel of the kingdom of God—he was giving us a call to action. It's not an easy call, for it requires that we enter into the heartache and suffering of the world. But Rich clearly illustrates through Scripture, as well as through his own experiences, that when we enter into that suffering, we find ourselves in the center of Jesus' mission and in the center of our own purpose for living. Every disciple of Jesus should read this book."

— Lynne Hybels
Willow Creek Community Church

"Every generation of Christians needs a wake-up call to remind us of how serious and strenuous are the demands of discipleship. May Rich Stearns's *Unfinished* be that alarm for our time."

— David Neff
Editorial vice president, *Christianity Today*

"Practicing what he preaches, Rich Stearns challenges us to cast aside our apathy, fears, wrong priorities, or other hindrances and pursue our individual Kingdom assignments with passion and purpose. You cannot read this book and return to life as usual."

— Deborah Smith Pegues
International speaker; and best-selling
author, *30 Days to Taming Your Tongue*

"*Unfinished* is a book that you will want to finish! And to live! It is more than one man's moving story and life view—compelling as these are, and it's more than the needs of the world—as urgent as they are. It is a call to each of us to find our true purpose in aligning our lives with God's great purpose. I believe—as has been true with Rich's first book—many will find themselves challenged, changed, and called in a way that will make their lives count for time and eternity."

— Leighton Ford
President, Leighton Ford Ministries,
Charlotte, North Carolina

"Do you ever battle with a deep sense of dissatisfaction in your life, a knowing that you were made for more? In a world that still peddles the lie that more *stuff* will fulfill us, Rich points us to the truth that in losing ourselves for the sake of the kingdom of God, we will find ourselves. Believing in Christ is just the starting line; running the race is what we were made for."

— Sheila Walsh
Author, *God Loves Broken People*

"*Warning: This Book Has Real-Life Consequences!* Once again Stearns has given us a broad and compelling work, a blend of relevant information, solid theology, and compelling stories. *Unfinished* is a clarion call to become true disciples of the Jesus who healed the sick, welcomed the outcast, and upended the paradigms of his day with the good news of God's coming kingdom. It is an invitation to become ambassadors and agents of this new kingdom—men and women who both proclaim and enact the love of God that is making all things new."

— Mike Yankoski
Refugee in the kingdom of God; itinerant speaker; and author, *Under the Overpass*

UNFINISHED

FILLING THE **HOLE IN OUR GOSPEL**

RICHARD STEARNS

W Publishing Group

An Imprint of Thomas Nelson

Published in Nashville, Tennessee, by W Publishing, an imprint of Thomas Nelson.

Author is represented by the literary agency of Alive Communications, Inc., 7680 Goddard Street, Suite 200, Colorado Springs, CO 80920. www.alivecommunications.com.

Thomas Nelson titles may be purchased in bulk for educational, business, fund-raising, or sales promotional use. For information, please e-mail SpecialMarkets@ThomasNelson.com.

Unless otherwise noted, all Scripture references are taken from the Holy Bible, New International Version®, NIV® © 1973, 1978, 1984, 2011 by Biblica, Inc.™ Used by permission. All rights reserved worldwide.

Scripture references marked CEV are from the Contemporary English Version. © 1991 by the American Bible Society. Used by permission.

Scripture references marked ESV are from the English Standard Version. © 2001 by Crossway Bibles, a division of Good News Publishers.

Scripture references marked MSG are from *The Message* by Eugene H. Peterson. © 1993, 1994, 1995, 1996, 2000. Used by permission of NavPress Publishing Group. All rights reserved.

Scripture references marked NASB are from the New American Standard Bible®. © The Lockman Foundation 1960, 1962, 1963, 1968, 1971, 1972, 1973, 1975, 1977, 1995. Used by permission.

Scripture references marked NKJV are from the New King James Version®. © 1982 by Thomas Nelson, Inc. Used by permission. All rights reserved.

Scripture references marked NLT are from the Holy Bible, New Living Translation. © 1996, 2004, 2007. Used by permission of Tyndale House Publishers, Inc., Wheaton, Illinois 60189. All rights reserved.

Scripture references marked KJV are from the King James Version.

AT THE AUTHOR'S REQUEST, ALL ROYALTIES DUE TO THE AUTHOR WILL BENEFIT WORLD VISION'S WORK WITH CHILDREN IN NEED.

ISBN 978-0-5291-0114-3 (trade paper)

ISBN 978-0-7852-3838-6 (IE)

Library of Congress Cataloging-in-Publication Data

Stearns, Richard E.
  Unfinished : believing is only the beginning / Richard E. Stearns.
    p. cm.
  Includes bibliographical references and index.
  ISBN 978-0-8499-4851-0
  1. Self-actualization (Psychology)—Religious aspects—Christianity. 2. Conduct of life. I. Title.
  BJ1581.2.S7325 2013
  248.4—dc23   2012040816

Printed in the United States of America

13 14 15 16 17 RRD 5 4 3 2 1

To the *FINISHERS*—
my thousands of World Vision colleagues
who labor so faithfully every day:

- that the love of Christ may be seen and felt by those with eyes to see, and
- that the truth of the gospel may be heard by all with ears to hear.

And to all those who have given sacrificially, loved unconditionally, and served Christ with humility . . . Those who have "left houses or brothers or sisters or father or mother or wife or children or fields" for Jesus' sake . . . Those who have gone to the broken places and the ragged edges of our world to seek the lost and to serve "the least of these" . . . Those who long for a day when they will hear the promised words:

"Come, you who are blessed by my Father; take your inheritance, the kingdom prepared for you since the creation of the world. For I was hungry and you gave me something to eat, I was thirsty and you gave me something to drink, I was a stranger and you invited me in, I needed clothes and you clothed me, I was sick and you looked after me, I was in prison and you came to visit me." (Matt. 25: 34–36)

They,

- who have laid down their lives,
  - who have loved what Jesus loves,
    - who have treasured what Jesus treasures, and
      - who have obeyed what Jesus taught.

They are the *Finishers*.

And this gospel of the kingdom will be
preached in the whole world as a testimony to
all nations, and then the end will come.

—MATTHEW 24:14

Jesus went through all the towns and villages, teaching in their synagogues, proclaiming the good news of the kingdom and healing every disease and sickness. When he saw the crowds, he had compassion on them, because they were harassed and helpless, like sheep without a shepherd. Then he said to his disciples, "The harvest is plentiful but the workers are few."

—MATTHEW 9:35–37

How, then, can they call on the one they have not believed in? And how can they believe in the one of whom they have not heard? And how can they hear without someone preaching to them? And how can they preach unless they are sent? As it is written: "How beautiful are the feet of those who bring good news!"

—ROMANS 10:14–15

As the Father has sent me, I am sending you.

—JOHN 20:21

CONTENTS

ACKNOWLEDGMENTS

I feel a need to begin by offering an honest disclaimer. I am no theologian. Though I have been a follower of Jesus Christ for more than thirty-five years, I have no formal theological education. So I suppose I am saying, "Read this book at your own risk." I am indebted to a long list of pastors and theologians who have inspired me through their books and sermons. Many of them surely swim in the deeper parts of God's ocean while I paddle much closer to shore. Yet I take encouragement from the fact that God's truth is simple enough to be grasped by a child but also deep enough to challenge the most brilliant minds.

Every book is truly the work of a great symphony of performers rather than just that of the conductor who brings them all together within the pages. I want to acknowledge first those whose stories appear on these pages, for inspiring me with their lives and examples. There are many more whose lives and examples are reflected here only indirectly. They include my World Vision colleagues in the United States and around the globe, pastors and authors who have shaped my thinking, and friends who have shared the journey. They have all served as sounding boards for many of the ideas found within these pages.

I want to thank my wife, Reneé, who, more than anyone in my life, has served as my spiritual anchor and whose deep faith, integrity, and commitment to Christ not only led me to faith as a young man but also have helped sustain me in my faith ever since. Her spiritual insights are found on every page. I am grateful also to our five children, Sarah, Andy, Hannah, Pete, and Grace, some of whom appear in this book in one way or another. Seeing each of them grow out of their childhood faith and into mature followers of Christ has given me great encouragement. After years of teaching them the things of faith, I now find myself more often being taught by them.

I am especially grateful to the thousands of people who read my first book, *The Hole in Our Gospel*, and have encouraged me by sharing how God used the book to catalyze some important decisions in their own lives. Their testimonies have shown me what is possible when God's people commit themselves to God's kingdom. Without their encouragement there likely would have been no sequel.

I must recognize, too, the many helpers and encouragers at World Vision who have supported me in my writing: Rob Moll, who offered valuable insights; Brian Sytsma, my indispensable right-hand man and chief encourager; Milana McLead, who walked with me from inception to completion; and Shelley Liester and Cheryl Plantenberg, who supported me and protected my calendar so I could focus on the writing. Others at World Vision who helped in one way or another include Kari Costanza, Jon Warren, Jane Sutton-Redner, Phil Manzano, Tom Costanza, Heidi Isaza, Laura Reinhardt, Nathalie Moberg, Elizabeth Hendley, Beth Dotson Brown, David Shaw, Andrea Peer, Abby Stalsbroten, and Keelyn Roman. I also want to thank my gracious board of directors, who granted me another sabbatical because they believed in the importance of this message, and my senior leadership team, who led the organization with great competence during my absence.

My friends Leighton Ford and Dr. Steve Hayner were generous enough to offer their time to read the manuscript for theological soundness and provided solid suggestions that greatly improved my work. I take full credit for any remaining gaffes in this book.

My agent, Lee Hough, also provided valuable insights, as did Matt Baugher, my publisher at Thomas Nelson. Thanks to the entire Thomas Nelson team: Julie Allen; Paula Major; and Kate Etue, my diligent copy editor.

Finally, I give thanks to God, who still uses "the foolish things of this world" to accomplish his mighty purposes. Mother Teresa's profound words are surely true of me and true of you: "I am a little pencil in the hand of a writing God, who is sending a love letter to the world." My prayer is that he will use you to write his next love letter.

INTRODUCTION

Over the past few years I have had the opportunity to meet and speak personally to thousands of people as I have traveled around the globe on behalf of the world's poorest people. Many of them have come up to me to tell me a bit about their own lives and how they have sought to put their faith into action. There is a powerful common thread of longing that I hear from them—a yearning for a deeper sense of purpose and significance in their walks with the Lord. They want to discover that *one thing* that God is calling them to do. They long to feel that they are doing something important for God and that their lives really count for something. Many of them tell me they feel incomplete, as if something about their lives is unfinished. They are young and old, male and female, wealthy and not so wealthy. They are lawyers and real estate agents, homemakers and students, accountants and engineers, receptionists and CEOs. All of them want to experience the satisfaction of really knowing that their lives matter and that they are living in "the zone" of God's calling and purpose for their lives. They want to feel complete and whole, living lives in which their faith is integral and not just something they do on Sundays.

But if I have learned anything about the purpose, meaning, and significance of life over the years, I have learned, for a Christian, it is not found in any job, even a job like mine. It is not found in any human relationship, no matter how important. Nor is it found in any accomplishment, no matter how significant. Meaning, purpose, and significance are found only by aligning our lives with God's purposes, in lives committed to following Jesus Christ. That bears repeating: *The meaning, purpose, and significance of our lives are found only by aligning our lives with God's purposes, in lives committed to following Jesus Christ.*

In other words, it is not our work that brings purpose to our lives, nor is it our spouses, families, educations, abilities, money, or accomplishments. Rather, it is the *purpose* of our lives that brings meaning to everything else. And we find that purpose only in Christ. Jesus said, "I have come that they may have life, and have it to the full" (John 10:10). So why is it that so many Christians seem to lack that sense of fullness of life? They go to church, read their Bibles, and say their prayers but still feel something is missing.

SO WHY IS IT THAT SO MANY CHRISTIANS SEEM TO LACK THAT SENSE OF FULLNESS OF LIFE? THEY GO TO CHURCH, READ THEIR BIBLES, AND SAY THEIR PRAYERS BUT STILL FEEL SOMETHING IS MISSING.

We all know the familiar expression "He can't see the forest for the trees." It is used to describe a person who is so absorbed in the things right in front of him that he has lost a sense of the bigger picture. I believe this is exactly what has happened to many Christians in the twenty-first century—we have become so absorbed by the "trees" of our everyday lives that we have lost a sense of the bigger story within which our lives take place. We grow up, go to school, begin careers, get married, have kids, and struggle daily with life's challenges. These are the trees of our lives that occupy most of our waking hours.

Our church lives are not all that different. We go to church each week, sing some songs, and listen to a sermon. Maybe we even pray before meals, read our Bibles daily, and participate in small-group Bible studies. But they can become just more trees in a life already cluttered with trees. What happened to the forest; what happened to the bigger story? Who are we? Why are we here, and where are we headed? How do we fit into God's big story? A hiker who no longer has a sense of the bigger landscape around him becomes lost and confused, often wandering in circles because he is disoriented and no longer knows where he has come from or where he is headed. If we are ever truly going to find purpose and meaning in our lives, we first have to rise above the trees to rediscover the forest—we have to understand what God is doing in the world and how we fit in.

Fortunately, as Christians we have a way out of this dilemma. If God is the Author of the bigger story within which our own stories take place, if he is the Creator of the forest in which we all walk, then we can find the deepest meaning and purpose of our lives only when we discover the role he uniquely created for us to play in his bigger purpose. Doesn't it make sense that the Author of the bigger story, the Author who created each of the characters in the story, would have a specific role for each of those characters to play?

> GOD CREATED YOU INTENTIONALLY TO PLAY A VERY SPECIFIC ROLE IN HIS UNFOLDING STORY.

The implication of this is profound. God created you intentionally to play a very specific role in his unfolding story. God didn't create any extras meant to just stand on the sidelines and watch the story unfold; he created players meant to be on center stage. And you will feel fully complete only when you discover the role you were born to play.

So just what is that unfolding story in which we are to play our parts? How do we discover it? Mary and Joseph played their parts. So did Peter, Paul, Luke, and John. But now, two thousand years after the resurrection, we seem to have lost the plot. Where are we now in the bigger narrative, and what is it that we are supposed to be doing?

As the title of this book suggests, there is some unfinished business for followers of Christ in our world:

> "And this gospel of the kingdom will be preached in the whole world as a testimony to all nations, and then the end will come." (Matt. 24:14)

This plain statement by Jesus in Matthew 24 lays out a simple premise: once the "gospel of the kingdom" has been satisfactorily taken throughout the world, the end will come. Jesus' promise that the end would come was not a bad thing. He was dangling a very large carrot in front of his church. He was referring to his grand promise to reconcile all things, to right every wrong, to wipe away every tear, to raise the dead to eternal life, to judge the wicked, to restore his creation, and to establish his wonderful kingdom forever and ever. He was promising to tie up all the loose ends of the big story and bring it to its amazing conclusion. But before all of this happens, Jesus called his followers to complete a crucial assignment he gave to them just before he left.

This assignment Jesus gave to the disciples just before his ascension appears in several key New Testament passages and is generally referred to as the Great Commission. It was revolutionary in its vision. It involved going into all the world to establish and build a different kind of world order—one that Jesus often called the kingdom of God. It was a clarion call to follow him by joining him in his mission to reconcile humankind to God's purposes. At its essence it was not a call to simply believe the right things; instead, it was a call to action to join God in his intent to form a new kind of kingdom that would become a blessing to all nations—one based not on land, politics, power, and dominion but on God's truth, love, forgiveness, and compassion—a kingdom within kingdoms. It was not a call to give up on the world, now holding our "tickets to heaven" firmly in our hands and retreating into our churches. It was a call to go into the world to reclaim, reform, and restore it for Christ. It was a call to launch a revolution that involved nothing short of the overthrow of the prevailing world system. And before Jesus left, he commissioned his church to lead this revolution, promising that the very gates of hell would not prevail against it.

It is not an overstatement to say that the sole reason the church exists at all is to carry out this assignment; for once it is completed, the church will be dissolved into God's eternal kingdom. Once the revolution is won, the revolutionaries are no longer needed. These were the marching orders that Jesus gave to his disciples. It was the single goal he gave them to accomplish. He told them he would return when the job was finished; and then Jesus left.

Those first disciples were on fire. Nothing could stop them. The gospel had implications they understood. Within three hundred years, the gospel revolution had conquered the Roman Empire and changed the known world. Their radical lifestyles were characterized by a sense of urgency and divine purpose. Nothing was more important, and no price was too high to pay. Many of the first disciples were martyred for the cause, and others rose to pick up the banner and lead the charge. But two thousand years later the Christian movement, especially in the global North, has lost its sense of urgency. We have lost a sense of the plot and the big story—the arc of history. Affluent, comfortable, and distracted, Christians today seem to have lost the fire to change the world. The work of God's kingdom lies unfinished, and God's people seem to have lost their sense of purpose in the world.

There is something terribly disturbing in this.

The very Son of God became flesh and lived among us. He died that we might find forgiveness and reconciliation with God. He commissioned us to bring this same good news to the nations of the world, yet we have failed to deliver. What happened to the revolution?

I believe there is a direct connection between the unfinished work of God's kingdom and our sense of feeling incomplete in our Christian faith because there is a connection between our story and God's story. If we are not personally engaged in God's great mission in the world, then we have missed the very thing he created us to do. We are like birds meant to fly but living in a cage, fish meant to swim but floundering on the beach. It makes sense when you think about it. If the Author of the universe created us to play a key role in his unfolding drama, but we have failed to find our place in that story, then of course we would feel incomplete.

IF WE ARE NOT PERSONALLY ENGAGED IN GOD'S GREAT MISSION IN THE WORLD, THEN WE HAVE MISSED THE VERY THING HE CREATED US TO DO.

But it doesn't have to be this way.

God created each of us uniquely, and he created us for a purpose. This book is an invitation to discover the life that God created you to live. It's not about failure and guilt but more about opportunities and joy because God doesn't coerce us—he invites us. He offers meaning, fulfillment, and significance in our lives but always gives us the option to decline, and sadly, many do.

Simply stated, the message of this book is that:

- God has invited you to join him in changing the world.
- God has a dream for this world that Jesus called the kingdom of God.
- God created you to play an important role in his kingdom vision.
- You will never find your deepest purpose in life until you find your place in building God's kingdom.

Listen carefully to these next few statements: You don't have to go to the Congo or to Uzbekistan to change the world. You don't have to be brilliant to change the world—or wealthy or influential or a spiritual giant. But you do have to say yes to the invitation. You do have to be available and willing to be used, and you may have to pay the price that comes with following Jesus because changing the world and following Jesus isn't easy, and it doesn't come cheap. There will be some sacrifice involved—there always is.

Our Christian faith is not just a way to find forgiveness for sin in order to enter eternal life, yet it is that. It is not just a system of right beliefs about ultimate truth and the order of things, though it is that. Nor is it just a way to find God's comfort in times of trouble or a helpful code of conduct for how to live a good and productive life, though it is those things too. Fundamentally, the Christian faith is a call to leave everything else behind, follow our Lord and Savior Jesus Christ, and join in the great mission of Christ in our world. It is a call to forsake all else and follow him. Only then will we become completed people—people living according to God's deepest purpose for our lives.

In the chapters that follow I will ask you to come with me on a journey to rediscover God's vision for our world and his call upon your life. I will ask you to follow me through life's most basic questions: Why are we here, what is our purpose, and what is God doing in the world? Then we will look at the pivotal significance of the life, death, and resurrection of Christ within the expansive arc of God's big story, from Genesis to Revelation. We will try to understand just why Jesus seemed obsessed by the coming of the kingdom of God and attempt to answer the perplexing question of why Jesus left so suddenly, just fifty days after his resurrection. We will then explore the implications of the remarkable mission he imparted to those he left behind. And all along the way we will seek to discover what all of this means for us today, the followers of Christ in the twenty-first century. Where do we fit into this big story of God, how can we discover the role God created us to play, and what are the implications of this for our lives, our worldviews, our careers, and our families? I invite you to revisit the breathtaking truth, the urgent mission, and the profound personal significance of our Christian faith as we seek to follow the One who died that we might have life and have it to the full.

We can rediscover this great calling upon our lives and reignite the revolution. The twenty-first-century church has everything required—the resources, the knowledge, the scale, the mandate, and the power of God's Holy Spirit. All we lack is the will. It is time to finish the job.

—Richard Stearns
Bellevue, Washington
June 2012

I

. . .

THE MEANING OF LIFE AND OTHER IMPORTANT THINGS

At the deepest level, every human culture is religious—
defined by what its inhabitants believe about some ultimate
reality, and what they think that reality demands of them.[1]

—ROSS DOUTHAT

I have come that they may have life, and have it to the full.

—JOHN 10:10

On Christ the solid Rock I stand;
all other ground is sinking sand.

—EDWARD MOTE

A few years ago a new word came into our lexicon that characterizes our human preference to bend the truth to accommodate our desires. In 2006, Merriam-Webster selected the word *truthiness* as its Word of the Year. The word was coined by Stephen Colbert on his late-night political satire show in order to describe how politicians could bend the truth to support their actions. Here is the Webster definition:

> *truthiness*, n. the quality of preferring concepts or facts one wishes to be true, rather than concepts or facts known to be true[2]

When announcing that *truthiness* had been selected, beating out candidates such as *google* and *terrorism*, Merriam-Webster president John Morse commented, "We're at a point where what constitutes truth is a question on a lot of people's minds, and truth has become up for grabs. 'Truthiness' is a playful way for us to think about a very important issue."[3] Important indeed.

WHAT IS TRUTH?

Two thousand years before Stephen Colbert, Pontius Pilate asked Jesus perhaps the ultimate question: "What is truth?" Jesus had been brought to Pilate because, as the Roman governor, only he had the authority to order Jesus' execution. Pilate didn't know what to do with this political hot potato. He ended up having a conversation with Jesus and asked him just what kind of king Jesus was claiming to be. After all, it was dangerous, and perhaps a little bit loony, for someone to call himself a king under the nose of Caesar, especially a man standing in shackles in front of a Roman governor. Jesus said to Pilate: "You say that I am a king. In fact, the reason I was born and came into the world is to testify to the truth. Everyone on the side of truth listens to me."

This prompted Pilate, perhaps a cynical politician, to reply with his timeless question, "What is truth?"[4]

"IS THERE ANY SUCH THING AS TRUTH?" People today are still asking that same question. Many more seem to be asking the question that comes before that question, "Is there any such thing as truth?" This is not a book on philosophy, so I won't endeavor to make the lengthy philosophical argument required to fully answer this question. Rather, I will just appeal to your common sense. Of course there is truth. How can you make the statement "There is no such thing as truth" and then assert that your statement is true? It is virtually impossible to live our lives at all unless we make some assumptions about what is true and what is false, what is right and what is wrong. Most of us live our lives based on our understanding that some things are true and good and other things are false and wrong.

Why is this matter of foundational truth so important? Because truth has implications. For example, if you believe human life to be of little value, you might become a murderer. Why not? But if you believe that human life is precious, you might instead choose to become a doctor. Every choice you make will be based on the foundational truths you have embraced. Everything in this book and, in fact, everything in almost every book that has ever been written, deals in some way with the ultimate question of truth and the meaning of life. Writers either speak directly to life's meaning, or they base their writing on some underlying assumption of meaning. Certainly every religious leader in the world represents his or her understanding of the true meaning of life to his or her followers. But the meaning of life is not a question only for religious leaders. Every talk show host, political commentator, journalist, schoolteacher, comedian, celebrity, politician, mother, father, and bartender in the world bears witness to some definition—their definition—of the ultimate meaning of our lives. In fact, as I will try to demonstrate, every person who has ever lived has been confronted with the question "What does it all mean?" and has answered it one way or the other.

We all build our lives on some foundational assumptions about truth and reality, and those assumptions matter a great deal. If we build on a weak foundation, then what we build won't stand firm. Jesus warned of this very thing in Matthew 7:

> "Therefore everyone who hears these words of mine and puts them into practice is like a wise man who built his house on the rock. The rain came down, the streams rose, and the winds blew and beat against that house;

yet it did not fall, because it had its foundation on the rock. But everyone who hears these words of mine and does not put them into practice is like a foolish man who built his house on sand. The rain came down, the streams rose, and the winds blew and beat against that house, and it fell with a great crash." (Matt. 7:24–27)

Building our lives on the wrong foundations has consequences, disastrous ones. That is why this first chapter is so important. It will become the foundation for understanding where we fit in God's overall plan. So before we jump into a more specific discussion of the Christian worldview and its relevance in our world today, we need to have a first-things-first conversation about this meaning-of-life question that every person grapples with.

We believe that things like freedom, kindness, love, justice, and the dignity of human life are good and right. Don't we even value honesty and truth-telling itself in a person's character? We form friendships with other people because we believe friendship is good. We work to earn a living because we judge that it is wrong to steal. We sacrifice for our children because it is the right thing to do. Our entire legal system is based on the notion that some things are true and right and others are false and wrong. How many tortured prime-time crime dramas spend their full sixty minutes painstakingly seeking to determine the truth that will decide a person's guilt or innocence?

People who say there is no truth are phonies; they actually live their lives based on things they believe to be true. And let's dispense with the notion that something might be true for you but not for me. That may be accurate when describing why we prefer different foods or different music but not for ultimate issues. The law of gravity is not true just for me but not for you. And when it comes to God you can't have it both ways. God either exists for both of us or God doesn't exist at all. Both can't be true.

The really annoying problem with the truth, though, is that it is true. And things that are true put boundaries around us in ways we don't always like. Truth is stubborn. Truth has implications. The law of gravity dictates that we can't jump off buildings without consequence. Moral truths require us to control our behavior. Who wants that? Human beings don't seem to like anything that acts to impose restrictions on our behavior. Wasn't that Adam and Eve's problem with the apple?

Pontius Pilate nailed the key question: "What is truth?" Truth was up for grabs two thousand years ago, and it is up for grabs today. And, yes, it is a very important issue.

Science Fiction

One of my guilty pleasures is collecting comic books from the 1950s and 1960s. I sometimes troll around eBay, seeking to reacquire that special comic I once owned fifty years back, long ago discarded by my well-meaning mother. Little did she know that if she only had saved them, I could have put my children through college by selling the comics for tens of thousands of dollars. The ones I liked best were in the science fiction and superhero genres. They had titles like *Journey into Mystery*, *Tales to Astonish*, and *Mystery in Space*. The most imaginative ones transported readers beyond their comfortable surroundings to perceive reality in some new way that often involved aliens or time travel or the supernatural.

I'd like to combine comic books and theology for a moment in order to invite you to take a little journey of the imagination with me, one that I hope will cause you to see your life from a different perspective. I want you to imagine for just a moment how strange it would be if you went to bed tonight in your own home but woke up tomorrow morning on a different planet in a different part of the universe without any idea how you got there. I really want you to mentally put yourself there and begin to feel your emotions and hear your mind racing. Imagine that you find yourself in a closed room with just one window. Outside the window is a foreign landscape with strange features, bizarre architecture, and a race of nonhumans moving to and fro. There is a certain orderliness to the scene and to the purposeful movement of the inhabitants, but who they are and where you now find yourself are baffling mysteries. Your pulse quickens, panic rises, and your mind races desperately to make sense out of this astonishing mystery. Where am I, how did I get here, and what's going to happen to me now? Can you imagine just how utterly shocked and perplexed you would feel? If this actually happened to you or to me, we would totally freak out. A thousand questions would rush through our minds as we tried to puzzle it all out. In fact, at that moment, figuring out the baffling mystery would be the single most important priority of your life.

Are you finding this hypothetical situation hard to imagine? Well, I have news for you: that exact thing actually did happen to you . . . and to every person who has ever lived. Sometime in the past one hundred years, you were born on the third planet from the sun in a solar system within the Milky Way galaxy, in a universe that is incomprehensibly vast. Think about it: all of us just woke up one day on Planet Earth with absolutely no idea how we got here. We woke up in a particular culture at a particular time among a group of people who were there before we arrived. We awakened in the middle of an ongoing story that started long before we showed up and will continue long after we are gone. Of course, because we come into the world as infants, our situation is not nearly as shocking or abrupt as if we suddenly appeared on earth as adults. Nevertheless, the mystery is just as profound, and every person must come to terms with it in one way or another, trying to make sense of it all.

And this mystery, our mystery, raises some pretty fundamental questions. Where did we come from? How did we get here? Why are we here? Who created all of this—the universe, the earth, the beauty and complexity we see in the world all around us? How did it all come into being? Who gave us the ability to think and reason? How is it that we have the ability to produce art and music, laughter and love, skyscrapers and iPads? What does it all mean anyway? What is truth? These are the deep questions of our very existence.

I want to suggest to you that our lives are part of a much bigger story— one that began in eternity and one that will continue indefinitely into the future. And unless we understand how our story fits into this bigger story,

we will live our lives with little sense of real purpose or significance, drifting through life like a
ship without a rudder.

UNLESS WE
UNDERSTAND HOW
OUR STORY FITS
INTO THIS BIGGER

These foundational questions—about Why and
How and Who—are common to all people from all
ages. Every human being who has ever been born
woke up into the same mystery. It doesn't matter if
we are referring to Pontius Pilate, Albert Einstein,
Martin Luther King Jr., or Lady Gaga; every one of
them also landed here in the middle of this mystery,

STORY, WE WILL
LIVE OUR LIVES
WITH LITTLE SENSE
OF REAL PURPOSE
OR SIGNIFICANCE.

and just like you or me, they had to struggle to make sense of it all.

So then, just how can we make sense of life's greatest mystery? Essentially,
there are only three choices people can make. Here they are:

Choice #1: Believe There Is No Story

> In the last days scoffers will come, scoffing and following their own evil
> desires. They will say, "Where is this 'coming' he promised? Ever since
> our ancestors died, everything goes on as it has since the beginning of
> creation." (2 Peter 3:3–4)

We can choose to believe that there simply is no story or mystery to
figure out and that everything we see and experience is totally random and
without meaning. There is no truth. We are just a meaningless species on a
meaningless planet in a meaningless universe. There is, therefore, no God
and no real defining purpose to our lives.

When I was in college, there was a popular bumper sticker that summed
this up succinctly—"Life sucks, and then you die"—quite a noble motto to
live by.

But I think the best summary of this worldview that I have ever read
came from an advice columnist named "Coquette," who writes for the
online newspaper *The Daily*. A reader wrote in to ask a question about the
significance of her life. Here's how Coquette answered:

Dear Coquette:

How do I accept that I won't ever be great or outstanding? I always thought I had talent, and maybe I'm not bad, but a great many people are far better. I can't stop thinking this and it's causing me great anxiety.

Coquette:

Kill your ego, because nothing you do will ever matter. That's OK, though. It's not just you. It's all of us. It's taken 100,000 years for our species to hump and grunt its way into momentary dominance on this pale blue dot, but nothing we've accomplished is all that outstanding when you consider that a Mall of America–sized asteroid is all it would take to turn humanity into the next thin layer of fossil fuels.

Greatness is nothing but the surface tension on the spit bubble of human endeavor. On a geological time scale, our measurable effect on the planet is a greasy burp. We are 7 billion tiny flecks of talking meat stuck to an unremarkable mud ball hurtling through space in an unimaginably vast universe for no particular reason. There is no difference between kings and cripples, my friend. We're all the same hodgepodge of primordial goo, and the pursuit of greatness is a fool's errand.

Pursue happiness instead. Find peace in your insignificance, and just let your anxiety go. Learn to savor the likely truth that the sum total of human achievement won't even register in the grand scheme, so you might as well just enjoy whatever talents you have. Use them to *make yourself and others happy*, and set aside any desire to be great or outstanding.

—Coquette (emphasis mine)[5]

What an inspiring philosophy to live by—we are just "7 billion tiny flecks of talking meat stuck to an unremarkable mud ball hurtling through space in an unimaginably vast universe for no particular reason." Now, that makes me want to jump out of bed each morning to greet the day! People who believe Choice #1, that there is no story, often just ramble through life doing whatever feels good until the clock runs out. They have a mentality of "eat, drink and be merry, for tomorrow we die."

But because we don't live in isolation, there are implications to Choice #1. A person's view of truth always has consequences. What happens when your actions and decisions come into conflict with mine? Since we are both just "tiny flecks of talking meat" spinning in the "same hodgepodge of primordial goo," there is really no such thing as right or wrong, so the only mechanism to resolve our disputes is force or power; survival of the fittest. If you really believe that human beings are no more than flecks of meat, then taking a human life has no more significance than picking a mushroom or squashing an ant. One "fleck of meat" could form alliances with others to achieve their aims by overpowering another group of "meat flecks" with different goals. The group with the most power wins; right and wrong don't even enter into the discussion. Choice #1 leads to a world without truth, and a world without truth leads to chaos. So what are the consequences of all of this? One just needs to look at the bloody and brutal course of world history to see the answer.

Coquette's worldview is essentially the worldview of someone who is an atheist—life is pretty much meaningless and there is no higher purpose to our lives. Most atheists wouldn't confess this philosophy as bluntly as Coquette does because it is almost too shocking to state out loud, and most reasonable people would think them mad. Frankly, I don't think most athe-ists ever live their lives according to the inevitable conclusions of their own belief system.

One can't really live a life faithful to a worldview of "meaninglessness" without substituting some makeshift assumptions about meaning that do allow a person to function. Note that even Coquette recommends pursu-ing happiness and the happiness of others (in italics above) as a solution. She is essentially creating her own meaning because she believes there is no meaning, which takes us to the next option for dealing with the great mystery of our existence.

Choice #2: Make Up Your Own Story

For the time will come when people will not put up with sound doctrine. Instead, to suit their own desires, they will gather around them a great number of teachers to say what their itching ears want to hear. They will turn their ears away from the truth and turn aside to myths. (2 Tim. 4:3–4)

True atheists, those who believe that there is no story at all, are actually quite rare. Far more common are people who make up their own stories and then live accordingly. They create views of reality that make sense to them; they develop value systems consistent with their views and then live out their own homemade realities. They decide not to think about the bigger mystery much at all, and they often don't really care exactly how they got here or why they are here. They make up their own stories about what's important and what brings meaning.

Donald Miller, in his book *Blue Like Jazz*, said that he realized one day as a young man just how self-centered he had become; that his life was like a movie in which he was the main star of every scene, and everyone else was just a character in his movie.

> Life was a story about me because I was in every scene. In fact, I was the only one in every scene. I was everywhere I went. If someone walked into my scene, it would frustrate me because they were disrupting the general theme of the play, namely my comfort or glory.[6]

God used this revelation to lead Miller on a humble path of understanding that "dying to self" meant putting the needs of others ahead of his own.

People in this category are not necessarily selfish or egotistical. They can be quite pleasant and even admirable and inspiring. At their core they are quite practical: "I'm here. I have a life to live, so I am going to make some basic decisions about what I believe, how I will live, and what values will best guide me as I walk through life." These are the "what's right for you may not be right for me" people. They essentially invent their own truth but don't require or expect that others will necessarily live by it. They often begin sentences with "I think that . . ." or "I believe that . . ." They fill in the blanks with their own home brew. Here are a few of the manufactured "truisms" that might undergird the worldviews of these folks:

- You should be able to do whatever you want as long as it doesn't hurt other people.
- The one who dies with the most toys wins.
- Winning isn't everything; it's the only thing.
- We can all find God in our inner self.
- It's a dog-eat-dog world, and only the strong survive.
- I think that all religions are just different roads to the same truth.
- Everyone should have an equal opportunity to pursue his or her dreams.

Note that some of these truisms are quite appealing while others are quite awful. The thing that they have in common is that they are all made up and arbitrary. They may or may not be true. They are made to create meaning for people who don't really believe there is such a thing as absolute truth. Here is where our 2006 Word of the Year, *truthiness*, comes in handy.

> *truthiness*, n.: the quality of preferring concepts or facts one wishes to be true, rather than concepts or facts known to be true[7]

To solve the great mystery of their lives, people who have chosen to make up their own stories do so to create the meaning and purpose that their lives lack. I believe this may also speak to something innate within us that compels us to seek truth and meaning. The fact that we long for it so universally suggests to me that there must be such a thing as a truth and meaning that satisfies that longing, just as there is such a thing as food that satisfies our experience of hunger.

So who are these people who have chosen to make up their own stories about truth? Actually, this "make up your own story" approach to life's great mystery can produce both monsters and saints. They could be drug dealers or human traffickers as easily as they could be homemakers or schoolteachers. They might be NBA all-stars or *Fortune* 500 CEOs. Usually they share the fairly universal human goal—happiness. It's just that some pursue it through violence and crime and others through hard work and education. Some even find it in helping their fellow man and being generous.

People can live an entire lifetime pursuing happiness and fulfillment without really worrying about whether there is some deeper truth or bigger story that they might be a part of. They are the stars of their own movies, writing their own stories and making their own rules. For seventy or eighty years they move from one event to the next, like balls in a pinball machine, bouncing off bumpers with lights flashing and bells ringing all the way. They are busy racking up points and bonuses until the ball finally goes down the drain, the noises stop, and the lights go out. Game Over!

Then there's the third option.

Choice #3: Become Part of God's Story

> Yet to all who did receive him, to those who believed in his name, he gave the right to become children of God. (John 1:12)

If you read a mystery novel, there is one thing you know for sure: someone wrote it; there was an author. The author creates the setting (the place where everything happens), the plot, and all of the characters in the story. The author gives each character unique traits and personalities and a role to play in the bigger story. And, perhaps the most significant aspect of this metaphor, every character is designed to play a key role. Let me underscore this one more time. If God is the Author of the big story and you are a character in that story, then it follows that the Author created you to play a key role in his story. This is the theme I will develop more fully in later chapters.

THE AUTHOR CREATED YOU TO PLAY A KEY ROLE IN HIS STORY.

You have probably seen The Lord of the Rings movie trilogy, and I hope you have read the books too. J. R. R. Tolkien, the author of those books, created an astonishing world called Middle Earth. It was a remarkable place filled with adventure and dragons and orcs and hobbits. It was a story of good versus evil, of kings and sorcerers, wizards and magic. And the characters in the book—Frodo, Arwen, Gandalf, Sam, and many others—were placed in the midst of a big story unfolding around them that went back into time for thousands of years. Tolkien had created each of them to play some role in his sprawling epic story. And as we read about them, we realize that each of them struggled to make sense of the story and to understand just what his or her role should be. They couldn't see the whole of the big story from the author's point of view; they could only see the part that was in front of them with occasional glimpses of the broader narrative. But each of them had to puzzle out the role he or she was meant to play, based on the information that character had.

Well, doesn't it make sense that our story has an author too—one who created the world and the universe we were born into, one who cast the vision for the expansive plot and story narrative that has unfolded over eons of time, one who began the story and also will bring it to its conclusion? Doesn't it also follow that this same Author/Creator gave life to each and every character in his story—to you and to me—and that he created each one of us with unique gifts, talents, and personalities; and that he placed us within his story in both space and time?

I want to be frank in stating that all of this requires a significant leap of faith. Philosophers have been debating the existence of God for millennia, and I will not bring an end to that debate here. But again, I want to appeal to your common sense—something philosophers don't always have in abundance. Doesn't it make more sense to believe that our story has an Author than to believe that everything we see and experience is meaningless and without purpose?

In college I majored in neurobiology and animal behavior. I had the thrill of studying both the intricacies of the human brain and the amazing variety and diversity in the animal and plant kingdoms. At that time in my life I was an atheist . . . maybe an agnostic. I didn't believe in God, and I didn't think one could prove the existence of God, so I made Choice #2. I decided to make up my own rules. But what kept nagging at me was that the natural world I was studying was filled with such beauty, complexity, and wonder that I could not help but speculate just how something so marvelous could have come into being. Did it really make any sense to think that all of this just showed up by accident, that the most beautiful painting I had ever seen didn't have a painter? I could have described to you the detailed steps in the life cycle of the monarch butterfly and the amazing fact that more than 100 million monarchs mysteriously migrate thousands of miles each year and find their way to the same pine forests in Michoacán, Mexico.[8] They weigh a fraction of an ounce, but they can navigate and fly several thousand miles to the same small patch of land every year. I could describe all of this, but I was at a loss to explain why and how there was such a thing as a butterfly to begin with. If you have ever watched TV shows such as *Planet Earth* or *The Frozen Planet* from the BBC Natural History Unit, you cannot come away without being in awe and wonder of the incredible artistry and magic in our world. Does it make sense that the millions of plants and animals we see today; the remarkable music and art of human beings; the incredible civilizations of Egypt, Rome, Western Europe, China, and Japan; the technologies that created television, cell phones, computers, and spaceships; and incredible cities like New York, Paris, Rio de Janeiro, and Tokyo just *happened*? And even if you can swallow all of that, how can you possibly believe that the incomprehensibly vast universe with its billions of galaxies, in which we float like a speck of dust, just appeared out of nothing?

I know that my little argument won't convince the academics who are battling this out in universities all over the world, but it usually makes sense to ordinary people who also can look at our amazing universe and reach a similar conclusion—there has to be a painter; there has to be an Author.

> What may be known about God is plain to them, because God has made it plain to them. For since the creation of the world God's invisible qualities—his eternal power and divine nature—have been clearly seen, being understood from what has been made, so that men are without excuse. (Rom. 1:19–20)

It takes a lot more faith to believe what Coquette believes—that there was no Creator and that we are carbon chemistry swirling around a meaningless universe—than it does to simply believe that "in the beginning God created the heavens and the earth" (Gen. 1:1).

We are told in the Bible that the crowning achievements of God's creation, the lead characters in his story, are men and women—human beings. In fact, the Bible tells us that God created human beings in his own likeness with the ability to think and reason, to create music and art and beauty, and with a spiritual nature that makes them different from everything else in creation (Gen. 1:27). We are, in a real sense, God's children.

> THE BIG STORY OF GOD CAME TO A CLIMAX IN THE LIFE AND DEATH AND RESURRECTION OF JESUS. HE IS THE TRUTH; HE IS THE STORY.

We started this chapter with Pilate's provocative question: What is truth? Now it's time to listen again to the amazing statement by Jesus that provoked Pilate's question: "The reason I was born and came into the world is to testify to the truth. Everyone on the side of truth listens to me." The big story of God came to a climax in the life and death and resurrection of Jesus. He is the truth; he is the story. "I am the way and the truth and the life," Jesus stated. "No one comes to the Father except through me" (John 14:6).

TRUTH MATTERS

The tragedy of modern man is not that he knows less and less about the meaning of his own life but that it bothers him less and less[9].—Vaclav Havel

As Jesus said, we all have the choice to build on sand or to build on the rock of God's truth. But Jesus doesn't state that simply believing the right things provides the foundation of rock. He states that we have to believe *his words* and put them into practice.

"Therefore everyone who hears these words of mine *and puts them into practice* is like a wise man who built his house on the rock. The rain came down, the streams rose, and the winds blew and beat against that

house; yet it did not fall, because it had its foundation on the rock."
(Matt. 7:24–25, emphasis mine)

Truth ignored is no better foundation for our lives than no truth at all. Jesus was proclaiming that truth has implications for conduct. Truth becomes the foundation for our worldview, and worldview becomes the basis for our actions and behavior. We had better stand on a foundation of rock because we live in a world where the rain beats down, the waters are rising, and the winds will blow and beat against us. It is a world that unrelentingly assaults our senses and confronts our values. It is a world filled with temptations—money, sex, power, fame, and pleasure. It is a world characterized by crime, violence, racism, poverty, injustice, inequality, and deceit. We live in a world that constantly challenges our understanding of truth and demands that we make choices. And those choices matter.

This is the world into which every one of us woke up. This is the world in which each of us is seeking meaning and purpose. This is the world we, as Christians, were commanded to win in Christ's name, armed with Christ's truth, and motivated by Christ's love.

2

...

God's Big Story

Even if there is only one possible unified theory, it is just a
set of rules and equations. What is it that breathes fire into
the equations and makes a universe for them to describe?[1]

—STEPHEN HAWKING, ASTROPHYSICIST

In the beginning God created the heavens and the earth.

—GENESIS 1:1

Flying Saucers

As I went up to the spare bedroom this morning to begin writing, I
announced to my wife that today I would try to explain the meaning of
life and God's big plan for the universe. I think that brought out a bit of
a chuckle. Her advice was to keep it practical and down-to-earth and to
tell some stories. Good advice. The only reason I want to talk about these
bigger concepts at all is that I am convinced the very real and practical
issues we face in our lives have to be understood as they relate to the larger
issues of meaning and order in the world. As I said in the previous chapter,
the choices we make about reality matter. Truth matters. Beliefs matter. It

matters whether Jesus was God's Son, and what he taught us about truth matters a great deal. The truth has profound implications.

When I was a senior in high school, I had a running feud with my English teacher. To be honest, I was a bit of a jerk, and I regularly made her life difficult by behaving badly and disagreeing with her in class. I was always the contrarian. We all had to write a major research paper that year, and she told us we could choose any topic we wanted to write about. Other students chose to write about great books like *Moby Dick* or *Crime and Punishment*. But, of course, I had to be difficult. So when I had my meeting with her to get my topic approved, I reminded her that she said we could write on any topic and announced that I intended to write about flying saucers. Yes, you heard me right: my senior English research paper topic was flying saucers. I could tell she was a bit peeved by this, but all she said was, "Stearns, it had better be good."

For the next several months I read everything I could get my hands on about UFOs. I reviewed newspaper accounts of sightings and interviews with people who claimed to have seen them. I even wrote to the US government to get the official report of Project Blue Book, a seventeen-year study by the US Air Force in which more than twelve thousand sightings were investigated to determine whether UFOs posed a national security threat. I really got into this. The more I read and learned, the more I wondered whether there really might be extraterrestrial life. I can even remember going out at night to gaze into the heavens for hours, hoping that maybe I might see one of these UFOs myself because if UFOs were real, it changed everything. It would change everything about our view of the world because it would mean we were not the only ones here and that something bigger was going on. So why am I telling you all of this? Be patient.

It was about five years later that I completed another research project. I was dating a young woman named Reneé, whom I loved very much. The only problem was that she was a committed Christian and I was an atheist. And to her, truth mattered a great deal—so much, in fact, that she would not marry someone who didn't share the same view of truth. To her, the truth that God had sent his Son, Jesus, to teach us, forgive us, and offer us a new way to live changed everything about her life—including, unfortunately for me, her choice of whom she would marry. Truth had consequences and implications for her life that were real and serious.

TRUTH HAD CONSEQUENCES AND IMPLICATIONS FOR HER LIFE THAT WERE REAL AND SERIOUS.

Now, I didn't fully understand this. I was one of those "what's true for you may not be true for me" kind of people. Why couldn't we all just be happy? But I couldn't believe in Jesus just because he was a nice person and he made me feel good. As a guy with his college degree in neurobiology, I needed evidence that Christianity was actually true because, to me, it seemed that Jesus wasn't asking people to believe in him; he was asking people to build their entire lives around him. He had claimed to be God, after all. And if I discovered that he was, in fact, God, then it changed everything. I couldn't just wake up the next morning, brush my teeth, and go to school as if nothing had happened.

So, prompted by my love for the girl I would someday marry, I decided to research the claims of this whole Christianity deal. I read about fifty or sixty books over the next few months, trying to learn as much as I could. I read everything from comparative religion and philosophy to archaeology, science, faith, apologetics, and history. My mind raced as I considered, maybe for the first time ever, the fundamental questions of our lives. Where did we come from? How did we get here? Is there a God? What happens when we die? How should we live? What does it all mean? This is not a book about apologetics, so I won't try to summarize all that I learned. But I will share my conclusion.

I came to believe that the most plausible explanation for the universe was that God was real and he had created all that we see; that there was a painter behind this incredible painting, an author behind this astonishing story. I also came to believe that Jesus of Nazareth was indeed God incarnate—that God had taken human form in order to inaugurate a new and deeper kind of relationship with us. I based my belief on both historical evidence for the resurrection and also the inherent ring of truth I found in Scripture. It felt right and felt true. It had a depth and solidity to it, a consistency that almost spoke for itself, kind of like what Jefferson wrote in the Declaration of Independence—that "we hold these truths to be self-evident." The truth of the teachings of Jesus felt somehow "self-evident." The evidence for the historicity of the resurrection of Jesus seemed as unimpeachable as the evidence that Julius Caesar had been the emperor of Rome. So I knelt before the God of the universe one day in West Philadelphia and said, "Yes! Yes, I am your child. Yes, I want to know you and learn from you, and yes, I want to live every day of my life with you, yes!" And I also knew that my life would never be the same because Jesus changed everything.

Okay, so where do the flying saucers come in? In those first few months after committing my life to the truth of the message of Jesus, I was irrepressible when speaking to others about what I had discovered. I was just so excited and so eager to share what I had found with those who hadn't found it. I felt as though I had found a cure for cancer and had to tell everyone the incredibly good news. I am sure that I was insufferable to be around. One night I was having a lengthy debate about all of this with a friend who didn't understand why I was so worked up. He was also one of those "what's true for you may not be true for me" people. So I came up with this example to try to get him to understand. I said, "I want you to imagine that tonight as you drive home, a real UFO appears in the sky ahead of you, and to your shock and dismay, it lands in the road in front of you. You stop the car, quivering in the presence of this astonishing and inexplicable sight. Then an extraterrestrial being actually comes out and walks toward your car. It communicates to you where it is from and why it has come. It tells you to communicate this same information to others and says that someday it will come back. Then it returns to its ship, lifts off, and disappears into the night sky."

I asked my friend what he would do if that happened to him. I suggested that it would be the defining moment of his life and that he would probably spend the rest of his life telling others what he had seen and heard, whether they believed him or not. I asked him if it wouldn't change everything. He agreed it probably would. "So," I said to him, "now you know how I feel about Jesus Christ."

A person who had the experience of meeting an extraterrestrial as just described would become a changed person. He could no longer wake up and brush his teeth and go to work like other people. He could no longer sit in an office or a classroom all day as if nothing had happened. It would truly change everything. It would change his understanding of reality, his fundamental worldview, and the very meaning, purpose, and mission of his life.

So if a UFO sighting would have such profound implications for someone's life, what about the appearing in time and space, in human form, of the Creator of the universe? What if this same God-man taught amazing truths, lived a remarkable life, and actually rose from the dead? Might that not also have some implications for life as we know it? No, after encountering Jesus you can't just go back to your old life. That is not an option. It changes everything. The apostle Paul had just such a supernatural encounter with Jesus on the road to Damascus. That encounter not only changed Paul; the changed Paul then changed the world. His encounter was that profound.

> NO, AFTER ENCOUNTERING JESUS YOU CAN'T JUST GO BACK TO YOUR OLD LIFE. THAT IS NOT AN OPTION. IT CHANGES EVERYTHING.

By the way, I received an A on my research paper. And I don't think anyone would be more surprised that I became an author than my high school English teacher.

MEET THE AUTHOR

In short, I had always believed that the world involved magic: now I thought that perhaps it involved a magician. . . . I had always felt life first as a story: and if there is a story there is a story-teller.[2]—G. K. Chesterton

In chapter 1, I outlined the three different choices people can make when confronted with the incredible mystery of our very existence: believe there is no story, make up your own story, or become part of God's story. If you have chosen one of the first two, the rest of this book won't be terribly relevant for you. So let me assume that you believe God is the Author of the big story. The question then becomes, how do I find out more about the story the Author is writing?

And here I have to make a practical leap. I will focus in this chapter on the narrative of the Christian faith and story. This is not a book on comparative religion, nor is it a book trying to prove the existence of God. There are many fine books on these topics you can read. Instead, I will assume that you are a person who has already accepted the basic Christian narrative as being true but wants to understand its implications for your life in a deeper way. If you haven't accepted the Christian story as true, you can still read on, of course, and maybe even learn some things about the Christian worldview you didn't know before.

So how do we begin to wrap our minds around the story of God? Perhaps you have heard the expression "We don't know what we don't know." I have used it in a business context for years, and it essentially means that when we face a major new challenge for which our understanding is woefully inadequate, we don't know enough to fully appreciate what we don't know. It's an expression that humbly confesses ignorance in the face of something very big and very complex. That's the way I feel about God. The God who created the universe is so big, so powerful, and so far beyond my ability to comprehend, that I don't know what I don't know about God. I can no more comprehend God's ways than my dog Sophie can comprehend my ways. This was said well by God himself through the prophet Isaiah:

> "For my thoughts are not your thoughts,
>> neither are your ways my ways,"
>>> declares the LORD.
> "As the heavens are higher than the earth,

so are my ways higher than your ways

and my thoughts than your thoughts." (Isa. 55:8–9)

The truth is that the only things we can really know about God are the things he has chosen to reveal to us in one way or another. We can discern things about God from observing what he created. When we see the world around us, we see vastness, complexity, power, order, beauty, creativity, precision, and majesty. And all of these words say something about the Creator. We can also, of course, understand God in spiritual ways as we pray and meditate on his Word and seek his company daily. But the most specific things we can learn about God come from those things he has chosen to reveal directly to us through the story of Scripture. The sixty-six books of the Bible, from Genesis to Revelation, were given to us by God as the record of God's dealings with mankind. Without them we would understand very little of God's character, his motives, or his plan, which is exactly why God had it written down for us.

A "dirty little secret" is that few Christians have read the Bible from cover to cover. One source claims that fewer than 10 percent of professing Christians have read the entire Bible. Many have set out with the best intentions only to spin off the road in a fog of confusion somewhere in the book of Leviticus. Many more of us have read the New Testament all the way through, probably because of the tightness of the storyline, the accessibility of its writing style, and the dramatic appearance of the main hero, Jesus. Most of us have sampled the Old Testament as we might a buffet dinner—a helping of Psalms, a few stories about David and Moses, and maybe a dollop of Esther or Nehemiah on the side. The result is that most Christians don't have a good grasp of the broad storyline from creation to consummation. But here is the problem with that: we can't really understand the mission of Jesus unless we understand that he was the fulfillment of the entire Old Testament story. And if we don't understand the mission of Jesus, we won't understand the mission he gave us to fulfill. We have to know the big story to understand where our personal story fits in.

In a moment I will try to summarize the broad outlines of God's big story in a simple way, but before I do it is important to make a few key points. First, we will always be tempted to ask the question "Why did God choose to do it that way?" We might ask, for example, why did he make the universe so large, or why does life seem so rare in the known universe? We might ask why he made the sky blue and the grass green. And we might also ask why he chose to allow evil to exist, why he gave us free will, why he chose to reveal himself so slowly over thousands of years instead of all at once. We always want to know why he chose to do things the way he did. There is an infinite number of scripts he could have written, but for reasons only God understands, he wrote this one. And here's the point: no matter which script he chose, we would always wonder why he didn't choose a different one, one that maybe made more sense to us. The only real answer is that he is God, and we are not. We are a lot like children who keep asking their parents, "Why?" And sometimes parents just have to answer, "Because I said so." So as you read more about the big story of God, focus less on the why and more on the how—how you fit into the amazing story of God's love.

Here is my attempt to summarize the plotline of the sixty-six books of the Bible. Obviously it can't include everything, but my hope is that it will help you see the bright line of God's incredible love for us and gain a sense of where the story is going next.

LOVE STORY

The story of Scripture is the story of a Father's love for his children. It is the story of a Father faithfully reaching out to the children who rejected him. It is the story of a loving God who never gives up.

In the beginning God created the universe and everything in it. And he took joy in all that he created. He created Adam and Eve—man and woman—in his own image with mind, body, and spirit to enjoy in relationship as a father enjoys his children.

God was present with them in the special place he had made for them to live, Eden, and his wish was that they would flourish as they enjoyed the great inheritance he had provided. He desired that his children would work as his partners to oversee and manage the kingdom he had created, to manage the family business. He gave them their assignment and explained to them the kind of relationship he desired, one governed by the respect and obedience the Father deserves.

But when tempted to disobey God by the evil one—a fallen angel whose bitterness compels him to attack all that the Father loves—they strayed and made a terrible choice, a choice to do it their way instead, a choice of disrespect. They weren't satisfied with God's way and wanted more power and more control. They broke off the good faith relationship with their own loving Father. This broke God's heart because their actions would have terrible consequences. They would tragically come to understand this as they lived apart from God and began to see the implications of their own willful behavior.

And the consequences were dreadful—broken relationships with their Father, broken relationships with each other and with their children after them, selfishness, greed, strife, and even murder and death in the family. They got just what they had desired, a chance to do it their way. And all God had created fell into brokenness with them. But God still loved them as a father always loves his children, and he was heartbroken.

As the years passed, despite their widespread disobedience and wickedness, God offered his children many opportunities to return to him and live under his loving authority once more. He called out one man, Abraham, and promised that he would become the father of a new nation, Israel, a nation of God's own people, set apart from the evil and rebellion that had consumed the human race like a virus. And he promised Abraham that this new nation would someday be a blessing to all of God's children. Israel could reestablish the goodness of God's kingdom and live as a nation of God's children under the authority of their Father-King again, as Adam and Eve once had. But Israel struggled, and they, too, strayed and made the terrible choice to do it their way instead, a choice of disrespect.

Abraham's great-grandson Joseph was sold into slavery in Egypt by his own brothers, and Israel spent the next four hundred years in captivity in Egypt. Israel would have to wait if they were to fulfill God's desire for them.

Then God heard their cries and sent another man, Moses, to free his people from their captivity. Moses intervened on their behalf and led them through the waters of the Red Sea to safety. But still they doubted, disobeyed, and complained.

Seeing their confusion and knowing the nation of Israel would need a constitution and laws to guide them into right behavior, God gave them the Law, the Torah, at Mount Sinai. If they were to become God's kingdom people, they would need to understand God's truth and God's justice. He taught them right from wrong, goodness and truth. He taught them symbolically, through the bloody sacrifices of bulls and lambs, that their sin had consequences, and he showed them what that meant. Blood crimes required blood sacrifice. This would remind them that their own sins would have to be dealt with if their relationship was to be restored. Sin has consequences. Moses then led them through the wilderness for forty years to teach them again how to trust, obey, and rely upon God. He led them to the brink of a new promised land, where they could live in safety and prosperity in relationship with their Father God. But even after all of this, Israel turned away from God's love, just as Adam and Eve had before them, and chose to disobey and live according to their own desires.

> IF THEY WERE TO BECOME GOD'S KINGDOM PEOPLE, THEY WOULD NEED TO UNDERSTAND GOD'S TRUTH AND GOD'S JUSTICE.

Then they demanded a king so they might be like the other nations. And God granted them a king, first Saul and then David, son of Jesse, who was the greatest of Israel's kings. But over hundreds of years most of their kings led them away from God. They were conquered by other nations. God was again heartbroken by their stubborn ways. Over the ensuing years God sent them prophets to warn them and correct them, but they wouldn't listen. Israel and her kings had failed again to submit to God's authority and become God's beloved kingdom that would restore God's rule and become God's blessing to the nations of the world.

So God went silent for almost five hundred years. He had a different way, which he would reveal at just the right time.

"For my thoughts are not your thoughts,
neither are your ways my ways." (Isa. 55:8)

He broke the silence with the cry of a baby, born in a manger in the town of Bethlehem, at the zenith of the Roman Empire, an empire that represented the epitome of mankind's corrupt rule over the earth, with its lust for power, violence, greed, and oppression. God decided it was time, time for a revolution, a revolution to overthrow, once and for all, the perverted kingdoms conceived out of mankind's selfishness and greed. It was time to reveal God's values, God's justice, and God's way. It was time to establish God's reign, build God's kingdom, and enthrone God again as king. It was time for a rescue mission for all God's children.

The story of Scripture is the story of a Father's love for his children. It is the story of a Father faithfully reaching out to the children who rejected him. It is the story of a loving God who never gives up.

And as the ultimate act of love, God's own Son, Jesus, would lead the rescue—fully God and fully man. God became flesh. It was too important to be entrusted to anyone else, too vital to be left to others. Born of the Holy Spirit, the babe in the manger would rescue God's children. Jesus would fulfill Israel's destiny to be a blessing to the nations.

"For God so loved the world that he gave his one and only Son, that whoever believes in him shall not perish but have eternal life." (John 3:16)

Jesus would lead the revolution. But it was not a revolution about land and power and control; it was a revolution of love, obedience, peace, and restored relationships. Jesus modeled a different way to live and a different way to love. He spoke of a new kind of kingdom in which conventional wisdom would be turned upside down. The hallmarks of God's kingdom would be love and forgiveness, sacrifice and service, justice and fairness. Love would be the coin of the realm, and people would love their neighbor as God loved them. The poor would be lifted up, the sick healed, the weak cared for. It was a vision of a different kind of society governed by God's values, and everyone, not just Israel, would be invited to become its citizens. His kingdom would now come; his will would now be done, on earth as it is in heaven.

It was the good news that the prophets had spoken of, the good news that a new king would arise out of the stump of Jesse, the line of David, who would sit on Israel's throne and be a blessing to the nations. God himself would do it by sending his own Son to take on human form and lead us out of our own darkness. It was a chance for a new beginning.

Jesus lived and taught and astonished by speaking with truth, showing compassion, and performing miraculous signs. He gathered around him disciples, the soldiers of his revolution, twelve men who would lead the charge. For three years he poured his life into them, teaching them the ways of this new kingdom. They were twelve men who would represent the twelve tribes of Israel. He was preparing them to proclaim his new kingdom after he had paid the price for sin and evil and after he had left them. Jesus demonstrated the hallmarks of God's new kingdom—feeding the hungry, healing the sick, caring for the poor, casting out evil spirits, and demonstrating the unconditional love of God to all he encountered. No man had ever lived or spoken this way. And he prepared the twelve to carry on after he left.

But mankind was so twisted in its rebellion that even God's own Son was rejected—by the world and by Israel. The evil one from the garden of Eden was again trying to thwart the goodness of God. But God knew that this would happen; he knew that his own Son would be rejected, but he had decided long ago that he would restore his relationship with his children in a costly way, by himself taking the punishment for their rebellion because he could not bear for them to be punished so harshly. God's justice was pure, and it required that the crimes of humanity be addressed. Taking the place of one of the lambs sacrificed in the temple for the sins of Israel, Jesus would pay the terrible price. He would be the Lamb of God sacrificed once and for all to pay for the sins of God's children.

So Jesus submitted to those who called for his head. The very leaders of Israel demanded his death, and he consented. They could not know it, but it was the only way to remove the horrible guilt of God's children, to pay the awful price, and to restore their relationship with their loving Father. Even one of the Twelve betrayed him.

Then his disciples watched in horror as he was arrested, beaten, tried, nailed to a cross, and brutally killed. And as he gave up his spirit, they gave up their hope. The revolution was over, and all was lost.

The story of Scripture is the story of a Father's love for his children. It is the story of a Father faithfully reaching out to the children who rejected him. It is the story of a loving God who never gives up.

But God . . . God was not finished. The plot took a dramatic turn. The good news of God burst forth in all its fullness. After three days in the cold tomb, life coursed again through the body of Jesus. The penalty now paid, justice now satisfied, and death now defeated, he arose. The story would not conclude here, and the revolution would not end. Indeed, it had just begun.

IT WAS THE ONLY WAY TO REMOVE THE HORRIBLE GUILT OF GOD'S CHILDREN, TO PAY THE AWFUL PRICE, AND TO RESTORE THEIR RELATIONSHIP WITH THEIR LOVING FATHER.

He rallied the astonished disciples, explained the incredible events, and showed them how all that had happened had been predicted by the prophets. The good news of God was that they could now proclaim and build God's beloved kingdom "on earth as it is in heaven." They were to go into the world to establish God's rule by announcing the good news of God's forgiveness and inviting all people to enter into this new way of living. A new Israel, fulfilled in the person of Jesus, would now become a blessing to the nations. A revolution to overthrow the kingdoms of this world and spread God's new kingdom would be launched—and they would lead it. A new kingdom of God's children would now be established, and it would demonstrate a new way of living, a new society under God's will. Jesus called it the church.

The Eleven were excited to have Jesus leading them once again. Now everything would be possible. But they did not fully understand what God had planned to do. Just forty days after he rose from the dead, Jesus left them again. But before he left, he gave them this job to do. He told them to build God's new kingdom to the far corners of the earth, proclaim the good news of God's forgiveness, demonstrate God's love through their lives and words and deeds, and make new disciples of all nations by teaching others all that he had taught them. He bid them to invite everyone to accept his good news and enter his kingdom. He told them that he would be with them always because he would send them his Spirit as their comfort, help, and guide, and he said he would return when the job was done. And then . . . Jesus left.

> HE TOLD THEM TO BUILD GOD'S NEW KINGDOM TO THE FAR CORNERS OF THE EARTH, PROCLAIM THE GOOD NEWS OF GOD'S FORGIVENESS, DEMONSTRATE GOD'S LOVE THROUGH THEIR LIVES AND WORDS AND DEEDS, AND MAKE NEW DISCIPLES OF ALL NATIONS BY TEACHING OTHERS ALL THAT HE HAD TAUGHT THEM.

For the first time since the garden of Eden, the dark shadow of sin and guilt had been removed, and the sunlight of God's grace and forgiveness shone. Our sin and guilt had been forgiven, erased. God's intervention had removed the one thing that had separated us from our Father. Our freedom had been won, our salvation secured. We, as God's children, could go into the world free and without guilt to proclaim the good news of forgiveness, demonstrate the Father's love to all, and invite all of God's children to come home to the Father's warm embrace. God's kingdom had come; God's will now could be done, on earth as it is in heaven.

Two thousand years later we are his children in this generation; we are his church. But the job he gave us to do remains unfinished. It is our turn now . . . our time to lead God's revolution.

3

. . .

WHY DID JESUS LEAVE?

The birth of Jesus is the sunrise in the Bible.[1]

—HENRY VAN DYKE

After he said this, he was taken up before their very eyes,
and a cloud hid him from their sight. They were looking
intently up into the sky as he was going, when suddenly two
men dressed in white stood beside them. "Men of Galilee,"
they said, "why do you stand here looking into the sky?"

—ACTS 1:9–11

One question that has captivated every generation of Christians since the first century is the question of when Jesus will return. Specific predictions of the actual date of Christ's return have been made in virtually every generation since Christ's departure at the ascension, but they became intense just before AD 1000 and AD 2000—at the end of each millennium. The Left Behind series, which told the story of the last days and the second coming of Christ, debuted in 1995 and became a publishing phenomenon, reportedly selling more than 65 million books. In 2011 there was media frenzy over

Harold Camping's prediction that the rapture[2] and judgment day would take place on May 21, 2011. When it did not, Camping revised his prediction to October. The fact that you are reading this book indicates that Camping was wrong again, for which he seemed to have sincerely apologized.

As exciting as the question of the Second Coming is, I have come to believe that there is an even more profound question that needs to be answered first. It is a question that is absolutely fundamental to the under-

WHY DID JESUS LEAVE? standing of our faith, but it is a question that I don't think I have ever heard anyone ask, and I don't remember ever hearing a sermon preached on it. This question is not when Jesus will return, but rather, why did Jesus leave in the first place?

Stop and think about this for just a moment. Why did Jesus leave?

If you consider the sweeping meta-story of Scripture that I described in the last chapter, it culminates in the most dramatic event in all of history, the incarnation of God in human form in Bethlehem.

We know the story so well: the babe in the manger, the shepherds abiding in the fields, the wise men and the heavenly host of angels declaring the long-awaited promise: "I bring you good news of great joy that will be for all the people. Today in the town of David a Savior has been born to you; he is Christ the Lord" (Luke 2:10–11).

This incarnational moment has been called the very "hinge of history"[3]— God coming to dwell among men. No other event and no other person has so shaped world history. The story of Christ has rightly been called "the greatest story ever told."[4] But we may know the story *too well*. We have heard it so many times and seen it commercialized in so many ways that it is difficult for us to truly hear it without our twenty-first-century filters.

Allow me to take you back in time to help you hear the story as the disciples might have experienced it. I want you to experience it as if it were a mystery unfolding. Remember, the disciples did not know how the story would end as we do today when we look back on it. I want you to see the sheer drama in this story with new eyes.

The once-great nation of Israel had been trampled by a succession of empires and now lived under the boot of what was the most powerful empire of all, Rome. For centuries they had cried out to God for deliverance from their oppression. The prophets had foretold a savior, a messiah, who would be a king again on David's throne. He would someday liberate and restore the fallen nation of God's chosen people, and they had been waiting and longing for hundreds of years for this messiah-king to appear. Then, just about thirty years after that miraculous night in Bethlehem, which very few people were even aware of, Jesus burst onto the scene, publicly declaring in the local synagogue in Nazareth that he was the fulfillment of those messianic prophecies, that he was the Christ the Jewish people had longed to see for centuries. He was the King who would restore Israel. It was shocking. But instead of reacting with joy, "they got up, drove him out of the town, and took him to the brow of the hill on which the town was built, in order to throw him off the cliff. But he walked right through the crowd and went on his way" (Luke 4:29–30).

To demonstrate indisputably that he was indeed the long-awaited Messiah, Jesus began to perform what would become a torrent of miracles— healing the sick, blind, and lame; feeding the thousands; casting out demons; walking on water; quieting a storm; turning water into wine; and even raising the dead back to life. His teaching and sermons were astonishing in that they cast a vision for an entirely different way for people to live, a radical new way that would be pleasing to God and attractive to all men and women. For three years he canvassed the countryside preaching, teaching, and healing. He shockingly claimed the power to forgive sins, something only God could do. Though the Pharisees and chief priests opposed him and felt their power threatened, Jerusalem and the surrounding towns were literally buzzing with news of these events, and thousands began to seek him and follow him. Jesus even made the outrageous claim that he was God's Son. Unimaginable. Unprecedented. Stunning.

He selected twelve men to live within his inner circle—to travel with him and be taught by him. These twelve had a ringside seat to the most amazing series of events the world had ever witnessed. Try to put yourself in their sandals. They, despite being ordinary men—fishermen, tax collectors, zealots—had been chosen to be discipled by Rabbi Jesus. They were witnesses to his miracles and were privy to his most private teaching. They imagined that Jesus would come to power, overthrow Rome, and free Israel from her captivity. They even argued over which of them would have a higher rank in Jesus' new kingdom. But they misunderstood.

Just when the disciples felt certain that Jesus would liberate the Jews from Rome, the unthinkable happened. There was a startling and unexpected twist in the developing plot. Jesus, Messiah and King of the Jews, was betrayed by one of the Twelve and arrested one evening near the Garden of Gethsemane, just outside the walls of Jerusalem, where he had gone to pray. Arrested? How could this be happening? Why didn't he use his powers to escape? What would become of the revolution to overthrow Roman oppression? What would happen to them, the disciples? In confusion and fear they scattered. Then to their growing horror, within a matter of hours, Jesus was brutally beaten, sentenced to death, nailed to a cross, and murdered. Not possible! It could not end like this. But his dead, cold, and mutilated corpse was anointed with oils and spices, wrapped and bound in linen, and sealed in a stone tomb. Game over!

I don't think we can possibly imagine the depth of the disciples' despair. Their hopes and dreams were crushed. Their teacher and friend was dead. The messianic King of Israel had been snuffed out like the wick of a candle. There would be no freedom for the captives, no day of the Lord's favor, no victory over Rome, no growing movement of followers with Jesus at the lead. Everything they had believed and hoped for was gone forever. (I can think of no story in all of history more tragic.) So they slinked away in their grief. They feared for their own safety, so they fled and hid. The bad guys had won. It was over.

We can only surmise what must have gone on over the next several days. Peter, the courageous one, had denied even knowing Christ, fearing that he, too, might be arrested and killed. Presumably the others had gone into hiding as well. Words like *devastated, grief-stricken, confused, fearful,* and *demoralized* don't even begin to capture their emotions. Everything they had hoped for was gone. But they misunderstood.

Three long days went by, and one last outrageous and totally un-expected twist of the plot took place. Inside the bleak stone tomb the cold corpse of the dead Messiah stirred. Energy coursed through it; a trans-formation took place, and Jesus stunningly rose from death that first Easter morning. The stone was rolled back; he emerged victorious from the tomb: "Where, O death, is your victory? Where, O death, is your sting?" (1 Cor. 15:55). Jesus had conquered death itself and returned to his disciples.

There is no more dramatic story in all the world. Can you try to picture first the awe and then the joy that the disciples must have felt? It would be hard to exaggerate the depth of their emotional reaction. Nothing like this had ever happened. Every hope that had been dashed was suddenly alive again. Jesus was indeed the Messiah-King, and his resurrection changed everything. It still does.

We are told in Scripture that over the next forty days Jesus continually appeared to them and spoke about the kingdom of God. God was about to do something totally new and different. Their sense of anticipation for what might come next must have been growing and building toward a fever pitch. Jesus was back, and the revolution was back on track. Then it happened.

Forty days after his miraculous resurrection, the risen Jesus led the disciples to a familiar place on the Mount of Olives. He spoke a few words about the promised Holy Spirit and about how the disciples were to be his witnesses to the ends of the earth. Then, as Acts 1:9 tells us, "He was taken up before their very eyes, and a cloud hid him from their sight." That's right. Jesus just left.

Seriously? After all of the incredibly dramatic events—thousands of years of prophecy fulfilled, the incarnation of God in human form, the public ministry and profound teaching of Christ, the astonishing signs and miracles, and, finally, Christ's brutal death followed by the unprecedented resurrection—he just left? That's it? That's how it ends?

I don't know about you, but I would have written a very different ending to this story. I would have expected that the resurrected Christ would now bring history to its conclusion. The atonement had occurred;

our sins had been paid for. Didn't Jesus himself say, "It is finished"? Why not just go directly to Matthew 25's judgment scene? Do not pass GO; do not collect $200. Gather the nations, separate the sheep from the goats, get the judgment behind you, and set up your eternal kingdom forever and ever, amen. Now, that makes sense. Why not tie it all up in a neat bow and end it right then and there?

> WHY NOT TIE IT ALL UP IN A NEAT BOW AND END IT RIGHT THEN AND THERE? BUT NO. INSTEAD, JESUS CHOSE TO LEAVE.

But no. Instead, Jesus chose to leave.

I want you to put yourself in the place of the disciples at that moment. Try again to imagine their confusion. Here is what Acts 1 tells us: "They were looking intently up into the sky as he was going, when suddenly two men dressed in white stood beside them. 'Men of Galilee,' they said, 'why do you stand here looking into the sky?'" (vv. 10–11).

They were astonished, bewildered, dumbfounded, flummoxed, flabbergasted, stunned, and stupefied. *This can't be happening! Now what will we do?* I have this mental picture of them staring blankly with mouths hanging open, looking at the sky. Would any of us have been any less perplexed? But if we are brutally honest about the church today, two thousand years later, many of us are still perplexed and staring blankly at the sky, not quite knowing what to do.

Why did Jesus leave?

When will he come back?

And why were we left behind?

I want to suggest to all followers of Christ that not only does the very mission and purpose of the church depend on the answers to those questions, but so, too, does the purpose and meaning of our individual lives. If we don't understand why Jesus left, then we will never understand the significance of our lives in Christ today.

Now listen because here is the answer: I believe Jesus left because there was something critical he intended for his disciples to do. There was some unfinished business for his church to take care of. He was very specific about just what he wanted done, and he said he would return when that business had been completed. This was not something new that he hadn't told them about. Jesus had spent three years preparing his disciples for this critical mission. He spoke about it constantly, and in his last days with them he promised them that the Holy Spirit, a helper and comforter, would come with power to be their guide.

As I stated earlier, "that thing" that Jesus left us to accomplish involved *establishing and building the kingdom of God on earth.* For three years Jesus had cast his compelling vision of a different kind of kingdom, one that did not involve land, control, or power. It was a vision of a new way for God's people to live under God's authority and rule. It would be different from every other earthly kingdom because it would turn the world's values on their head. It meant revolution; not a revolution of force and violence but a revolution of values and ideas. Just as the fall in the garden had resulted in sin, death, and separation, Jesus' revolution would result in peace, love, and reconciliation. Men and women could now live in a restored relationship, not only with God but also with each other.

The kingdom of God would be comprised of God's people, forgiven and empowered, living according to God's values in communities he called *church.* And Jesus' dreamed-of kingdom would explode like a mustard seed, which begins as "the smallest of all seeds, yet when it grows, it is the largest of garden plants and becomes a tree, so that the birds come and perch in its branches" (Matt. 13:32). I believe Jesus envisioned his new kingdom transforming the world much as the coming of spring transforms the frozen landscape after a long and brutal winter; the snow and ice retreat, the waters flow again, and new life springs forth with an outrageous display of beauty, blossoms, and fruit. The kingdom of God would launch a peaceful assault on the power structures that ruled human empires, but they would resist that assault with violence. The revolution would be bloody, but Jesus assured the disciples that the very gates of hell would not prevail against it. After spending three years equipping them for this great task and showing them the way, he took them up to the Mount of Olives and gave them their marching orders:

"Therefore go and make disciples of all nations, baptizing them in the name of the Father and of the Son and of the Holy Spirit, and teaching them to obey everything I have commanded you. And surely I am with you always, to the very end of the age." (Matt. 28:19–20)

Then Jesus left.

HOW DOES THIS CHANGE THE WORLD?

A penny will hide the biggest star in the universe if you hold it close enough to your eye.[5]—Samuel Grafton

So what does the sudden departure of Jesus two millennia ago have to do with us in the twenty-first century? How should it affect the way we live our lives and our understanding of purpose and meaning? The answer lies in our worldview. As Christians we must see the world and our purpose in it differently than others do. The Brazilian theologian Frei Betto made the observation, "The head thinks where the feet stand."[6] This is profoundly true. If you are North American or European, think of how different your worldview might be if you had been born and raised in Afghanistan, China, Gaza or the West Bank, Russia, North Korea, or Ethiopia.

Different cultures, different economies, different governments, different religious roots, different languages, different foods, different realities. No wonder there is conflict in our world. Even within the USA, someone born and raised in Beverly Hills is going to have a very different worldview from someone raised in rural Mississippi. But geography is not the only thing affecting worldview. Your race, economic status, gender, health, and family situation deeply affect your worldview. Stand in another person's shoes, and your head will think differently. The notion of worldview turns out to be profoundly important as we seek to see the world more like God sees the world. Here's a definition:

worldview: the overall perspective from which one sees and interprets the world

Whether we acknowledge it or not, every one of us has a worldview, and it influences almost every dimension of our lives: our attitudes, our values, our decisions, and our behavior. It influences the way we relate to our neighbors, our communities, and even other nations. It influences our education, our career choices, and the way we use our money. Perhaps most importantly, our worldview even influences the way we understand our faith. That is why the key issue of foundational truth discussed in chapters 1 and 2 is so very important.

So what then do this "forest" or big picture of God's story and the mission of Jesus now tell us? How should they shape and inform Christians in the twenty-first century? I have tried to establish that the very meaning of our lives ultimately depends on understanding the big story that the Author of the universe is writing. If we are characters in this story, created specifically to play a key role, then the ultimate meaning in our lives must be found by discerning where our stories intersect with God's big story. Authors do not create characters with no purpose and no role to play. We looked at the sweep of what God has been doing in our world from creation and the subsequent rift between God and his children through the many overtures of our patient Father God to pursue reconciliation with his children.

Finally, we looked at the dramatic sending of God's own Son, Jesus, on a rescue mission to offer forgiveness and a new way of living in God's kingdom and under God's rule. But remarkably, God chose not to complete the story and tie up all the loose ends with the death and resurrection of his Son. Though Jesus' work of atonement was complete and the forces of evil had been dealt a fatal blow, the story did not end with the resurrection. Instead, the triumph of Jesus from the grave actually started a new chapter. And this new chapter began with the startling decision of Jesus to physically depart, leaving all of his followers behind. His one final act was to give them a mission in the world, an assignment he wanted them to undertake. There were specific tasks he wanted them to finish. And they could accept this mission with all of its consequences or they could walk away and return to their previous lives as fishermen, laborers, and tax collectors. He gave them a choice.

And they made it. They chose obedience. The once scattered and fearful disciples returned to Jerusalem, gathered together and prayed constantly, selected Matthias to replace Judas, and then waited for the gift of the power of the Holy Spirit whom Jesus had promised. Ten days later, just as Jesus had said, the dramatic arrival of the Holy Spirit occurred on Pentecost. From that day on, as we read in the book of Acts, the disciples proclaimed the gospel with revolutionary fervor throughout Jerusalem, Judea, and Samaria, and to the ends of the known world. They were driven. Nothing was more important. Their worldview had been shattered by the amazing events of Jesus' death and resurrection, the new truths he taught about God, and the urgent mission he had given them to accomplish. The gospel, the good news of Jesus as King and Messiah, had implications they now understood. None of them just went back to the lives they'd had before Jesus called them; how could they? That was no longer an option. Everything had changed. The truth had implications.

In the twenty centuries that have followed, nothing has changed, and everything has changed. The vital mission given by Jesus to his followers is still in force. Every single teaching and instruction is still in effect. Truth doesn't change, but the world does. Today our worldviews have been assaulted by a thousand competing influences. It is so very easy to be seduced away from God's truth, even when we have tried to build our foundation on the rock.

As followers of Christ, we should want to embrace his view of the world. We should want to see the world as he must see it, love the world as he loves it, and live in the world as he would want us to live. We should weep for what he weeps for and treasure what he treasures. But if we are to see the world through God's eyes we have to see through different lenses. The truth still has implications.

4

...

MAGIC KINGDOM, TRAGIC KINGDOM, AND THE KINGDOM OF GOD

We see people and things not as they are, but as we are.[1]

—ANTHONY DE MELLO

Most Americans are still drawing some water from the Christian well. But a growing number are inventing their own versions of what Christianity means, abandoning the nuances of traditional theology in favor of religions that stroke their egos and indulge or even celebrate their worst impulses.[2]

—ROSS DOUTHAT

When he saw the crowds, he had compassion
on them, because they were harassed and
helpless, like sheep without a shepherd.

—MATTHEW 9:36

TWO CHURCHES, TWO SUNDAYS

Jesus wept. (John 11:35)

Sunday, December 5, 2010—Port-au-Prince, Haiti

We left early that morning to make the circuitous drive through the rubble-strewn streets of Port-au-Prince to a tent camp a few miles outside of the earthquake-ravaged city. The Corail Camp was just one of the locations to which earthquake refugees had been moved after losing their homes to the devastating January 12 quake. More than two hundred thousand had died that day.[3] Eleven months later, these refugees were the "lucky ones."

We entered the Corail Camp just before 9:00 a.m. Crude tents sprawled as far as the eye could see. Perhaps ten thousand people now lived on this barren patch of dust and dirt, a city of victims, a city of pain and loss. We watched as hundreds of people, dressed in their best white shirts and blouses, found their way through the maze of tents toward a larger tent structure—a makeshift church of scrap lumber, corrugated tin, and UN tarps with a rugged cross atop it. Reneé and I entered this little chapel with perhaps three hundred souls gathered to worship. And worship they did. We were about to learn a transformative lesson about the power of the gospel. For more than two hours they poured out their praise—and their pain—to the One who was pierced for our transgressions and crushed for our iniquities and through whose wounds we are healed.

It was hard to comprehend. *How,* I thought, *could these broken people, who had lost so much, still sing their praises to God?* Sitting in the front row on rough wooden benches were not one but six amputees. Men, women, even a little girl of six; each had lost a limb that day eleven months earlier. Still they sang praises. One strong and dignified woman led the choir; we would later learn that her name was Demosi. She stood out above the others in her bearing, passion, and fervent praise. But she stood on just one leg and clapped with just one arm. Demosi had lost both an arm and a leg on that day. But there she was, leading the choir with energy and clapping her one hand to her shoulder in praise to her Lord. What a beacon, what a light for her people. She who had lost more than all the others, showing them how to live in their new normal.

After two sermons by two pastors and a lengthy period of worship and praise, we walked with Demosi back to her small tent. Eight feet long by six feet wide and perhaps five feet tall, this structure was where this single mother of two now lived and raised her two young girls.

HOW, I THOUGHT, COULD THESE BROKEN PEOPLE, WHO HAD LOST SO MUCH, STILL SING THEIR PRAISES TO GOD?

Sensing we were in the presence of one of God's great servants, Reneé and I sought to understand. Her smile was infectious. Demosi had lost more than just two limbs that day. She had also lost her home and her job and had then spent the next eleven months living in this tiny tent. How, then, could she smile? We could detect no bitterness or depression. Instead, she was grateful—grateful to God because he had spared her life that day. He had given her a second chance. Demosi was filled with hope, not bitterness. She looked forward to receiving a prosthetic arm as she had received a prosthetic leg, to becoming a seller in the market, and perhaps to receiving one of the twenty-by-twenty slab homes World Vision was building nearby.

She was so much better off than those who had died, she told us, because she had been spared and given another chance to raise her girls and serve her Lord. Demosi knew there was work to be done, and she was thankful that God had given her an opportunity to do it. She could now be the light in this dark place, giving hope to the others who had also lost everything. Her suffering could now be used as a blessing to others.

As we sought to understand this great soul, Reneé asked her what she would want us to say about her to people back in America. Demosi smiled her great smile and said, "You tell them you've met Lazarus, and she is back from the dead!" Back from the dead to serve the God she loves with the life she has been given.

Sunday, December 12, 2010—Seattle, Washington

Seven days later we were back in Seattle and on the way to our very different church.

It was Advent, and our sanctuary was stunning: adorned with garlands and poinsettias, candles in each of the stained glass windows, festive banners draped from the ceiling, and two twenty-five-foot Christmas trees up front, each festooned with hundreds of lights. One of the largest pipe organs in America filled the church with beloved Christmas hymns—"Hark! The Herald Angels Sing" and "Joy to the World." The adorable children's choir came in dressed in their Sunday best and sang "Go, Tell It on the Mountain." It was beautiful. On any other Sunday this would have been a blessing to me and Reneé. But somehow, seven days after the worship service in Haiti, it felt wrong.

As the service ended, with lots of smiles and Christmas best wishes, people streamed out of the church and into their cars. Undoubtedly many of our fellow worshippers left the church that day and went to the shopping malls to finish Christmas shopping; others went home to watch football games on their large-screen TVs.

Two different churches on two different Sundays. Something just felt wrong, and I imagined a tear running down the face of God as he looked upon these two very different expressions of his church. This couldn't have been what God had in mind when he sent us into the world to build a new kind of kingdom by establishing his church.

A CLASH OF KINGDOMS

If you are a Christian or even if you are not, you can't help but feel some moral discomfort in reading this little parable about two Sundays and two churches. Human suffering always makes us uncomfortable.

What must God think? What must God feel? How would God want us to respond? Surely my illustration raises profound questions for those of us living and worshipping somewhere like Seattle. But most of us are so far removed from the Demosis of our world that we no longer see them.

Our worldviews have become distorted because of our contexts. Truly, as Frei Betto observed, "The head thinks where the feet stand."[4] How can we compensate for this distortion within our worldviews? How can we hold in one hand the truth that Jesus loves the poor, the widow, and the orphan yet hold in our other hand the tickets to our upcoming Disney vacation? Disparity makes us uncomfortable, especially when we know we could do something about it. So what does our faith mean in the face of this kind of disparity? Again, if we are to build our lives on the foundation of God's truth, we must learn to see the world as he sees it. Should we not weep for what he weeps for and treasure what he treasures? Should we not "seek first his kingdom and his righteousness" (Matt. 6:33) rather than kingdoms of our own making?

> DISPARITY MAKES US UNCOMFORTABLE, ESPECIALLY WHEN WE KNOW WE COULD DO SOMETHING ABOUT IT.

THE MAGIC KINGDOM

Prosperity knits a man to the World. He feels that he is "finding his place in it," while really it is finding its place in him.[5]—C. S. Lewis, *The Screwtape Letters*

Watch out! Be on your guard against all kinds of greed; life does not consist in an abundance of possessions. (Luke 12:15)

As the father of five children, I was often asked by my kids when could we all go to Walt Disney World. Every time one of their classmates would go there on a family vacation, we could expect to hear their impassioned nagging. I thought that I was actually quite shrewd in the way I handled this. I always promised that our family would go as soon as the littlest brother or sister was out of diapers. I explained that it wouldn't be much fun if we had to deal with a baby the whole time we were there. Of course, just as the youngest was turning three and seemed old enough to go, we would have another baby. Sarah, our oldest, finally concluded that she would never go until she was married with children of her own. But when Sarah turned sixteen, our fifth and youngest, Gracie, was turning three and finally old enough to go. And so we went.

Walt Disney World has been called "the happiest place on earth," and its owners take great pains to make sure that every variable is controlled to make your visit the best possible experience. And of course, when you enter the gates, you do enter a magic kingdom that really lives up to your highest expectations, especially if you are a kid. It is a world filled with dazzling attractions: costumed characters, adventure and thrill rides, entertainment experiences, evening fireworks, tempting foods, and astonishing buildings and structures epitomized by Cinderella's Castle. Even for a grown-up it is a pretty exciting experience. Inside the park everything is controlled. The streets are perfectly laid out, and everything is spotlessly clean. Every aspect has been created with enjoyment in mind so that "guests" can leave their cares at the door and escape whatever challenges they have left behind outside the gates to the Magic Kingdom park. Here's an odd thought: What would people be like if they had been born and raised inside the Magic Kingdom park and had never seen the outside world? Since our worldviews are shaped by our contexts, imagine what a distorted worldview they might have.

Any wealthy country can easily produce what I call Magic Kingdom Christians—Christians who have been sheltered and shaped by their affluent culture. Magic Kingdom Christians tend to see the world as a gigantic theme park. It is a world filled with all kinds of rides, attractions, and destinations to enjoy. They live in comfortable houses or apartments and own one or more cars. They have two hundred channels of cable TV. They enjoy going to movies and out to dinner. Magic Kingdom Christians live in a reasonably safe, predictable, and orderly world in which their government oversees the national interests, laws are generally respected and enforced, schools are provided for all children, and the basic necessities of food, water, and medical services are generally available. With those things taken care of, they can now channel their energies enthusiastically toward "the pursuit of happiness."

They may enjoy golfing or skiing or tennis and might very well belong to a health club. They often take wonderful vacations, sometimes to a lake or the shore or a resort nearby but sometimes to places like Hawaii, Paris, Rome, Hong Kong, or Bermuda—exciting destinations with enchanting sights, scrumptious restaurants, luxurious hotels, and fabulous entertainment. For those with more adventurous tastes, there are African safaris, ecotourism, and other exotic expeditions. It's all there to enjoy.

Magic Kingdom Christians live in a world of art, literature, and beauty . . . a world of culture, knowledge, human achievement, and technology . . . a world of business, entrepreneurship, wealth, and capitalism. It's a world of possibilities. Their children have rooms full of toys, video games, computers, and iPhones. They play on soccer, basketball, or baseball teams, depending on the season, and they often take lessons in piano, dance, or kung fu. Magic Kingdom kids are encouraged to dream about what they might become and then to go chase their dreams.

In the Magic Kingdom people struggle with "first-world" problems: where to go for dinner, how to best decorate their homes, where to invest their excess money, what kind of car they will drive, where to go on their vacations, which diet and workout regimen are most effective, and how much money to leave to their children. It is pleasant in the Magic Kingdom. In fact, it's one of the happiest places on earth.

IT IS PLEASANT IN THE MAGIC KINGDOM. IN FACT, IT'S ONE OF THE HAPPIEST PLACES ON EARTH.

Magic Kingdom churches can be quite appealing as well. They sometimes have fabulous buildings, state-of-the-art sound systems, and multimedia projection systems. Sunday morning can feel like a glorious concert or a Broadway production. Some even have coffee bars and restaurants to entice people to come and spend the day. Their youth groups have summer camps and winter ski weekends. Each Sunday a parade of shiny new cars fills their parking lots as the faithful come to worship and praise God for all his goodness. Magic Kingdom churches are great places to escape from all of the ugliness we read about around the world.

Yes, life in the Magic Kingdom can be a pretty sweet ride. The great thing about the Magic Kingdom is that it is open to everyone—that is, as long as you were born in the right country and can afford the price of admission. Living in a Magic Kingdom society profoundly shapes a person's worldview. It affects the way we look at every dimension of our lives: our values, our expectations, our priorities, our money, our politics, and yes, even the way we see our Christian faith.

When we visit Walt Disney World, we understand that we have entered an insulated bubble that does not reflect the reality of the world outside its gates. Those of us who live in Magic Kingdom countries need to understand that we, too, have lived our lives within an insulated bubble that does not reflect the reality of the rest of the world. After an hour or two at Walt Disney World, we can almost forget what lies outside its gates. Imagine how much we can forget if we spend our whole lives there.

THE TRAGIC KINGDOM

There was a rich man who was dressed in purple and fine linen and lived in luxury every day. At his gate was laid a beggar named Lazarus, covered with sores and longing to eat what fell from the rich man's table. (Luke 16:19–21)

Outside the borders of the Magic Kingdom there is another reality. Demosi and her two daughters in Haiti live in what I sometimes call the Tragic Kingdom. They live on the very margins; each day is a struggle just to survive. Many who live here are followers of Christ as well, worshipping and praying to the same God and reading the same Bibles. Let me take you on a brief tour of the Tragic Kingdom.

We can begin with the ravages of natural disasters such as the earthquake that struck Haiti in 2010 and devastated Demosi's family. If you watch or read the news at all, you certainly are aware that in recent years we have witnessed debilitating floods, earthquakes, famines, and tsunamis that have traumatized millions, not to mention the wars, civil wars, and insurgencies that also ravage people's lives. World Vision responds to more than eighty natural and man-made disasters every year, affecting between 100 and 200 million people. But these numbers don't even begin to describe the scope and the scale of the numbing amount of human suffering in our world.[6]

In the Tragic Kingdom millions of people go to bed hungry each night.[7] In fact, about 1 billion people today are chronically short of food, many slowly starving to death. That's three times the population of the United States. More than one out of four of the world's 2 billion children are underweight or stunted.[8] Today, as I write, there are severe food shortages in Somalia, Niger, Mali, North Korea, and Sudan, to name only a few.

Lack of clean water may be an even worse problem for Tragic Kingdom citizens, as 783 million have no access at all. Instead, they walk miles each day to dip their buckets in filthy, bacteria-ridden water that makes them sick and kills their children.[9]

Let's add to our list of woes the violence and tension in the Middle East, nuclear tensions with Iran and North Korea, the ongoing conflict in Darfur, and the twenty-year war in the Congo, where tens of thousands of women have been brutally raped; it's a war that has taken 5 million lives, but most Americans have never heard of it.[10]

In the Tragic Kingdom people struggle with the consequences of ethnic and religious hatreds and violence; the blight of human trafficking; pandemic diseases, such as AIDS, cholera, and tuberculosis; the serious effects of climate change; and the staggering problems faced by the world's 18 million orphaned children.[11]

Are you feeling the heaviness yet? I'm not done. To fully appreciate the sheer dimensions of the suffering in our world, we must understand how broadly the pain extends. More than one-third of the world's population lives on less than two dollars a day, and more than three-quarters live on less than ten dollars a day—three-quarters![12] That bears repeating: 75 percent of the people on our planet survive on less than ten dollars a day. What does this do to alter your worldview? If you earn an income of forty thousand dollars, you make more money than 99 percent of the people in the world. An income of just thirteen thousand dollars places you in the top 10 percent.[13] The Tragic Kingdom is much, much larger than the Magic Kingdom.

And, finally, the most terrible statistic of all: nineteen thousand children under the age of five die every single day of largely *preventable* causes simply because they are poor.[14] That's almost 8 million children every year, one every four seconds. This is something God sees every moment of every day. Is this what you see?

Churches in the Tragic Kingdom often don't even have a building or Bibles to read, let alone sound systems, PowerPoint screens, and latte bars. Some pastors of Tragic Kingdom churches perform funerals more often than they hold worship services—many for toddlers who have died of malnutrition, respiratory infections, or, unbelievably, simple diarrhea. In the Tragic Kingdom there aren't any vacations from the hard work of daily survival. Sick, hungry, downtrodden, and often persecuted and oppressed, these church members gather each week on the very brink of survival to praise God while crying desperately that he will send help.

Surely something is very wrong in a world where these tragedies play out daily and with such staggering frequency. Yet this is the same world into which one half of the world's children will be born, a heartbreaking world that kills their hopes and dreams. Most Magic Kingdom Christians don't know much about the Tragic Kingdom; in fact, they go out of their way to avoid it. That's because it is terribly unpleasant, and even acknowledging it takes them out of their comfort zones. Back in the days when Haiti was a resort destination, vacationers would be picked up at the airport by the resort's shuttle bus. The bus windows were blacked out to prevent people from looking out. It was just too disturbing for the guests to see the awful poverty en route to the beach resorts. Most of us who live in the Magic Kingdom have blacked out our windows too.

THE KINGDOM OF GOD

I have come that they may have life, and have it to the full. (John 10:10)

As you sent me into the world, I have sent them into the world. (John 17:18)

There is a third way. God's way. God's worldview. The kingdom of God.

The world doesn't have to be this way. In fact, God does not want the world to be this way. There is a different way of living, a different vision of human thriving. Jesus called it the kingdom of God.

In the gospel accounts Jesus spoke without ceasing about the kingdom of God or the kingdom of heaven. You could say he was almost obsessed with this single topic. It is mentioned more than 125 times in the New Testament, and most of the mentions are by Jesus himself. If you picked up your Bible and read just the four Gospels, looking only for references to the coming kingdom, you would come to perhaps a surprising conclusion: the central mission of Jesus' incarnation was to launch God's kingdom on earth.

In sermon after sermon, parable after parable, Jesus cast a breathtaking vision of this kingdom to everyone who would listen. It was Jesus' vision of a new way of living, a new dream for human society that turned the values of the world upside down. Men and women would live under God's authority and be governed by God's rules. It was to be a kingdom without borders, a kingdom within kingdoms, which would survive, grow, and flourish apart from the rise and fall of human kingdoms.

Every citizen of this new kingdom would be equally loved and valued: rich or poor, slave or free, Jew or Gentile, male or female, black or white. The rich would share with the poor; the healthy would care for the sick; the strong would protect the weak. His kingdom would be characterized by the attributes and values of God himself: integrity, mercy, compassion, forgiveness, faithfulness, justice, and love. Jesus' followers would love their enemies, be generous with their money and possessions, live lives of integrity, and seek justice for all. It was not some pie-in-the-sky dream of a kingdom in the clouds; it was a concrete vision of communities of God's people established in every nation of the world. God's people living in God's way would be a blessing to their neighbors, resulting in people of all nations being drawn into God's expanding kingdom.

Jesus had come to fulfill the covenant that had been established with Abraham, that through Israel all nations would be blessed. The Messiah had come to provide open access to God's kingdom—one not based on land, politics, power, and dominion but a kingdom based on God's truth and God's values.

Just how central was the idea of the kingdom to Jesus' thinking? In Luke 4, after Jesus had performed several miracles, the people of Capernaum tried to get him to stay with them, but Jesus rebuked them, saying, "I must proclaim the good news of the kingdom of God to the other towns also, *because that is why I was sent*" (Luke 4:43, emphasis mine).

Did you catch that? Jesus was sent to "proclaim the good news of the kingdom of God."

I will write much more about the kingdom of God and the invitation of God in chapters 5 through 7, but let me point you now to two more references. The first is from Acts 1: "After his suffering, he presented himself to them and gave many convincing proofs that he was alive. He appeared to them over a period of forty days *and spoke about the kingdom of God*" (Acts 1:3, emphasis mine).

Jesus had risen from the dead and had just forty days left with his disciples, but the key thing he wanted to speak to them about was *the kingdom of God*.

Then, as we saw in the last chapter, before Jesus left, he commissioned his followers to take this good news of the kingdom of God to the whole world and to make it a reality. He essentially said, "Go, do what I've told you to do, teach what I've taught you to teach, act as I've taught you to act, and love as I've shown you to love. Build my kingdom in all the nations. This is what you were made to do" (Matt. 28:19–20, author's paraphrase).

Let me underscore the breathtaking significance of this. The Son of God, the Creator of the universe, the Author of life, gave this specific assignment to every one of his followers just before he left. And he said he would return when it was completed. The implication was that this specific command of Jesus not only would become the central mission of our lives but also would provide for us the deepest purpose and meaning we seek for our lives. Just as God created birds to fly and fish to swim, he created us to live as citizens in his emerging kingdom and to invite others to join us. That is the assignment he gave to us. The corollary of this is that if we are not fully engaged in this great mission of God in our world, we will miss the very thing he created us to do.

JUST AS GOD CREATED BIRDS TO FLY AND FISH TO SWIM, HE CREATED US TO LIVE AS CITIZENS IN HIS EMERGING KINGDOM AND TO INVITE OTHERS TO JOIN US.

Jesus was clear. He did not commission us to return to our old lives as if nothing had happened. He did not commission us to become financially independent and retire to Boca Raton. And he did not commission us to simply go to church on Sundays and sing songs. He called us to go into the world and change it by proclaiming the good news of the kingdom of God, modeling a different vision of community, and inviting others to join it. It was nothing less than a calling to partner with God in establishing a new world order. That was the mission.

The first disciples did change the world. In fact, no movement in the history of human civilization has changed the world more profoundly than that born of the small band of men and women who followed the carpenter from Nazareth. Within three hundred years the gospel revolution had conquered the Roman Empire and changed the known world. Their radical lifestyles were characterized by a sense of urgency and divine purpose. Nothing was more important, and no price was too high to pay. Churches were established wherever the gospel was preached, and we are told that the number of believers grew geometrically. The revolution swept through the Roman Empire like a virus. The early church was aggressively opposed by the Jewish authorities and brutally persecuted by Rome. As evidence of this, history records that all but one of the twelve disciples died as martyrs for their faith. The revolution was costly. But the exuberant expansion of the church dramatically altered the course of world history as it spread across the Middle East, East Asia, Europe, and North Africa. The kingdom of God that Jesus imagined had established outposts and penetrated thousands of national, tribal, and ethnic groups across the globe. Those first disciples had fought the good fight, run the good race, and passed the baton to the next generation and that generation to the next.

Two thousand years later we now hold the baton. But the passion and vision seem to have faded. In large swaths of the church, the fire has died down, and the trail seems to have grown cold. It should be disturbing to us that somehow this central mission of Christ, this compelling vision of God's kingdom breaking through, this call to overthrow the values that govern human society, this radical call to discipleship, has become tamed, domesticated, and polite. In the twenty-first century the revolution has dissipated because we have deserted the front lines and retreated to the safety of our careers, our families, and our one-hour Sunday services. What if Peter and Andrew had returned to their fishing, Matthew to his tax collecting, Paul to his prestigious role as a Pharisee? Many of our churches are no longer the boot camps established to equip us for battle; they're spiritual spas designed to enhance our well-being and give us a glow at the beginning of our week. We sing a few songs, shake a few hands, and listen to a pleasant homily. The call of Jesus to lay down our lives, take up our crosses, and share in his suffering seldom echoes from our pulpits.

We, as followers of Jesus Christ, have failed to do this one thing he commanded us to do. We have failed to obey Christ's commands to live radically different lives, to build and establish the kingdom of God, to make disciples of all nations, and to demonstrate his love to a hurting world. And in failing to do these things, we have failed not just our Lord but also the Demosis of this world . . . and we have failed ourselves. Christ did not call us to retreat from the world's pain but to enter it. He called us to go. The twenty-first-century church has everything required to finish the job—the resources, the knowledge, and the mandate. But the great mission given to us by Christ lies *unfinished*.

It is time to relaunch.

5

. . .

THE MISSION OF GOD

And this gospel of the kingdom will be
preached in the whole world as a testimony to
all nations, and then the end will come.

—MATTHEW 24:14

God leaves us here because He has a mission for us to fulfill.
We aren't here by accident; neither are we here simply to
enjoy the good things life has to offer. We are here because
God put us here, and He has a sovereign purpose in keeping
us here. It's true for us as individuals, and it's true for His
body, the Church, in all of its fullness. As Jesus prayed just
before His arrest and trial, "I am not praying that You take
them out of the world . . . As You sent Me into the world,
I also have sent them into the world" (John 17:15, 18).[1]

—BILLY GRAHAM

"The time has come," he said. "The kingdom of God
has come near. Repent and believe the good news!"

—MARK 1:15

How is it that so many of us have missed this central message of Jesus—
that the kingdom has come near? These were the very first words of
Jesus recorded in the very earliest gospel, the gospel of Mark. It is first an
announcement of an astonishing new development (the kingdom of heaven
has come near) followed by the response required (repent and believe the
good news). Just five verses earlier Mark tells us that immediately after John
baptized Jesus "he saw heaven being torn open" (Mark 1:10). In a very real
way God demonstrated that he was breaking into human history in a literal
as well as spiritual sense; the kingdom of heaven was now accessible, torn
open, and his Son, Jesus, was making this possible. Jesus' call to repent was
more than merely a call to feel remorse or regret for our sins; it was a call to
change our minds, to exchange our agenda for his; it was a call to reorder
our lives in the face of God's dramatic news that his kingdom was now
available to all. Eugene Peterson paraphrases Mark 1:15 this way: "Time's
up! God's kingdom is here. Change your life and believe the Message"
(MSG). Jesus called us not just to believe but also to change our lives.

I argued in the last chapter that Jesus seemed to be obsessed with this
notion of the coming of the kingdom of God. He spoke about it inces-
santly, illustrated its characteristics using multiple metaphors, and literally
declared that the main mission of his incarnation and death on the cross
was to open the way for men and women to gain access to God's kingdom.
Then before he left, he commissioned his disciples to take his kingdom
message to the four corners of the earth, to make more disciples, and to
establish kingdom outposts called churches wherever they went. So why is
it that the kingdom of God plays so small a role in the thinking of twenty-
first-century Christians? In all my years as a Christian, I have listened to
thousands of sermons, and I can't remember even one that fully explained
to me that the central mission of Christ and the purpose he gave to his
church was to proclaim, establish, and build God's kingdom on earth. Nor
have I ever heard that the sole purpose of my life as a follower of Jesus is to
join him in this mission; that this is the very reason I was created. Somehow
that baby got thrown out with the bathwater in my Christian education.

I want to be careful here, not to be too harsh on the earnest and sacrificial efforts of the church to build, establish, and model Christ's king-dom either now or in the past. Today there are more than 2 billion people who identify themselves as Christians in our world, making the Christian faith the largest of the world religions.[2] It would be virtually impossible to overestimate the cumulative impact for good in our world that followers of Christ have had in his name over the centuries. And while it is popu-lar to criticize Christians for the evil done in the name of Christ, any truly objective analysis of the positive influence of Christians on human society would decisively dwarf the negatives. But we also have to be honest and ask whether the twenty-first-century church is as committed to Christ's kingdom-building mission as was the church of the first century. We live in a unique time in history, in

> THE CENTRAL MISSION OF CHRIST AND THE PURPOSE HE GAVE TO HIS CHURCH WAS TO PROCLAIM, ESTABLISH, AND BUILD GOD'S KINGDOM ON EARTH.

which virtually every dimension of human endeavor has been advanced: communications, travel, education, medical solutions, agriculture, nutri-tion, child development, economics, and even government. Christians themselves have more access to Scripture and biblical teaching in hundreds of languages than in any previous generation as well. Today more is possible than ever before.

So why then has progress stalled, particularly in the churches of the global North? I want to argue that we have misunderstood one of the core tenets of our faith—the gospel story itself—and that this misunderstand-ing has derailed the achievement of Christ's Great Commission. We have misunderstood the gospel to be simply the good news that our sins can be forgiven and we can enter eternal life by believing in Jesus Christ, period. And while this is an important element of the gospel, it is not the whole gospel.

THE HOLE IN OUR GOSPEL

In my first book, *The Hole in Our Gospel*, I argued that most American Christians have embraced a diminished view of the fullness of the gospel, or good news, of the story and message of Christ. I argued that if we saw the gospel as simply a quick transaction with God in order to have our sins forgiven so that we might get our ticket to heaven, we had embraced not the whole of the gospel but rather a gospel with a hole in it—a fairly gaping hole. Yet that is exactly how many Christians view the gospel of Christ. I do a deal with God, buy the fire insurance policy, put it in my drawer, and then I can go back to the party. Sure, it wouldn't be a bad idea to go to church now and then to dip my feet into spiritual waters, and it wouldn't hurt to pray from time to time, but, basically, with my salvation secured I can now get on with my life. This is what Dallas Willard refers to as the "gospel of sin-management."[3] We simply have a personal sin problem, and this gospel offers a quick and easy solution. Just take the antidote and get back to living your life. I am a bit less polite and call it a dumbing down of the gospel.

Scot McKnight talks about the difference between a *disciple* and a *decider*: "Most of evangelism today focuses on getting someone to make a decision; the apostles, however, were obsessed with making disciples."[4] Jesus called us to be disciples and make disciples, not just be deciders.

Deciders just believe the right things; disciples seek to do the right things. Disciples are dedicated to learning their Master's truths so they can imitate their Master's life. Disciples seek to embrace their Master's mission and serve their Master's purposes. Disciples try to plan their entire lives around Jesus' teaching and commands. Deciders have their own plans for their lives and invite Jesus to bless them. Jesus had some harsh things to say about deciders.

"Why do you call me, 'Lord, Lord,' and do not do what I say?" (Luke 6:46)

"Not everyone who says to me, 'Lord, Lord,' will enter the kingdom of heaven, but only he who does the will of my Father who is in heaven. Many will say to me on that day, 'Lord, Lord, did we not prophesy in your name and in your name drive out demons and in your name perform many miracles?' Then I will tell them plainly, 'I never knew you. Away from me, you evildoers!'" (Matt. 7:21–23)

Deciders are like those in Jesus' parable of the sower who "hear the word; but the worries of this life, the deceitfulness of wealth and the desires for other things come in and choke the word, making it unfruitful" (Mark 4:18–19). Deciders have repeated the sinner's prayer and have simply said "I do" or "I will" to the Master's invitation. But merely saying the sinner's prayer no more leads to a life-changing relationship with Christ than simply saying "I do" leads to a long, successful marriage.

A marriage is built on thousands upon thousands of daily expressions of love and sacrifices made for the ones whom we love. In strong marriages we reorder our entire lives around the desires and expectations of our spouses. Everything changes. We can't just say "I do" and then do whatever we please. Can we put ourselves first, be unfaithful whenever we want, spend our time and our money to suit our whims, ignore the deepest desires of our spouses, and still claim that we have fulfilled our wedding vows? Of course not. Neither can we say "I do" to Jesus and then live our lives ignoring his desire for obedience and service. There are dramatic and serious implications to saying "I do" to our spouses,

IT IS NOT ENOUGH TO BE SIMPLY A DECIDER; JESUS WANTS DISCIPLES.

and there are dramatic and serious implications to saying "I do" to the Lord of the universe. It is not enough to be simply a decider; Jesus wants disciples.

This same sin-management understanding of the gospel also dumbs down the Great Commission. If the gospel just requires someone to make a decision, then the Great Commission is about making more deciders, not disciples—it's about selling more fire insurance policies.

> "Therefore go and make *deciders* of all nations, baptizing them in the name of the Father and of the Son and of the Holy Spirit, and teaching them that obeying everything I have commanded you is optional. And surely this fire insurance policy will remain in force always, even to the very end of the age."

Now it's simple. We don't have to bother with that part about "make disciples" and "teaching them to obey everything I have commanded"

(Matt. 28:19–20). We can accept Jesus as Savior, but we don't have to accept him as Lord. This dumbed-down gospel is a lot easier to swallow than the high-fiber, whole-grain version. It's a gospel quite comfortable with the status quo. It doesn't make any demands on our lifestyle or behavior, and it lets us do whatever we want with our money; feeding the hungry, clothing the naked, caring for the sick, or taking a stand against injustice in our world—all strictly optional. If only the disciples had understood this, they surely wouldn't have had to give their lives for the cause. Why so radical? Selling cheap tickets to eternal life needn't upset anyone. All they had to do was just simply say "I do."

There's only one problem with this gospel; it wasn't the gospel Jesus preached, and it lacks the power to change the world and win it for Christ. What happened to Jesus' vision of the kingdom of God coming now, on earth as it is in heaven? What happened to the great mission of Christ to transform human society, model the values of God's kingdom, make disciples of all nations, love our neighbors, and care

WITHOUT REAL DISCIPLES THE REVOLUTION DIES.

for the poor? And what about his assertion that his church would storm the very gates of hell? What happened to the revolution? Surrendered. That is why it is so very important to get the gospel right, the *whole* gospel, because without real disciples the revolution dies.

I have to make a confession here. I spent most of my Christian life understanding very little about the significance of God's kingdom to the mission of the church. I had also distilled the gospel down to the simple good news that Christ had died for my sins and I could now be forgiven. And because I was forgiven, after I died, I would be admitted into God's kingdom. I had reduced the Great Commission down to the idea that all Christ wanted us to do was to tell others the same good news. I had embraced the call to make a *decision* for Christ rather than the call to become a *disciple* of Christ. To be sure, becoming a disciple of Christ begins with a decision, but it must be followed by a radically new way of living under God's authority, God's truth, and God's values.

In other words, the good news of the gospel is not that I can enter God's kingdom when I die; it is that Christ's death and resurrection opens the kingdom of God to me *now*. For the first time since the fall, men and women now have direct access to God and can live under God's rule with God's Holy Spirit in their hearts to guide them and teach them. The good news of the gospel is that the doors to God's kingdom have been flung open, and we have all been invited in!

> For he has rescued us from the dominion of darkness and brought us into the kingdom of the Son he loves, in whom we have redemption, the forgiveness of sins. (Col. 1:13–14)

THE WHOLE GOSPEL

So if the gospel is more than just a fire insurance policy or a sin-management strategy, what is it? The gospel is the whole story of Jesus, that God's kingdom has now come and that Jesus is king. It is the whole story I told in chapter 2:

> The story of Scripture is the story of a Father's love for his children. It is the story of a Father faithfully reaching out to the children who rejected him. It is the story of a loving God who never gives up.

Ever since the garden of Eden and the broken relationship caused by the sin of Adam and Eve, God has longed to reestablish direct fellowship and communion with men and women. He has desired to reconcile and restore his relationship with his children. If you think about it, every overture made by God from that moment forward was an invitation, calling his children back into relationship with their Father.

EVER SINCE THE GARDEN OF EDEN . . . GOD HAS LONGED TO REESTABLISH DIRECT FELLOWSHIP AND COMMUNION WITH MEN AND WOMEN.

- Abraham was called out of the nations to become the father of a new people, Israel: a people whom God would invite back into fellowship and who would live again as God's children.

- Moses rescued Israel from captivity and called them out of one kingdom, Egypt, to become a new kind of kingdom: a kingdom of God's children living in accordance with God's truth.
- The Law was given to them at Sinai, constituting the legal system of God's new kingdom and providing the moral and ethical guidelines that would govern them.
- Israel was then cleansed in the wilderness and led to a promised land, a place where God's new kingdom could thrive and flourish.
- First the tabernacle and then the temple were established that God might again dwell in the midst of his children.
- Priests were established and animal sacrifices were ordained to remind God's children that their sins were serious and still required atonement.
- Kings were anointed to govern God's children with righteousness and justice and to uphold God's laws and values.
- Prophets were sent again and again to call God's children to obedience and to warn them about the consequences of disobedience.

I want you to see that every one of these gestures was an attempt by God to give his children a second chance, and a third and a fourth, to live again in harmony with their Father in a way that would enrich their lives as they were meant to be lived. Every overture was a call away from the kingdoms that men had established to rule the world and into the kingdom that God sought to establish, in which he would reign with love and justice. And each time God's children rejected his offer.

I don't know why God chose to do this so many times over so many years. Surely he knew what the outcome would be. I imagine that God did it so we might realize the futility of our efforts to earn our way back into fellowship with him. As a parent I sometimes allowed my children to do things their way just so they could learn for themselves that their way was not the right way or the best way. Sometimes those lessons are only learned the hard way.

So, finally, after hundreds of years of failed attempts by God's children to establish a kingdom in which they might live under God's rule under God's terms, remarkably, God intervened. The arrival of the kingdom of God in Jesus was like that of a government in exile breaking through to establish its rightful authority, to overthrow the established regimes and liberate the people living in bondage. God undertook a rescue mission that would offer his children a final chance to be reconciled. The rescue mission would leave nothing to chance. God would lead it by taking on human form; he would send his own Son to accomplish it. And it would be costly.

> You see, at just the right time, when we were still powerless, Christ died for the ungodly. Very rarely will anyone die for a righteous man, though for a good man someone might possibly dare to die. (Rom. 5:6–7)

Like Moses before him, Jesus would lead his people out of captivity. His blood, shed on Passover, would protect them from the angel of death just as the lamb's blood had protected Israel's firstborn on that first Passover. And just like Moses, Jesus would lead his people to the promised land, where they could finally establish a kingdom under God's rule. But this time the result would be different.

God's invitation to enter his kingdom was something the Jewish prophets had dreamed of and longed for. It was something new, something not before possible. For the first time since the fall in the garden, it was an opportunity to become truly reconciled with God. But it was not possible until God made it possible. All previous attempts at reconciliation had failed because they had relied on man's efforts. This time it could succeed for three reasons. First, God removed the dividing barrier that had separated us from his love in the past by offering a full pardon for our sins and substituting his Son to pay our penalty. Second, the life and teachings of Jesus modeled how men and women could enter his kingdom and live differently than they had before. And third, God's Spirit would now literally dwell within us, giving us the power to actually live this way.

This third point is no small thing. Ever since the fall the relationship between God and men and women had been broken. We no longer had unfettered access to God. In the Old Testament God's presence was confined symbolically to the holy of holies, behind a thick curtain within the temple. A priesthood was established to be the intermediary between God and man. And only the high priest of Israel on the Day of Atonement each year, after sacrificing a perfect lamb, could enter the holy of holies in God's presence to seek the forgiveness of sins for the nation.

Just as God had announced at Jesus' baptism that the kingdom of heaven had now been torn open, so, too, would Jesus' atoning death for our sins tear open and restore open access to God by removing the barrier that separated us—our sins. So at the very moment of Christ's death on the cross—the perfect sacrifice—something astounding happened in the temple in Jerusalem:

> It was now about noon, and darkness came over the whole land until three in the afternoon, for the sun stopped shining. And *the curtain of the temple was torn in two*. Jesus called out with a loud voice, "Father, into your hands I commit my spirit." When he had said this, he breathed his last. (Luke 23:44–46, emphasis mine)

The curtain, the temple, and its priests and sacrifices were no longer needed. Nothing now separated God from his children. The perfect sacrifice had been made, and the payment for sin had been paid in full. Now men and women could enter freely into God's presence and live securely under his authority. At Pentecost, just a few weeks later, the Holy Spirit of God came with power. Now God would dwell within each of his children. Our bodies, not the temple, would become the new dwelling place of the Spirit of God, and we could now enter fully into God's kingdom in a new relationship with God, to live again in harmony with his purposes. We had been rescued.

NOTHING NOW SEPARATED GOD FROM HIS CHILDREN.

Consequently, you are no longer foreigners and aliens, but fellow citizens with God's people and members of God's household, built on the foundation of the apostles and prophets, with Christ Jesus himself as the chief cornerstone. (Eph. 2:19–20)

The gospel of the kingdom, then, is the whole story of Jesus:

- the Messiah, the king of Israel, sent by the Father, has come
- he fulfilled God's promise that through Israel all the nations would be blessed
- he has died so our sins are forgiven
- he has risen, so death is defeated
- he has given us direct access to the kingdom of God, the rule of God in our lives through the Holy Spirit
- he has taught us how to live
- he has commanded us to obey
- he has invited us to join him in proclaiming and establishing his kingdom in all the world:
  - announcing God's forgiveness,
  - demonstrating God's love,
  - upholding God's justice, and
  - inviting others to join his kingdom
- he has commanded us to "go and make disciples of all nations" (Matt. 28:19)

The gospel is not just one part of this story; it is the whole story. It is the whole story of Jesus as the fulfillment of God's promise to Abraham that his descendants would be a blessing to the nations. The "gospel," or "good news" of the kingdom, was the story that the king had come and that the kingdom was now open and available to all. We cannot cherry-pick the parts we like and ignore the parts we don't. Forgiveness and salvation are crucial parts of the whole story of Jesus, but they are not the

THE GOSPEL . . . IS
THE WHOLE STORY
OF JESUS AS THE
FULFILLMENT OF
GOD'S PROMISE TO
ABRAHAM THAT
HIS DESCENDANTS
WOULD BE A
BLESSING TO
THE NATIONS.

whole story. We cannot limit Jesus to being our Savior but not our Lord and King. When we say yes to Jesus, we say yes to his forgiveness, but we also say yes to his commands and yes to his kingdom. We merge our stories into his story and join the unfolding plan of God to establish and grow his kingdom—"Thy kingdom come. Thy will be done in earth, as it is in heaven" (Matt. 6:10 KJV). We must renounce our citizenship in this world and irrevocably enter his kingdom.

6

. . .

THE INVITATION OF GOD

It may be hard for an egg to turn into a bird: it would
be a jolly sight harder for it to learn to fly while
remaining an egg. We are like eggs at present. And
you cannot go on indefinitely being just an ordinary,
decent egg. We must be hatched or go bad.[1]

—C. S. LEWIS

Who then is the faithful and wise manager, whom the
master puts in charge of his servants to give them their food
allowance at the proper time? It will be good for that servant
whom the master finds doing so when he returns. Truly I
tell you, he will put him in charge of all his possessions.

—LUKE 12:42–44

In Philippians, Paul speaks of Jesus' followers as citizens of heaven: "Above
all, you must live as citizens of heaven, conducting yourselves in a manner
worthy of the Good News about Christ" (1:27 NLT). This metaphor is helpful
in understanding God's expectations of us as we seek to live as good citizens

of the kingdom of God. Persons who apply for citizenship in the United States first make a *decision* that they want to leave their former countries behind and become citizens of this new country called the United States. After satisfying the requirements of citizenship, they are then issued a certificate of citizenship, which gains them free access not only to their new country but also to all of the rights and privileges of its citizens with the expectation that they will strive to fulfill the responsibilities citizens are expected to bear. These include abiding by the laws of the land, paying taxes to support the costs of the country, and contributing to the collective good—for example, working, volunteering, raising responsible children, and being good neighbors. But imagine for a moment if a person, having decided to become a citizen of the United States, never moved in, never took up residence, never took advantage of the many rights and privileges of citizenship, and never performed any of the duties of citizenship. He has his certificate, but he has chosen not to use it. He is, in effect, still living as a citizen of his former country. Technically, he has become an American, but he is so in name only.

Regarding entrance into the kingdom of God, Jesus' death on the cross to atone for our sins made it possible for us to get our "certificate of citizenship" in his kingdom. But his expectation is that we will not only move in but also renounce our former citizenship; that we will become fully engaged citizens, enjoying our new rights and privileges, abiding by the laws of his kingdom, contributing to its growth and prosperity, and even becoming its ambassadors to those who live outside of God's kingdom. Jesus wants us to enter into a new way of living in the here and now, empowered by the Holy Spirit, living under God's rule and authority, forsaking the influence of other kingdoms, and taking up the full responsibilities of our citizenship. Tragically, many Christians make the decision, get their certificates, but never really move in to become full citizens of God's kingdom.

Perhaps an even better metaphor is that of enlisting in the army during a time of war. When a soldier enlists, he (or she) makes a commitment to turn his life over to a higher authority. From that date forward, everything about his life is governed by that authority. He doesn't get to decide where he will live, how he will spend his days, or what his priorities will be. All of those former rights are relinquished at the time of enlistment. He goes where the army sends him, wears what the army gives him, is trained according to the army's purposes, and embraces the army's goals and mission. His mission is to win the war, and he is expected to die for the cause if necessary.

When one enlists in the military, he gives up his rights as they pertain to his career, time, money, priorities, and even his family and identity. Imagine someone enlisting and then informing his superiors that he has decided to live in Hawaii, work as a stockbroker, join a country club, and take a monthlong vacation every year to travel abroad. Can you spell *court-martial*?

> Join with me in suffering, like a good soldier of Christ Jesus. No one serving as a soldier gets entangled in civilian affairs, but rather tries to please his commanding officer. (2 Tim. 2:3–4)

How much more serious, then, is our commitment to follow Jesus Christ, to embrace his mission in the world, and to take up our crosses daily as we serve and obey the One who laid down his life so that we might be able to live in his kingdom? It is not enough for us to simply enlist; we are called to join the battle.

IT IS NOT ENOUGH FOR US TO SIMPLY ENLIST; WE ARE CALLED TO JOIN THE BATTLE.

So let's now look at what we have enlisted in. Just what is involved with this business of building and establishing God's kingdom? There are three dimensions for us to consider in answering the question of just what God expects of us as followers of Jesus Christ who are committed to his mission in the world. These are the things that separate *deciders* from *disciples*:

1. SUBMITTING TO GOD'S RULE IN OUR LIVES

"Whoever finds their life will lose it, and whoever loses their life for my sake will find it." (Matt. 10:39)

It begins with our own personal transformations. Jesus taught us a very different way to live based on his truth, his values, and his priorities. We begin by submitting, by replacing our wills with God's will for our lives. We commit to the lifelong process of becoming more like Christ. We make that commitment to be his disciple the top priority in our lives, organizing every other aspect of our lives to support that goal.

When I committed my life to Christ at the age of twenty-three, I understood that if Jesus was, in fact, God's Son, nothing in my life could ever be the same again. I understood that this new realization required me to order my entire life around God's truth. Jesus couldn't be just another person I admired, such as Martin Luther King Jr., Abraham Lincoln, or Bishop Desmond Tutu. No, the Son of God is in an entirely different category. He doesn't just speak the truth; he is the truth. He didn't just live an admirable life; he led the perfect life and also gave us the instructions we needed to live as God intended for us to live. He not only knows us intimately at the deepest level; he literally brought us into existence and wrote the owner's manual. He demanded to become my North Star as I journeyed through life, providing meaning and purpose to everything I now do. And he invited me to become his partner in offering life in the kingdom of God to others. This is how Paul described the One who has invited us to live in his kingdom under his rule:

> The Son is the image of the invisible God, the firstborn over all creation. For in him all things were created: things in heaven and on earth, visible and invisible, whether thrones or powers or rulers or authorities; all things have been created through him and for him. He is before all things, and in him all things hold together. And he is the head of the body, the church; he is the beginning and the firstborn from among the dead, so that in everything he might have the supremacy. For God was pleased to have all his fullness dwell in him, and through him to reconcile to himself all things, whether things on earth or things in heaven, by making peace through his blood, shed on the cross. (Col. 1:15–20)

So we need to dispense with any notion that we can take this Jesus on our own terms, that we can simply add him to the structure of our lives, fit him into our plans, worship him once a week for an hour or so, and offer him a prayer whenever we find ourselves needing something. No, Jesus demands the total commitment of our lives in his service. We are called to enlist in his army and lay down every other priority in our lives at his feet. Our ambitions, our careers, our relationships, our possessions, even our families must be laid at his feet to do with as he wishes.

John Stott, the eminent theologian and church leader, whose book *Basic Christianity* was instrumental in my own coming to faith, came to this simple conclusion in the last book he wrote before his death:

> I want to share with you where my mind has come to rest as I approach the
> end of my pilgrimage on earth. It is this: God wants his people to become
> like Christ, for Christlikeness is the will of God for the people of God.[2]

That was his simple summary of the sole purpose of mankind. Indeed, once we understand that Jesus came to inaugurate God's kingdom on earth and that he has invited us to join him, it has profound consequences for all of us as Jesus' followers. Simply stated, living in the kingdom of God means we must try to live as Jesus lived, love what Jesus loved, and obey what Jesus taught.

2. FORMING COMMUNITIES GOVERNED BY GOD'S VALUES

> Every day they continued to meet together in the temple courts. They
> broke bread in their homes and ate together with glad and sincere hearts,
> praising God and enjoying the favor of all the people. And the Lord added
> to their number daily those who were being saved. (Acts 2:46–47)

Every kingdom is organized into communities—states, counties, cities, villages, neighborhoods. The church is the organizing principle of God's kingdom. The local church creates the framework for followers of Jesus to come together around worship, discipleship, and mission. These church communities, because they seek to live under God's rule and according to God's truth, should be shining examples of a radically different way for people to live.

Jesus cast a vision of how men and women could live in this new kingdom reality. The Sermon on the Mount, by itself, represents perhaps the most revolutionary vision ever cast for the thriving of human society living in harmony with God. Along with the rest of Scripture, it serves as a blueprint for this new way to live in God's kingdom.

In his discourse Jesus starts by encouraging the down-and-out—those who mourn and suffer, the meek, the merciful who hunger and thirst for righteousness, the persecuted, and the peacemakers. In his church they— the excluded ones, the insignificant ones—are now included, not just the rich, the powerful, and the prominent, as is so typical of kingdoms established by men. He goes on to redefine right and wrong, suggesting that not only are murder, adultery, divorce, and revenge wrong, but the very attitudes of anger, lust, and selfishness that lay behind the actions are also sins. Jesus sets a new standard for purity that requires us not just to be clean on the outside (legalism) but rather to be pure on the inside (sanctified). It is not just the outward action that matters to God but also the inner attitude of the heart and spirit. He tells us that we are to love not just those who love us but our enemies as well. We are to walk the extra mile, turn the other cheek, and pray for those who persecute us. He addresses generosity and compassion. Jesus teaches us to store up real treasure in heaven by not storing up earthly treasure for ourselves. We are to be generous with our money and care for the needy.

Lastly, we are told not to worry but rather trust God and not judge others but first look to our own lives. He summarizes all of this by stating that all the Law and the Prophets can be summed up by this: "in everything, do to others what you would have them do to you" (Matt. 7:12). Jesus finishes his discourse with the story we looked at in previous chapters, of the man who built his house on the foundation of rock because he heard Jesus' words *and* put them into practice: "The rain came down, the streams rose, and the winds blew and beat against that house; yet it did not fall, because it had its foundation on the rock" (Matt. 7:25). The Sermon on the Mount encapsulates the heart of the good news of God's kingdom, a new vision of human flourishing in which men and women can build a different kind of community based on the foundation of God's truth, governed by God's principles, unified by God's Spirit, and committed to being God's ambassadors in the world.

> "I will put my law in their minds
>   and write it on their hearts.
> I will be their God,
>   and they will be my people." (Jer. 31:33)

Authentic churches truly living together in this way offer a radically different and beguilingly attractive alternative to every other model of human community. Indeed, we are told that the first-century church was compellingly attractive in just this way:

> They devoted themselves to the apostles' teaching and to fellowship, to the breaking of bread and to prayer. Everyone was filled with awe at the many wonders and signs performed by the apostles. All the believers were together and had everything in common. They sold property and possessions to give to anyone who had need. Every day they continued to meet together in the temple courts. They broke bread in their homes and ate together with glad and sincere hearts, praising God and enjoying the favor of all the people. And the Lord added to their number daily those who were being saved. (Acts 2:42–47)

3. GOING INTO THE WORLD AS GOD'S AMBASSADORS

> We are therefore Christ's ambassadors, as though God were making his appeal through us. (2 Cor. 5:20)

The third dimension for us to consider is how people of the kingdom, organized into communities of the kingdom, must now embrace the mission of the kingdom. I want to again underscore that the entire story of Scripture is that of a rescue mission—God seeking to reconcile and restore fellowship with his children. The very incarnation of Christ and his resolute march to the cross were solely conceived by God as a mission to rescue all of humanity once and for all from their bondage to sin and rebellion. By tearing open the kingdom of heaven and ripping asunder the curtain in the temple, Christ literally threw open the gates to God's kingdom; then he invited people to come in. And we who have responded to Christ's invitation, we who have been rescued and have become disciples, we who have chosen to live under God's rule in kingdom communities called churches are now called to go and invite others to come too. As World Vision's late president Ted Engstrom loved to say, "Our job is simply to populate the kingdom of heaven."

WE . . . ARE NOW CALLED TO GO AND INVITE OTHERS TO COME TOO.

So let's return to the question, "Why did Jesus leave?" The answer is that he left so we could go into all the world and invite people to come—to expand his rescue mission. Just before he went to the cross, Jesus prayed for his disciples:

> "My prayer is not for them alone. I pray also for those who will believe in me through their message, that all of them may be one, Father, just as you are in me and I am in you. . . . Then the world will know that you sent me and have loved them even as you have loved me." (John 17:20–21, 23)

So in a real sense the verses we know as the Great Commission command us to join God's rescue mission by inviting people in all nations to become citizens of God's expanding kingdom.

Finally, let's look more closely at this last charge by Jesus to his followers in the context of Jesus' larger message of God's coming kingdom. It is found in multiple passages but is most often quoted from Matthew 28:19–20. I have also included Matthew 24:14, which speaks more clearly of the "gospel of the kingdom":

"And this gospel of the kingdom will be preached in the whole world as a testimony to all nations, and then the end will come. . . . Therefore go and make disciples of all nations, baptizing them in the name of the Father and of the Son and of the Holy Spirit, and teaching them to obey everything I have commanded you. And surely I am with you always, to the very end of the age." (Matt. 24:14; 28:19–20)

The Commission involves . . .

- ANNOUNCING the gospel, or "good news" of the kingdom, the whole story of God, that the king has come, our sins are forgiven, and a new way of living under God's rule as citizens of God's kingdom is now open and available to all;
- INVITING people to enter the kingdom of God by believing in Christ and his kingdom and repenting—reordering their lives around the values and priorities of the kingdom;
- DISCIPLING AND TEACHING these new citizens of the kingdom how to live differently and how to obey the teachings of Christ;
- BAPTIZING THEM IN THE NAME OF JESUS so that they might be filled with the Holy Spirit, connecting them directly to God in relationship and guiding them into this new way of living; and
- ESTABLISHING outposts of the kingdom (churches), communities of kingdom citizens throughout the nations of the world, that will also embrace and implement the coming kingdom.

Even when we read perhaps the strongest statement in Scripture of salvation by faith alone and not by works, we find in the very next verse the outline of our kingdom mission to then go and do good works:

For it is by grace you have been saved, through faith—and this is not from yourselves, it is the gift of God—*not by works*, so that no one can boast. For we are God's handiwork, *created in Christ Jesus to do good works, which God prepared in advance for us to do*. (Eph. 2:8–10, emphasis mine)

HE CHOOSES US   We are saved *by* faith, and we are saved *for*
FOR A MISSION,   works. And God himself has prepared specific
AND HE CHOOSES   people for specific good works. He chooses us for a
A MISSION FOR US. mission, and he chooses a mission for us.

ALL YOU NEED IS LOVE

And now these three remain: faith, hope and love. But the greatest of
these is love. (1 Cor. 13:13)

I once made this rather unconventional declaration to a group of World
Vision donors at a large conference: "God's deepest desire is not that we
would help the poor"—I then paused, knowing that this would get their
attention, and continued—"God's deepest desire is that we would love the
poor; for if we love them, we will surely help them."

Above all else, Jesus loved people. He didn't see them merely as tar-
gets for his preaching and his healing. Everything he did flowed out of his
incredible love. And love, of course, cannot be demonstrated if it is not
expressed in tangible ways. Ask your spouse how she or he would feel if
your love was only spoken but never expressed.

Everything Jesus did was an expression of his love for the Father and
his love for people. He embodied love as no one else ever has. It is important to see, then, that the Great Commission calls for much more than
a mechanical repetition of the doctrines of salvation to anyone who will
listen. It involves much more than convincing people to recite the sinner's prayer. It requires much more than just preaching and evangelism.
It starts with loving people; then it blossoms into caring about every
dimension of people's lives: caring, sharing, helping, healing, giving,
comforting—telling people of God's good news after showing people
God's great love.

When John the Baptist sent his disciples from prison to ask, "Are you the
one who is to come, or should we expect someone else?" Jesus replied, "Go

back and report to John what you hear and see: The blind receive sight, the lame walk, those who have leprosy are cleansed, the deaf hear, the dead are raised, and the good news is proclaimed to the poor" (Matt. 11:3–5). While Jesus loved all people, he had a particular concern for the poor, the sick, the weak, the persecuted, and the downtrodden—"the least of these"—and he demonstrated it through his actions. Yes, the good news was proclaimed, but Jesus always cared about the whole person and demonstrated to them both his love and his compassion:

> Jesus went through all the towns and villages, teaching in their synagogues, proclaiming the good news of the kingdom and healing every disease and sickness. When he saw the crowds, he had compassion on them, because they were harassed and helpless, like sheep without a shepherd. (Matt. 9:35–36)

In fact, if you had to summarize Jesus' approach to other people, you could characterize it with just one word: *love*. He loved them. And he told us to do the same: "As I have loved you, so you must love one another" (John 13:34). John gives the simplest definition of God in the entire Bible: "God is love" (1 John 4:8, 16). And this is totally consistent with my characterization of the story of Scripture as a love story featuring a loving Father reaching out to his children. Jesus was an ambassador of the Father's love. The most quoted verse in the Bible is about love, God's love: "For God so loved the world that he gave his one and only Son, that whoever believes in him shall not perish but have eternal life" (John 3:16). This tells us that God loved the world so much that he acted (he did something), and that something involved a great sacrifice. God's love resulted in action and sacrifice. And when Jesus was asked what the greatest commandment is, he offered two—both about love:

> "'Love the Lord your God with all your heart and with all your soul and with all your mind.' This is the first and greatest commandment. And

the second is like it: 'Love your neighbor as yourself.' All the Law and the Prophets hang on these two commandments." (Matt. 22:37–40)

GOD'S EXPECTATIONS OF US CAN BE SUMMED UP SIMPLY—LOVE GOD AND LOVE OUR FELLOW MAN. God's expectations of us can be summed up simply—love God and love our fellow man. The teaching and example of Jesus and the bright thread of compassion for others that runs through all of Scripture underscores God's desire that followers of Jesus will be recognized by their tangible expression of his love for all people:

If anyone has material possessions and sees a brother or sister in need but has no pity on them, how can the love of God be in that person? Dear children, let us not love with words or speech but with actions and in truth. (1 John 3:17–18)

What good is it, my brothers and sisters, if a man claims to have faith but has no deeds? Can such faith save him? Suppose a brother or sister is without clothes and daily food. If one of you says to him, "Go, I wish you well; keep warm and well fed," but does nothing about his physical needs, what good is it? In the same way, faith by itself, if it is not accompanied by action, is dead. (James 2:14–17)

"'Truly I tell you, whatever you did for one of the least of these brothers and sisters of mine, you did for me.'" (Matt. 25:40)

In other words, love always requires tangible expression. It needs hands and feet. As followers of Christ we can too easily become overwhelmed by the complexity and depth of our Christian faith, and we can become confused by doctrine and theology. But the beautiful simplicity of our faith is that it distills down to the exact same bottom line for both the brilliant theologian and the five-year-old child: love God and love each other—period. Everything else derives from that.

SPIRITUAL MUSCLES

If you are reading this book, it likely means that you consider yourself a "serious" Christian. You read Christian books because you want to learn more about Scripture and want to become a better disciple. You probably go to church regularly, attend a Bible study group on a regular basis, listen to Christian music, and spend time daily or weekly reading the Scripture and praying. All of these activities are good exercises that help us build spiritual muscles, but what will you do with the muscles you are building?

My son Pete works as a junior high youth pastor in a large church in the suburbs of Chicago. As a dad, I have been proud of Pete's calling to ministry and his commitment to be the man God has called him to be. Pete has a knack for explaining spiritual truth to kids in ways they easily relate to. He had a particularly good insight about Christians who spend a lot of time building their spiritual muscles. Here is an excerpt from one of his messages, titled "Spiritual Body-builders":

> When I think about body-builders, I think of massive muscles and glistening tans. These guys dedicate their entire lives to getting huge. I heard an interview with a body-builder who admitted to eating eighteen meals a day. That is incredible! This man is dedicating everything he has—his health, his money, his energy, and his time—to becoming the "strongest looking" man in the world. So why do these body-builders do it, you might ask? This is a question I struggle to answer. They don't play a sport; they don't use their muscles to pull trucks and lift cars, as they do in the World's Strongest Man competition. They are not prison guards, firemen, or rescue workers; no, these men use their muscles just to don a Speedo and strut around a stage, flexing their muscles to a choreographed routine of blaring hip-hop music. It's all for show. What a waste of their incredible strength, and what a waste of their time and effort.

Pete goes on to tell his kids that this is exactly what Christians do when they build all of their spiritual muscles just for show but never use them to do anything significant. What a waste, indeed. But these Christians sure do look good and feel quite pleased with their impressive spiritual physiques.

As a follower of Christ you can fall into the trap of believing that a deeper knowledge of Christ will automatically make you a better disciple of Christ. You can read scores of Christian books, attend conferences, and participate in various Bible studies to deepen and broaden your understanding. But head knowledge of theology no more makes you an effective disciple than knowing the rules of tennis turns you into Roger Federer or Serena Williams. It's only when you take that head knowledge out onto the playing field and invest thousands of hours putting into practice what you have learned that you actually become more like the one you seek to imitate. "Do not merely listen to the word, and so deceive yourselves," said James, the brother of Jesus. "Do what it says" (James 1:22).

WE ARE INVITED

So then, as ambassadors for God's kingdom sent into all the world, what should our approach be? How must we put what we know to be true into practice? We are called above all to love people in the name of Christ. And if we love them, we will demonstrate that love through . . .

- PROCLAMATION: explaining to them the good news that their sins can be forgiven and the kingdom of God is now open to them through Jesus' death on the cross;
- COMPASSION: caring about their physical, emotional, and relational needs;
- JUSTICE: taking a stand against persecution and every form of exploitation; and
- RESTORATION: making disciples by teaching people how to live differently by entering the kingdom of God.

The revolutionary power of the gospel is rooted in the fact that it is good news for every dimension of human life. It is not simply a system of beliefs for us to study and then proclaim; it is a different way of living we are called to adopt and demonstrate. Mere words without accompanying deeds carry far less power than both together. As John pointedly said, "Whoever claims to live in him must live as Jesus did" (1 John 2:6). We are to live as Jesus lived, love as Jesus loved, and proclaim the good news of the kingdom of God as we are sent into the world as his ambassadors.

The Great Commission represented the last words of Jesus to his disciples, and, as such, it is pregnant with significance. It cast Jesus' vision for human thriving within God's emerging kingdom. This was the whole work of the gospel and the whole mission of God. It directed all followers of Christ to embrace a specific mission—to go, to make disciples, to baptize, and to teach—in order to expand this new kingdom of God. No one was exempt. "As the Father has sent me," Jesus said, "I am sending you" (John 20:21). The gospel message of Jesus was not just an offer of forgiveness; it was his call to enlist; it was a recruitment to join the great mission of God in reclaiming his world from enemy occupation. It was not a call to withdraw into our churches with our salvation secure, to await our rescue from this fallen world. No, it was a call to arms in a revolution to overthrow the other kingdoms that control the lives of God's children; it was a call to rescue them from their captivity. It was an invitation to become God's partner in restoring, reforming, and redeeming every dimension of human life.

THE GOSPEL MESSAGE OF JESUS WAS NOT JUST AN OFFER OF FORGIVENESS; IT WAS HIS CALL TO ENLIST.

But invitations must be accepted. God invites us, but he will not force us. You can choose to refuse. You can decide to stand on the sidelines as a bystander to the great mission of God to restore his kingdom and rescue his children. You can let God's great purpose for your life pass you by. But how sad to live your life as a bystander.

7

. . .

RSVP

He sent his servants to those who had been invited to the
banquet to tell them to come, but they refused to come.

—MATTHEW 22:3

The truth is not that God is finding us a place
for our gifts but that God has created us and our
gifts for a place of his choosing—and we will
only be ourselves when we are finally there.[1]

—OS GUINNESS

An invitation requires a response. Reneé and I have hosted our share of parties and gatherings over the years. For the last two or three decades, wherever we have lived, we have had an annual Fourth of July barbecue and a Christmas open house that we always invite a group of our good friends to enjoy. Also, having been a CEO of several different organizations, we have done our share of business entertaining, hosting events for different teams of people I have worked with. One of the things that always astounds us is that there are invariably a few invitees who don't RSVP at all. We would probably all agree that it is a bit rude not to respond to a personal invitation from someone you know well. It is especially puzzling to me that some people don't respond to a personal invitation from their boss. Worse still is the person who says yes and then never shows up. While saying no to an invitation is fairly simple and requires only a note or an e-mail, saying yes to an invitation requires more. It requires both a decision and a commitment: the decision to accept the terms of the invitation—date, time, location, and amount of time and effort required to attend—and the commitment to clear our schedules of conflicts, set aside the time, and go to the place where the event is being held.

In 2009, I was invited by President Obama to become a member of his White House Council on Faith-Based and Neighborhood Partnerships. This council was assembled to give the president advice on how the government can best partner and relate to faith-based organizations and other nonprofits. About twenty-five key secular and religious leaders were invited. I remember clearly that the invitation came via a phone call immediately after the Super Bowl ended. I was told that the appointment would last about one year and that I would have to attend at least four to five meetings in person and many more by phone. Since the meetings were held in Washington, DC, each one required two long flights back and forth from Seattle, so each demanded about three days of my time. I was also told that the president needed an answer within a week so that someone else could be invited if I declined. It was an honor to be asked, and even though I knew it would be demanding and would require some sacrifice, I accepted.

I can still remember the reaction from one politically conservative friend who, after hearing that I had decided to serve, asked why on earth I would serve on a council formed by such a "liberal" president. My response: "When the president of the United States asks me to use my skills and abilities to serve my country, the answer is yes, period!" He is the president, after all.

Jesus Christ has invited us to join his great mission in the world to proclaim the good news of his kingdom and to invite others to join. He is the Creator of the universe, after all. Of all the invitations we might receive in our lifetimes, surely an invitation from God should carry with it the very highest priority. Jesus expects an RSVP.

In Matthew 22, Jesus tells a parable of just such an invitation from a king. He compares his invitation to join the kingdom of God to a wedding banquet that a king had prepared for his son. Listen to his words:

> Jesus spoke to them again in parables, saying: "The kingdom of heaven is like a king who prepared a wedding banquet for his son. He sent his servants to those who had been invited to the banquet to tell them to come, but they refused to come.
>
> "Then he sent some more servants and said, 'Tell those who have been invited that I have prepared my dinner: My oxen and fattened cattle have been butchered, and everything is ready. Come to the wedding banquet.'
>
> "But they paid no attention and went off—one to his field, another to his business. The rest seized his servants, mistreated them and killed them. *The king was enraged.*" (Matt. 22:1–7, emphasis mine)

Perhaps most striking here is that anyone would refuse an invitation from the king. In ancient Rome an invitation from Caesar would have been a command performance of the highest order. Yet the insulted king here was gracious enough to give them a second chance. But they ignored the invitation the second time, and we are told that one went off to his field and another to his business. They apparently had more important priorities in their lives than obeying the king. They then took their refusal to the ultimate level by mistreating and killing the king's servants. We should not be surprised to learn in verse 7 that "the king was enraged."

It is significant to note to whom Jesus was telling this parable. We are told in the previous chapter that Jesus was teaching in the temple courts and that he was being challenged by the high priests and elders. This was the religious establishment of the Jews, the very people who should have been most devoted to the King. Of course, the deeper point Jesus was making is that God's chosen people were rejecting the Messiah and his invitation to join the kingdom of

EVEN WITH OUR GREATER UNDERSTANDING, WE STILL INSULT THE KING, GOING OFF INSTEAD TO PURSUE OUR OWN PRIORITIES— OUR CAREERS, OUR LIFESTYLES, OUR SOCIAL LIVES, AND OUR HAPPINESS—EVEN AS THE KING BECKONS US.

God: "The kingdom of God has come near. Repent and believe the good news!" (Mark 1:15).

While these religious leaders did not yet grasp Jesus' true identity, today, two thousand years later, we have no excuse for failing to RSVP. We have the benefit of knowing who Jesus is, that he rose from the dead to forgive our sins and that he has invited us to join him in his great mission to invite people from all nations to the wedding banquet of the King. But even with our greater understanding, we still insult the King, going off instead to pursue our own priorities—our careers, our lifestyles, our social lives, and our happiness—even as the King beckons us. I have no doubt that our King is also enraged . . . and brokenhearted as well.

Jesus said to his disciples, "If anyone would come after me, he must deny himself and take up his cross and follow me. For whoever wants to save his life will lose it, but whoever loses his life for me will find it." (Matt. 16:24–25)

THE MOST VALUABLE THING YOU POSSESS

What is the most valuable thing you possess? Would you be willing to offer it to Jesus? I'd like you to really stop and think about this for a moment because the answer to this question has profound implications for your walk with the Lord. This most valuable possession might be something you own: a home, a business, or a treasured possession. It might be your accumulated wealth or a six-figure income. It could also be your career, your position, your accomplishments, or your credentials. It may be your reputation, your self-image, or your sense of identity. Christians can so easily fall into the trap of spiritual identity theft, letting ourselves be defined by what we do or what we own instead of by the One we follow. Jesus understood the idols of the human heart: "For where your treasure is, there your heart will be also" (Matt. 6:21). The call to follow Jesus is a call to lay down our lives and everything in our lives that might compete with our commitment to follow him. It is a sacrificial call to lay down the most valuable things we possess at Jesus' feet.

I recently met a young woman who taught me a profound lesson about sacrificial love. Reneé and I traveled to Cambodia in February 2012 to see the work that World Vision was doing in the area of human trafficking and what we call *child protection*. Thousands of children in Cambodia, often because they are poor, are funneled into the sex trade to literally become slaves. I will not soon forget the twenty-two-year-old woman Reneé and I met there. I will call her Ruse—not her real name—to protect her identity. Ruse had spent three years trapped in a Cambodian brothel before being rescued and sent to World Vision's trauma recovery center in Phnom Penh. This is where these broken children are taken to heal and to be restored. World Vision's trauma counselors try to put these girls back together one piece at a time, like beautiful vases that have been shattered. There were more than thirty girls in recovery there at the time of our visit, some as young as eight years old.

Ruse's story was both heartbreaking and inspiring. The eldest of three children, Ruse grew up in a family that was extremely poor. Her father had abandoned them, and when Ruse was just thirteen, her mother became seriously ill and needed medical care. But there was no money. Ruse had a neighbor who knew a brothel owner who would pay a lot for a young virgin, and she approached Ruse and her mother with a terrible proposition: sell your virginity and save your mother. You see, there are men—often American or European men—who will pay a great deal to have sex with a young girl, especially a virgin. Virginity is the most expensive prize in the sex-trade business. A night with a virgin might be sold for more than one thousand dollars while a night with a nonvirgin would bring only five dollars.

As Ruse told us her story that day, she said something I will never forget: "My virginity was the most valuable possession my family had." Can you try to imagine being so poor and desperate that you would actually count your daughter's virginity as the most valuable asset your family owned? Thirteen-year-old Ruse was confronted with a terrible choice. These were her exact words to us: "I finally decided to sell my virginity because I wanted my mother to be healthy and I wanted to help my family's living conditions to be improved so that we could have enough food to eat. My two younger siblings were so small, as I am the oldest daughter, and I had to do whatever I could to help my family."[2]

So Ruse sold herself for four hundred dollars and spent the next three years in a brothel, having sex with more than seven hundred men a year. I find great poignancy in this story of a young girl who loved so much that she would give herself to save her mother and her siblings. This is the same kind of love that Christ lavished on us: "For even the Son of Man did not come to be served, but to serve, and to give his life as a ransom for many" (Mark 10:45).

What is the most valuable thing that you possess? And would you be willing to offer it to Jesus? This call to follow Jesus requires that we first lay down our treasured possessions in his service.

Ruse was rescued and restored by what I would describe as a veritable bucket brigade of Christian love. She was first rescued by the International Justice Mission in a brothel raid. Then she was initially received by another Christian organization called World Hope before being transferred to World Vision's trauma recovery center. After two years of care and healing from her trauma in a safe environment with loving counselors, Ruse was ready to move on. Today she has a small apartment and a job as a nanny. She is now raising her younger brother and sister, the ones for whom she sacrificed her most valuable possession. She also has committed her life to Christ and is being discipled at a local Baptist church. Ruse is an example of the great "rescue mission of God" in action, the one that we have been invited to join. For this young girl the kingdom of God has come near, and she has become one of its newest citizens.

GOD CALLING

Rarely is the invitation to join God's rescue mission as direct and overt as it was for me in 1998. At the time I was living my version of the American dream as the CEO of Lenox, the venerated American china company. I had one of those jobs that most people just dream of, leading a prestigious company with four thousand people working for me, a huge salary, and all the perks. It had taken me twenty-five years and a whole lot of long hours and hard work to get there. And on the day that I received this dramatic invitation from God, I certainly wasn't thinking about changing the world or building his kingdom. I was mostly concerned with my own success: my family, my career, my reputation, and my lifestyle. Oh sure, I was a Christian. I was one of those deciders who had made the decision to accept Christ as my Savior while in graduate school. But I can't say I had truly become a disciple. I hadn't yet laid down my most precious possessions at Jesus' feet. I looked the part—went to church every Sunday, attended a weekly Bible study group, sat on the board of a Christian school, and had a big Bible sitting on my big CEO's desk for everyone to see. I had some glistening spiritual muscles. I had my fire insurance policy, and now I was just enjoying the good life. I hadn't really understood that Jesus had called me to enlist, to replace my agenda with his agenda, to repent, and follow him—until the phone rang one morning.

The call was from an executive recruiter retained by the huge Christian relief and development organization World Vision to find their new president. I won't tell the story in detail here since it is contained in its entirety in *The Hole in Our Gospel*. But the point I want to make is that on that morning in 1998, in a phone call from a recruiter, Jesus was inviting me once again to follow him, to become his disciple. He was giving me an opportunity to partner with him in changing the world by proclaiming the good news to the poor that "the kingdom of God has come near." World Vision, with its forty-five thousand staff members in almost one hundred countries, represents one of the great battalions in God's kingdom advance. I was being offered the astounding privilege of a command post at the front lines of the battle. There was only one problem: I didn't want to join the battle. I was enjoying civilian life far too much, and I didn't want to drop what I was doing, quit my job, cut my pay, sell my house, move my family, and go to the front lines. Jesus seemed to be asking me for the most valuable things I possessed.

Do you remember a similar "phone call" about two thousand years back, which came to Simon Peter and Andrew as they were fishing on the Sea of Galilee?

> As He was going along by the Sea of Galilee, He saw Simon and Andrew, the brother of Simon, casting a net in the sea; for they were fishermen. And Jesus said to them, "Follow Me, and I will make you become fishers of men." (Mark 1:16–17 NASB)

THERE WAS ONLY ONE PROBLEM: I DIDN'T WANT TO JOIN THE BATTLE. I WAS ENJOYING CIVILIAN LIFE FAR TOO MUCH, AND I DIDN'T WANT TO DROP WHAT I WAS DOING, QUIT MY JOB, CUT MY PAY, SELL MY HOUSE, MOVE MY FAMILY, AND GO TO THE FRONT LINES.

I try to imagine Peter and Andrew saying something like this to Jesus: "We'd love to come, Jesus, but you need to understand that the fishing business is just starting to take off. We've found some new investors, and we're about to expand our fleet to four boats. We've rented some retail space and are planning to expand to ten new market locations. Besides, Andrew has just broken ground on a brand-new house and is carrying two mortgages. We'd love to join you, Jesus, but now is just not a good time. You understand." That pretty much sums up what I wanted to say to that recruiter that morning. In fact, I did say something pretty similar—that I wasn't interested or available. But that's not what Peter and Andrew said. We are told that Peter and Andrew immediately dropped their nets and followed him. No hesitation and no questions asked. "Jesus, we're all in. Just show us what you want us to do."

As we saw in the parable of the king's wedding banquet, Jesus knew that his invitation would be refused by many. When Jesus invited the rich young ruler of Matthew 19 to "go, sell your possessions and give to the poor, and you will have treasure in heaven. Then come, follow me" (v. 21), the ruler couldn't do it. He could not lay down his most precious possession if that was what was required to follow Jesus. Instead, we read, "When the young man heard this, he went away sad, because he had great wealth" (19:22). Thanks for the invitation, Jesus, but the cost is just too high.

In Luke 9, Jesus invited another man to follow him:

> But he replied, "Lord, first let me go and bury my father." Jesus said to him, "Let the dead bury their own dead, but you go and proclaim the kingdom of God." Still another said, "I will follow you, Lord; but first let me go back and say goodbye to my family." (Luke 9:59–61)

Each had good excuses.

I had plenty of excuses too. I had five kids to put through college. Reneé and I were living in our dream house. My career was in high gear and promised some big financial rewards in the next few years. Besides, my identity, my security, and my reputation were all tied up together in that job and that lifestyle. "I'd love to join you, Jesus, but it's just not a good time; you understand." Jesus understands quite clearly. It's always a matter of priorities: "No one can serve two masters. Either you will hate the one and love the other, or you will be devoted to the one and despise the other" (Matt. 6:24).

Although I lacked the immediate enthusiasm of Peter and Andrew, I ultimately did make the difficult choice to follow Jesus. I reluctantly quit my job. We sold our house, pulled our kids out of school, moved across the country, and began what would become the greatest adventure of our lives. After saying yes to God, I experienced the privilege of serving on the front lines of the kingdom, the satisfaction of joining God's great mission, the wonder of discovering gifts and talents I had never before used, and the joy of feeling for the first time in my life that I was doing what I was created to do. While it is trite to say, I had "found myself," I had found myself by losing myself in God's service: "For whoever wants to save his life will lose it, but whoever loses his life for me will save it" (Luke 9:24).

I often wonder what became of the two men who told Jesus they couldn't follow him quite yet. Nothing more is written about them. But we do know that Simon Peter and Andrew went on to change the world. They weren't extraordinary men by any measure, nor were any of the twelve

THEY WERE DISCIPLES, NOT MERELY DECIDERS, AND THAT MADE ALL THE DIFFERENCE. disciples. Peter and John were described in the book of Acts as "unschooled, ordinary men" (Acts 4:13). I believe that Jesus selected them precisely because they were ordinary to demonstrate the amazing things he can accomplish through average people. But while they may have been ordinary, they were also willing. They were available. They left their nets and followed Jesus without hesitation. They were willing to be used of God. They were disciples, not merely deciders, and that made all the difference.

8

. . .

LET'S MAKE A DEAL

For whoever wants to save their life will lose it, but whoever
loses their life for me and for the gospel will save it.

—MARK 8:35

And everyone who has left houses or brothers or sisters or
father or mother or children or fields for my sake will receive
a hundred times as much and will inherit eternal life.

—MATTHEW 19:29

Like the rich young ruler and the many others who made excuses when
confronted with Christ's call to deny themselves, take up their crosses,
and follow him, we may find that our first reaction is defensive—we make
excuses. In almost every case our excuses stem from the fact that we don't
want to give up control of our lives. Even when our lives aren't going so
well, we still want to do it our way. Yet Jesus tells us that if we are to find
our lives we must first lose our lives. In chapter 1, I stated that the only
way we can find the deepest meaning in our lives is to understand the big
story that God is writing and then to see how our individual stories fit in

to that big story. But there is a corollary to that truth: if we are to find our story in God's, we must first give up our right to do as we please or to write our own stories. In *The Lord of the Rings*, Sam and Frodo had to forsake their comfortable lives in the Shire in order to undertake the great calling on their lives. They had to take risks and move out of their comfort zones. Peter and Andrew had to leave the financial security of their fishing business. Jesus asked the rich young ruler to do the same. But the young man turned and walked away because he was not willing to give up what he had in order to get what Jesus was offering.

Have you ever watched the game show *Let's Make a Deal*? This show took on new significance for the Stearns family this year as our daughter, Hannah, actually appeared as a contestant on the show. A third-year law student at the time, Hannah hoped she might win a little money to help with her tuition expenses. So she got tickets to the show, and in order to increase her chances of being chosen as a contestant, she dressed up as a law book—a torts book, to be precise. She felt a bit foolish, but it worked, and she was picked to come out of the audience to be a contestant. Hannah did well. She ended up winning a motorbike, a laptop computer, and a couple of nice backpacks. To her parents' great relief, she sold the motorbike to get cash to pay her bills.

Let's Make a Deal is a great little metaphor for the choices God requires us to make. In the show contestants are brought up on the stage and offered a wide range of prizes, both good and bad. But the real essence of the show, and the thing that makes it so compelling, is the agonizing choices the contestants are forced to make. The host might first offer someone one thousand dollars in cash, with no strings attached. The contestant can quit right there and go home one thousand dollars richer. But then the fun begins. He offers a trade-in of the cash for the unknown prize that lies behind the curtain on stage. Of course, the contestant doesn't know what lies behind the curtain. It could be a brand-new Corvette; a two-week, all-expenses-paid vacation to Hawaii; or a case of dill pickles. It's the contestant's choice: trade what he has already won for the promise of something better, or play it safe and keep what he already has. The drama of the show is increased as winners are constantly offered opportunities to improve their prizes but always with the risk of dill pickles.

In a real way the decision to follow Christ and to lay down our lives to follow him is quite similar. Jesus was playing *Let's Make a Deal* with the rich young ruler: "Go, sell everything you have and give to the poor, and you will have treasure in heaven. Then come, follow me. I'm offering you the great adventure of your life. I am inviting you to partner with me in my great kingdom mission. I promise you will find your deepest purpose and your greatest fulfillment in life in doing what I created you to do. All you have to do is lay down what you've already won, and I will replace it with treasures beyond your imagination" (Matt. 19:21, author's paraphrase).

It's that last sentence that's the hard part—"lay down what you've already won."

"Can't I keep it all, Jesus?"

"No, my child, because no one can serve two masters—you will either hate the one and love the other, or be devoted to the one and despise the other" (Matt. 6:24, author's paraphrase).

In my own case I had won the CEO position at Lenox, the big salary, and the dream house. I had won financial security, prestige, and comfort. I had written my own story, and I liked the way it was turning out. "Let go of all that, Rich. Follow me, and I will take you on the great adventure of your life. Let me show you who I created you to be. Trust me, Rich." My own mother, when I called her to say I had decided to accept the job with World Vision, said, "But you've got it made! Why on earth would you give all of that up to go work for a charity?" I tried to explain to her that as a follower of Christ, it was no longer about me and my life; it was about Jesus and the life he intended me to live. But it is so very hard to trust, so hard to let go, and so easy to cling to whatever it is we have clutched in our hands.

What are you clinging to? There are so many things that compete with God in our lives. Perhaps a career that you have invested decades in building or maybe a business you have started. Surely it can't be wrong to pursue a career or build a business? It could be money, wealth, and the ability to create wealth that have their hold on you or, perhaps, the many things that money can buy. The more you have, the harder it is to sell everything you have and give it to Jesus. That may be why so many people give their lives to Christ when they have nothing left to lose.

You might be clinging to an unhealthy relationship or an identity you have shaped. Maybe you have an addiction you have not been able to let go. Lots of people cling to a physical place. Do you live somewhere you love that you aren't willing to leave? Do you love your house, your friends, your comfort, and the familiarity of your life? These are not bad things unless you place them above God.

> DO YOU LOVE YOUR HOUSE, YOUR FRIENDS, YOUR COMFORT, AND THE FAMILIARITY OF YOUR LIFE? THESE ARE NOT BAD THINGS UNLESS YOU PLACE THEM ABOVE GOD.

The common thread behind all of these attachments is control. We want to control our lives and our choices, and we don't like anyone who threatens to take that away. Remember my comparison between following Jesus and enlisting in the army? When you give your life to following Jesus, he asks you to give control to him. As one bumper sticker aptly put it: "If God is your co-pilot . . . switch seats!" Jesus wants to drive; he wants to lead, but he cannot until you "lose your life" for his sake so he can give you the life he always meant for you to live. What are the most precious things you possess? Are you willing to offer them to Jesus?

Now, here is a really important thing to understand. If you lay down all of these things in the service of Christ and his kingdom, he won't necessarily take them away from you. He doesn't ask us all to quit our jobs, leave our homes, and have an estate sale to liquidate all our earthly possessions. No, he only asks that we turn all of those decisions over to him. If you have built a business that can generate great wealth, he may leave you right there so that the business can be used to his glory and to accomplish his purposes. If you are an investment banker at Goldman Sachs, he may want you to stay put and become a kingdom builder right where you are stationed by letting your light shine in a place where a shining light may be desperately needed. If you love your community, he may use you to help transform it and reclaim it for his kingdom. He might even use your addiction as a powerful testimony of his restorative power to transform human lives. But he does require that the certificates of title be signed over to him. He becomes the owner, and we become the stewards, not of our possessions but of the Master's possessions. I know many followers of Christ who are serving him in powerful ways, who have not been called to sell, leave, forsake, or abandon the lives they have built. But they have been called to use the lives they have built for Christ and his kingdom. Sometimes he does take the things we have laid down at his feet, but, unlike the game show host on *Let's Make a Deal*, he always replaces them with something better.

As a final postscript to my decision to leave Lenox and join World Vision, God gave me an extraordinary opportunity to glimpse the life I might have had. Ten years after I left, I returned. I was traveling in the Philadelphia area and e-mailed an old colleague at Lenox to ask him if I could drop by and say hello to any of the old-timers who might remember me. As about a dozen old friends gathered in a conference room that day to "catch up" on all that had happened in the decade since I had left, I listened as they recounted a horrific tale of sadness and pain. Though Lenox had enjoyed record sales and profits in the first couple of years after I left, things started to unravel in the years that followed. In those ten short years Lenox had a succession of five CEOs as the market contracted and sales and profits fell. They were forced to close five of their six US factories and lay off thousands of employees. Finally, they were divested by their parent company and merged into a smaller company. It had been a nightmare of changes and downsizing for those who had endured and survived through the decade. I have no doubt that had I stayed at Lenox, I would have been one of the casualties of that dreadful economic downturn.

When it was my turn to share, I told them of the amazing opportunity I'd had to travel the world, helping children and communities. I told them of a board of directors who prayed for me and a leadership team who had all taken huge cuts in pay to join what God was doing in the world. I shared what it felt like to get up each morning knowing that God was using me to make the world a better place. Hearing the excitement in my voice, one of my former colleagues blurted out: "It sounds like heaven. Do you have any job openings there?" Heaven, indeed; the kingdom of heaven, in fact. God had invited me into his vision for human thriving. He had invited me to the front lines of his revolution to change the world, and, thankfully, I had said yes. As I look back on that decision now, I have the acute realization that I could have said no; I could have walked away. Jesus wasn't forcing me; he was inviting me. But first I had to let go of the things I was clutching so tightly in my hands so he could replace them with something so much more precious. I had to lay down my old life for the new life that was behind the curtain *before* I really knew what the curtain would reveal. I am quite sure that if I had said no he would have called someone else. Someone else would have been offered the incredible opportunity to partner with Jesus by serving at World Vision. "Those who cling to worthless idols forfeit the grace that could be theirs" (Jonah 2:8).

Two weeks after my reunion visit, Lenox declared bankruptcy. A few weeks after that I received a letter saying that the Lenox executive pension I had been receiving for several years had been canceled. In case I had any remaining doubts, God was showing me with great finality that I should rely on him alone for my security.

MORIAH RANCH

Again, the kingdom of heaven is like a merchant looking for fine pearls. When he found one of great value, he went away and sold everything he had and bought it. (Matt. 13:45–46)

A couple of years ago I was in Michigan, and a good friend of World Vision's ministry, Stu Phillips, offered to drive me from Grand Rapids to the Detroit airport to catch my flight home. During the drive, Stu startled me with a surprising statement. He said, "You know, you're not very popular around the Phillips household these days." Ouch! What had I done? I couldn't think of anything I might have said that would make me unpopular with Stu and his family. Stu then smiled and explained. I learned that Stu and Robin owned a fourteen-thousand-acre ranch in the Laramie

Mountains in Wyoming. It was a very special "piece of heaven" that meant the world to their whole family. On this magnificent piece of God's creation, Stu and his sons, Jordan and Stephen, had spent countless hours when the boys were teenagers, fishing for trout and hunting elk from the herd that roamed their ranch. Robin, an avid painter, had used the ranch as her most beautiful subject. Stu and Robin had built a special home there as a family retreat.

Stu explained that he and Robin had both read my book *The Hole in Our Gospel*, and it had convicted them a great deal about God's concern for the poor and their responsibility to love the poor as God does. He said that he and Robin were spending a few days at the ranch and that he had been praying and reading my book for a second time when he clearly felt God was speaking to him.

I asked Stu and Robin if they would share their very private story as an encouragement to others. They reluctantly agreed and first shared it at a World Vision event. Here are Stu's own words:

Then I heard a still, quiet voice: I heard God speaking to me. It was a voice I had heard before. God asked me two questions. First, he asked, *What do you value most?* He wasn't talking about my family and friends. The question was, what *possession* did I value most? One of the challenging aspects of God speaking to you is that he knows the answers, even when you don't or don't want to admit that you do. The answer was clear; it was the ranch.

He then asked the second question: *Given what you now know about the needs of the poor, how does that balance with the four months a year you spend at the ranch and the resources you have tied up here?* I knew the answer instantly. I was stunned.

My next reaction was to doubt what I had heard. Maybe I had just imagined it. Then I tried, hopefully, to negotiate with God. We already gave significant resources to poverty programs. We

> ONE OF THE CHALLENGING ASPECTS OF GOD SPEAKING TO YOU IS THAT HE KNOWS THE ANSWERS, EVEN WHEN YOU DON'T OR DON'T WANT TO ADMIT THAT YOU DO.

already used the ranch for *godly* purposes: hosting college groups from church, sharing time with friends in need of solitude, and appreciating God's handiwork. Perhaps we could just increase our commitment to using the ranch for those purposes. Maybe that would satisfy God. And maybe it would, but it wasn't his plan; it wasn't his request. Robin and I put the ranch up for sale.[1]

So now I understood why Rich Stearns might not be such a popular topic of conversation around the Phillipses' dinner table. I was stunned.

"Stu," I said, "are you sure you want to do this?" Stu said God had been clear, and he was committed. He said that he and Robin intended to use all of the proceeds to do "God's kingdom work." If you think that somehow it was easy for Robin and Stu to lay down their most precious possession, you need to think again. The whole family struggled and agonized over the decision.

> It took some time for me, for us all, to digest what had occurred. After hearing our plans, Stephen, our youngest son, put it this way: "God may have told you to sell the ranch, but he didn't tell me." You see, the questions God had posed to me that day were in direct conflict with all of our plans as a family. But God then took hold of the situation as only he can. In the worst recession since the Great Depression, we received a serious offer the first week, twice our original purchase price.[2]

I didn't hear any more about the ranch for months, and then one day I received an e-mail from Stu and Robin with a photo attached. It was a photo of Stu, Robin, one of their sons, and the governor of Wyoming sitting at his desk and signing the commitment to purchase Moriah Ranch. The deal closed in April 2012. What is perhaps most remarkable about this story of faithfulness and obedience is that Stu and Robin's greatest sacrifice became their greatest blessing. They had exchanged their will for God's will, their plans for his plans.

In our minds the ranch was now even more valuable, and the potential for dedicating more resources to help the poor even more intense. *Our hearts had crossed over; Robin and I were now more excited to see what God would do with these resources than we were saddened by the loss of the ranch.*

It is important to be clear: "to God be the glory." We should have no illusions regarding the spiritual significance of our gifts. God has told us what impresses him, and our checks, regardless of the size, don't do it. However, our obedience may. God isn't impressed by a rich guy giving up a luxury that is well beyond the wildest dreams of those in poverty. He is impressed by the single mom who gives of the little she has to help her neighbor or the widow on a fixed income who sponsors a child. Their offerings are more selfless and more sacrificial than ours.[3]

Stu and Robin had learned to love what Jesus loves, treasure what Jesus treasures, and value what Jesus values. They had played *Let's Make a Deal* with God. When asked whether they would trade their most precious possession for what was behind God's curtain, they said yes! You see, this was not some game show host looking for a laugh at their expense. This was the Son of God who had given his life that they might live. This was the One who said he had come to heal the sick, free the captives, bind up the broken-hearted, and preach the good news to the poor. This was the Lord of the universe, inviting them to join him in his great kingdom mission to reach into the world's pain with the good news of God's love. They had RSVP'd with a resounding yes!

Some time later God tested Abraham. He said to him, "Abraham!"

"Here I am," he replied.

Then God said, "Take your son, your only son, whom you love—Isaac—and go to the region of Moriah. Sacrifice him there as a burnt offering on a mountain I will show you."

Early the next morning Abraham got up and loaded his donkey. He took with him two of his servants and his son Isaac. (Gen. 22:1–3)

It cannot be a coincidence that Stu and Robin's ranch was named Moriah Ranch. Mount Moriah, of course, was the place God asked Abraham to go to sacrifice his most precious possession, his son Isaac. For Abraham it was a test to see whether he would trust God or trust himself; whether he would hold back in his relationship with God or let go. Stu and Robin had been tested too. God had rewarded Abraham's faithfulness with a great promise; because of Abraham's sacrifice his descendants would be as numerous as the stars and become a blessing to the nations. I have no doubt that Stu and Robin will be blessed also as God uses their sacrifice to become a blessing to many.

> The angel of the LORD called to Abraham from heaven a second time and said, "I swear by myself, declares the LORD, that because you have done this and have not withheld your son, your only son, I will surely bless you and make your descendants as numerous as the stars in the sky and as the sand on the seashore. Your descendants will take possession of the cities of their enemies, and through your offspring all nations on earth will be blessed, because you have obeyed me." (Gen. 22:15–18)

9

. . .

WE WERE MADE FOR MORE

The mass of men lead lives of quiet desperation.[1]

—HENRY DAVID THOREAU

Alas for those that never sing,
But die with all their music in them.[2]

—OLIVER WENDELL HOLMES

Therefore, if anyone is in Christ, the new creation
has come: The old has gone, the new is here!

—2 CORINTHIANS 5:17

How do you see your life? Does it sometimes feel like you are just going through the motions of the daily grind to answer the alarm clock, go to work or school, come home, and do it all over again the next day—just so you can put food on the table and a roof over your head? Are you mired in a torrent of bills that never seems to end? Does your life sometimes feel like it's just an endless series of problems and struggles punctuated by the occasional relief of a holiday, a round of golf, or a vacation? Do you feel insignificant as just one of 7 billion human beings going through the same daily struggle that you are? Have you come to the realization that the dreams you had when you were younger have now died? Sadly, many people, even followers of Christ, might describe their lives in just this way. They have, as Henry David Thoreau once penned, resigned themselves to living "lives of quiet desperation."

Or maybe you are much more upbeat about your life. You may be basically happy, with a great circle of friends and family and a job you like. You may have an optimistic outlook and gratitude for all that God has given you. But you still may lack that sense of greater purpose and significance. In fact, you might feel as if you are missing something, just marking time, trying to enjoy the life God has given you but without much sense of a higher calling. Many of the hundreds of people I meet around the world inevitably share something like this with me and ask how they can really find God's purpose for their lives. Though they are happy, they feel as though something is missing, as if they are just standing on the sidelines, watching the game, longing for the coach to put them in.

> THOUGH THEY ARE HAPPY, THEY FEEL AS THOUGH SOMETHING IS MISSING, AS IF THEY ARE JUST STANDING ON THE SIDELINES, WATCHING THE GAME, LONGING FOR THE COACH TO PUT THEM IN.

I spoke to about eight hundred men in 2012 at the annual retreat of the New Canaan Society, a national men's organization whose goal it is to connect men in relationship and to equip them to have a powerful impact for Christ on their families, their communities, their workplaces, and the wider world. The theme of their retreat was "We Were Made for More." I love this phrase because it captures so well the message of God's kingdom. The God who made the universe, the Author of the big story in which we all are living, created you and me uniquely. There is no other human being who has ever lived who is exactly like you or me; we are each one of a kind. We were not created to live lives of quiet desperation or to just pass the time as we shamble through our eighty years on earth. God created us for a divine purpose, to play a role in his unfolding story. We are children of the King, and we were made for more.

This phrase "we were made for more" truly captures the significance of the transformation that occurs when a person repents and believes as he or she responds to the gospel. Jesus said, "God's kingdom is here. Change your life and believe the Message" (Mark 1:15 MSG). Our lives are to be transformed in every way by the power of the gospel story. Our stories become joined with God's bigger story as we become citizens of God's expanding kingdom. And just as Peter could no longer simply return to his fishing nets after his encounter with Jesus, we cannot just return to life as we knew it either. The essence of what Scripture teaches us about our transformation as followers of Christ is, "Therefore, if anyone is in Christ, the new creation has come: The old has gone; the new is here" (2 Cor. 5:17). We are new creations who have been given a new purpose, a new mission, and a new calling: "As the Father has sent me, I am sending you" (John 20:21). Jesus is sending us into the world to continue the work that he began. He is calling us to the front lines of the gospel revolution to man the barricades as we join the great rescue mission that the Father has launched to invite all of his children back into the fellowship of his inexhaustible love. There is no such thing as an ordinary follower of Christ with an ordinary life; every one of us was made for more.

KNOWING WHERE YOU'RE GOING

I have had the privilege of speaking at several college graduations and have attended the graduations of all five of my own children. These are exciting moments in the lives of young people. It feels as though we are all gathered around them in support as they stand at the starting line of their adult lives. A graduation marks the beginning of life's long journey—not of a sprint but of a marathon. At no other time in a person's life are there so many possibilities open to him or her. It is truly one of life's momentous occasions.

In my commencement addresses I usually ask the graduates about their goals in life. People beginning a race or a journey need to have a finish line or a destination in mind before they begin. And don't we as parents, family, and friends always ask them those destination questions: What will you do after you graduate? Where are you headed? What do you aspire to? What do you want to become? Many graduates dread the questions because they don't really know the answers yet.

In one of my commencement addresses, I emphasized just how important it is for them to have the right goal or destination in mind for their lives since they will have to invest so much time, energy, and effort in pursuing it. Can you imagine running a marathon only to find out that after all of your training, sacrifice, and effort you crossed the wrong finish line? But that's exactly what so many people do. "Wouldn't it be great," I asked, "if you had a kind of GPS device that could guide you on your life journey, giving you explicit driving directions all along the way?"

A GPS is a great thing to have; I don't know how we all used to get from A to B without it. I know before I had a GPS, I typically spent a lot of time driving in circles until my wife chided me into stopping to ask for directions. Here's how a GPS works: The very first thing you need to do is establish a starting point and a destination. The starting point is pretty easy; it is generally where you are right then. I usually know where I am; I just don't know how to get where I'm going. The second input is the most important: the destination. Once the GPS has both a starting point and a destination, it will provide a long list of driving directions, mapping out each twist and turn along the way. What a great invention! Now we no longer have to get lost on our journey. But here's the catch: if you enter the wrong destination, then all of the steps along the way will be wrong as well. In other words, the GPS will give you precise and detailed turn-by-turn directions to the wrong destination. So knowing where we're going turns out to be the one critical decision we need to make first.

Life works the same way. If we select the wrong destination, the wrong life goals, we will very likely go through life making decision after decision on a road that is leading us precisely to the wrong place. Most people are able to articulate some of their life goals, and on the surface these goals seem quite lofty and desirable. Let me list just a few of the life goals that are typically expressed:

1) BECOME A SUCCESSFUL _____. (Fill in the blank: teacher, lawyer, politician, pastor, carpenter, homemaker, doctor, soldier, pilot, business owner, physical therapist, landscaper, and so on.) This seemingly admirable goal of career success is almost universally embraced. Who doesn't want to be successful? Isn't that why college graduates go to college in the first place?

2) ACHIEVE COMFORT AND SECURITY. Usually one of the core benefits of becoming successful is that we can become comfortable and secure. For some, this is really their most important goal, and success is just a means to achieving it. For others it is just a nice by-product of success. We don't want to have to worry about whether we can pay the rent or go out to a movie, and we want to have enough to be comfortable when we retire.

3) BECOME WEALTHY. Okay, admit it. Don't you really want to be wealthy? Don't you feel a pang of envy when the *Forbes* 400 list of the wealthiest people in the United States comes out each year? Why else do annual US lottery ticket sales exceed $50 billion? At one dollar a ticket, that works out to an average of about 175 tickets per person per year.[3] Wealth is a very popular dream. Sure, money isn't everything, but it can sure buy almost anything. Most of us wouldn't say out loud that we want to become wealthy, but we are definitely thinking about it.

4) BECOME FAMOUS. This is another one that few people admit to, but it lingers in the back of a lot of minds. We obsessively follow the lives of the rich and famous in our culture, from athletes to movie stars to business leaders. Andy Warhol famously predicted in the 1960s that in the future everyone will have their "fifteen minutes" of fame.[4] Certainly the proliferation of media and the incredible phenomena of Twitter, YouTube, Facebook, and other social networking vehicles have made at least fleeting fame available to the masses.

5) BE HAPPY. Who can argue with this one? I suppose being happy is what people hope for when they achieve their other goals of comfort, wealth, success, or fame. Happiness might be considered

a goal, but it is more often a derivative of all of the other choices people make in life.

I could list many more. The life goals of any given person might well contain a combination of the above. On the surface most of these are deceptively attractive aspirations. We live in a culture that rewards the successful, envies the wealthy, and affirms the ambitious. If reality TV has revealed anything about our nature, it has revealed the almost universal human desire for fame, wealth, success, and significance. Why else would someone appear on *Survivor*, *American Idol*, or *The Bachelor*? But I digress.

What I want you to see is what happens to us when we enter destinations like those listed into the GPS device of our lives. Essentially we get driving directions that steadily and methodically direct us to the achievement of our goals. So let's say for a moment that we enter something like *success* or *wealth* into our GPSs. What driving directions might we get?

- Look out for number one.
- Drive hard and fast, and stay on the highway at all costs.
- Become a workaholic.
- Neglect your family and friends when the demands of success require it.
- Don't stop to help people broken down at the side of the road— the poor, the sick, and the needy; it's every man for himself. They will just distract you.
- Spend your money to get all the things you want because you've earned them.
- Keep your faith in the safe zone. Don't let it sidetrack you.
- Turn off your moral compass; it can be so annoying and inconvenient.
- Let the ends justify the means.

We have all seen the wreckage in the lives of people who have entered the wrong destination and then single-mindedly pursued it without regard to any of the warning signs. I read a story online of a man in Bedford Hills, New York, who slavishly followed his GPS onto some train tracks without first looking left and right. The car got stuck, and the train crashed into the car at sixty miles per hour, turning it into a gigantic fireball and pushing it one hundred feet down the track. Fortunately the man escaped just before the car was struck. But five hundred train passengers were delayed for hours, and 250 feet of track were destroyed.[5]

Sometimes people who obsessively pursue their goals at all costs cause collateral damage in the lives of others. The apostle Paul gave this same warning to his young protégé, Timothy:

> Those who want to get rich fall into temptation and a trap and into many foolish and harmful desires that plunge people into ruin and destruction. For the love of money is a root of all kinds of evil. Some people, eager for money, have wandered from the faith and pierced themselves with many griefs. (1 Tim. 6:9–10)

Paul made the point that wealth—and we might add fame, success, and even happiness—are illusory goals and that the ardent pursuit of them is at best harmful and at worst catastrophic, leading us away from God and into ruin. We need only look at most Hollywood marriages to see what the pursuit of fame can do or read the stories of people who actually won the lottery to see what achieving their goal of wealth did to them. But if we keep reading, Paul went on to tell Timothy what he should pursue instead:

SOMETIMES PEOPLE WHO OBSESSIVELY PURSUE THEIR GOALS AT ALL COSTS CAUSE COLLATERAL DAMAGE IN THE LIVES OF OTHERS.

> But you, man of God, flee from all this, and *pursue righteousness, godliness, faith, love, endurance and gentleness.* Fight the good fight of the faith. Take hold of the eternal life to which you were called when you made your good confession in the presence of many witnesses. (1 Tim. 6:11–12, emphasis mine)

In other words, "Timothy, you were made for more."

So what if we entered a different life destination—not success or happiness or comfort but, instead, a destination involving God's plan for our lives? What if, as Paul recommended, we "take hold of the eternal life to which you were called" (1 Tim. 6:12) when we commit to become followers of Jesus Christ? In light of the past few chapters, what if we were to enter this destination into our GPSs: *follow Christ, live as Jesus lived, love as Jesus loves, and proclaim the good news of the kingdom of God as we are sent into the world as his ambassadors*? Isn't this, after all, the life goal given by God himself to every follower of Christ? With this new destination, the GPS would likely spit out a very different set of driving directions:

- Put the needs of others ahead of your own.
- Take detours when someone needs your help.
- Get off the highway to spend time with family and friends, even though it slows you down.
- Pick up hitchhikers.
- Use your money to build God's kingdom, not yours.
- Don't confuse career success with being a successful person.
- View your work as a means to the end of serving God, not as an end in itself.
- Invest your time, talent, and treasure in being rich toward God rather than getting rich yourself.
- Stop to help those broken down on the side of the road who need a little help on their journey.
- Pay close attention to your moral compass.
- Keep your relationship with God as your North Star.

There is a very important truth in this little metaphor, and it is this: As followers of Jesus we are expected to . . . well, follow him. We must put him first in our lives and not simply try to fit him around our goals and priorities. The call of Jesus is not to merely fit him into our agendas; it is to *replace* our agendas with his, to enter his destination into our GPS devices. And his agenda is nothing short of a revolution that will change the world and rescue his children. His agenda is to invite people into a new way of living within the ever-expanding kingdom of God. God is at work in our world, and he bids us to set our GPSs to join him.

> "I have been crucified with Christ and I no longer live, but Christ lives in me." (Gal. 2:20)

THE ENDS VERSUS THE MEANS

So the obvious question becomes, *What does this really mean for your life?* What does it mean to a graduating senior who has studied hard to become an engineer, an accountant, or a teacher? What does it mean for someone who has worked for twenty or thirty years as an engineer, accountant, or teacher? The answer lies in the difference between *ends* and *means*. If your life goal is to be a successful _____, then I want to argue that you have the wrong life goal. Your life goal and mine should be the same: to follow Christ, live as Jesus lived, love as Jesus loves, and proclaim the good news of the kingdom of God as we are sent into the world as his ambassadors. But being an engineer, accountant, or teacher might just be a very good means to that end. Everything we have and everything we are can be used in service to the Lord and to further his kingdom goals. It is important to remember that he created us with the very gifts and talents that enable us to become good engineers, accountants, and teachers. If God's kingdom mission is to demonstrate a totally new way of human flourishing governed by God's truth and God's values, and we are called to go into the world to show others what this looks like, then it is important to show the world what a kingdom engineer, accountant, or teacher looks like. God's kingdom needs every skill and capability that every other kingdom needs: farmers, lawyers, builders, plumbers, economists, politicians, investment bankers, and hairstylists.

There is no difference for the follower of Christ between the sacred and the secular. All work is sacred if it does not violate God's laws and

THERE IS NO DIFFERENCE FOR THE FOLLOWER OF CHRIST BETWEEN THE SACRED AND THE SECULAR. ALL WORK IS SACRED IF IT DOES NOT VIOLATE GOD'S LAWS AND IF IT IS OFFERED IN THE SERVICE OF BUILDING HIS KINGDOM. if it is offered in the service of building his kingdom. When we speak of God's calling on our lives, it is a calling away from our own agendas, a leaving behind of our hopes and dreams to embrace his hopes and dreams for our lives. It is a putting to death of our purposes and priorities, and at the same time it is a coming alive to God's purposes and priorities. We may still be engineers, accountants, and teachers, but we are now kingdom engineers, accountants, and teachers. We may still have great financial wealth, but we are no longer owners but instead stewards, not of our wealth but of God's wealth, entrusted to us to use in building his kingdom. And we may still be mothers and fathers, but we are now kingdom mothers and fathers, raising our children to take their places in God's great rescue mission.

Are You Sure, Andy?

Last year my son Andy, who was twenty-nine at the time, called me and told me that he intended to run in the Nairobi marathon to raise money and awareness for the needs of children. Andy works for American Express, and his wife, Kirsten, works at World Vision, coordinating our Team World Vision program, which mobilizes people across the country to run marathons or triathlons in order to raise money to help kids. Team World Vision had organized a special group of runners to go to Kenya for the Nairobi marathon in 2011. But in order to participate each runner had to commit to get fifty children sponsored. After the race the runners would get to visit World Vision projects and meet some of the kids they were helping. So Andy and Kirsten had to reach out to all of their friends to ask them to support Andy's commitment to run by sponsoring these fifty children. I was a proud dad listening to the excitement in Andy's voice as he shared his determination to make this happen. But then he told me something that startled me. He said that he and Kirsten had decided they would offer an incentive to every one of their friends who would sponsor a child; they would match each friend's sponsorship commitment with a substantial donation of their own. I did the math and was shocked at the size of Andy and Kirsten's commitment.

Before I had time to really let this sink in, I said, "Andy, are you sure you want to do this? That's a lot of money, and you and Kirsten are just in your twenties. Don't you want to save some money to someday buy a house? Isn't this a little reckless?"

I will never forget Andy's response: "Dad, isn't this what *you* taught us?" Ouch! Of course, Reneé and I *had* taught our kids that our money is not ours to do with as we please, that we are stewards of what God has entrusted to us, and that we need to be generous in reaching out to the poor and in supporting God's kingdom work. We tried to set that example as the kids were growing up, even to the point of involving them in our giving decisions. I think what shocked me is that Andy and Kirsten were demonstrating a commitment that was pretty radical. They were trusting God so much it frankly made me a little uncomfortable. Andy went on to say, "Dad, we don't need this money. We have all that we need, and besides, how can we let this money just sit in a bank account when so many kids are in desperate circumstances? We can make more money, but these kids need help now." Wow!

A few months later, after he and Kirsten had succeeded in getting their fifty kids sponsored, Andy called me again. "Well, Dad," he said, "today we mailed the big check to World Vision. I have to tell you that writing a check that big hurt. But it's supposed to hurt, isn't it, Dad?" Yeah, Andy, I think it is supposed to hurt a bit. You see, Andy and Kirsten were following their inner GPSs. They had set their destination to live their lives in service to God's kingdom, not for wealth or success or bigger bank accounts. And the driving directions they were following told them that this was exactly the right road to take. That's what a young kingdom couple looks like.

Andy and Kirsten are just one example of how followers of Christ, working full-time in secular jobs, can be soldiers for the kingdom of God right where they are planted. In fact, a number of those kids were sponsored by

Andy's colleagues at American Express. And as I have suggested, if we think of the coming kingdom of God as a revolution intended to overthrow the prevailing value systems in our world, doesn't it make sense that we need soldiers of the revolution stationed at the very places where those battles are being fought: in businesses, in schools and universities, in the arts, in the media, in Hollywood, in nonprofits, in hospitals, in the cities, in the suburbs, in the prisons, on Wall Street, in town halls, and in the halls of Congress?

In my eleven years in senior leadership positions at Lenox, I tried to begin every day with a prayer that God would use me in this place to love, serve, and obey him, that I might be his ambassador, and that I might let my light shine in that place. I was by no means a perfect ambassador, and I had many moments when I felt I had failed to represent the Lord well, but I tried to make serving Christ in that place my top priority. Selling china and crystal was secondary; it was a means to an end. Perhaps the greatest affirmation I ever received came six months or so after I had left my position at Lenox. It came in a phone call from my former secretary, Maureen. She said, "Rich, I can't really explain it, but things are different here now that you've left. There is a whole different atmosphere. People seem cruder, more mean-spirited, and more aggressive; people just feel devalued here now. We miss you." I like to think that she was noticing the difference I had been able to make as Christ's ambassador, shining a little light into the darkness and influencing the culture of an organization by living according to the values of God's kingdom: integrity, truth, love, respect, compassion, justice, and valuing all people as God's children. If God is sending his servants out to invite people to fill his kingdom banquet hall, then those servants need to take those invitations everywhere people are gathered.

In the end being a follower of Christ in our world today is not defined by two or three momentous events in our lives, and it's not about what happens on Sunday mornings or in our weekly Bible study groups or our daily devotional times. It's about the thousands of daily twists, turns, detours, and choices that make up the very fabric of our lives. It's about a life well lived for Christ by those who know their destination and take seriously the role God has given them to play as full participants in his kingdom work.

Jesus told us to "seek first his kingdom and his righteousness, and all these things will be given to you as well" (Matt. 6:33).

God offers all of us the amazing opportunity to join in this sacred work. We have the great privilege of being the hands and feet of Christ in a hostile and hurting world, and there are countless ways to participate. We can work with joy in the face of difficulty, speak the truth in a place of deceit, choose integrity when corruption is the norm, offer comfort in a time of grief, challenge injustice to protect its victims, and offer forgiveness in the midst of brokenness. God invites us to mentor a young person who needs a role model, visit with a lonely senior citizen, provide food to the hungry and water to the thirsty, welcome an immigrant family, comfort the sick and afflicted, bring the good news of the gospel to someone who's never heard it, comfort a coworker going through a crisis, or pray for those in need, who happen to live ten thousand miles away. These are sacred things, privileged things, kingdom things. They are profoundly meaningful

THESE ARE SACRED THINGS, PRIVILEGED THINGS, KINGDOM THINGS.

and significant, deeply human and moral and right; they are the very things that demonstrate that we all are made in God's image; we are children of the King with the capacity to love, give, grieve, and rejoice. These are the things in which we find our true significance and purpose. We were made for more.

10

. . .

GOD'S SPIRITUAL GPS

"Whoever believes in me, as the Scripture has said,
streams of living water will flow from within him." By
this he meant the Spirit, whom those who believed in
him were later to receive. Up to that time the Spirit had
not been given, since Jesus had not yet been glorified.

—JOHN 7:38–39

But when he, the Spirit of truth, comes, he
will guide you into all the truth.

—JOHN 16:13

It is impossible to overestimate the significance of the Holy Spirit in the life
of a follower of Jesus Christ. The Spirit is the third person of the Godhead,
as fully God as the Father or the Son. It was the coming of the Holy Spirit
on Pentecost, ten days after Jesus ascended into heaven, that transformed
the first disciples from a confused and frightened circle of has-beens, cow-
ering for fear of their lives with no hope and no vision for the future, into
a bold, cohesive, revolutionary band of leaders whose lives changed the

course of history. The difference between the former and the latter was just one variable, the Holy Spirit. Without the Holy Spirit they were a bunch of mere men with no power to change much of anything; with the Holy Spirit they became the most influential force in world history. This coming of the Holy Spirit was so important that just before he ascended, Jesus instructed them to do nothing until the power of the Holy Spirit was given to them:

> "Do not leave Jerusalem, but wait for the gift my Father promised, which you have heard me speak about. For John baptized with water, but in a few days you will be baptized with the Holy Spirit. . . . You will receive power when the Holy Spirit comes on you; and you will be my witnesses in Jerusalem, and in all Judea and Samaria, and to the ends of the earth." (Acts 1:4–5, 8)

For most of us the Holy Spirit is one of the great mysteries of our faith. I truly believe it is impossible for us to fully comprehend the profound significance of God literally dwelling within us in the manifestation of his Holy Spirit. And it is beyond the scope of this book to fully explore the nature of the Spirit or the many dimensions in which the Spirit of God is at work in us and in the world. But it is absolutely critical that we understand a few basics.

I spoke in a previous chapter about how, in the Old Testament, direct access to God was limited. After the expulsion from the garden, men and women lived in exile, their close relationship with God broken and severed. God's people could still cry out to him through prayer and try to discern his will, but their access was limited by a kind of spiritual "curtain" symbolized by the curtain in the temple that closed off the holy of holies. But even in the Old Testament there are numerous times when we are told that the Holy Spirit was specifically made available to certain people at certain times. We are told that Moses was guided by the Holy Spirit. Gideon, Joshua, Saul, David, Isaiah, Zechariah, and many others are said to have had the Spirit of the Lord upon them. Sometimes this was for a brief period of time and sometimes for many years. Almost always the Spirit was given when power or discernment or courage or prophecy was needed. The Spirit always enabled them to do something that they could not otherwise do or discern something they could not otherwise discern. But the Spirit was not given to everyone—until Jesus. But we do see throughout the Old Testament prophetic books the great promise that the day would come when the Spirit of the Lord would be freely given:

> "I will pour out my Spirit on all people.
> Your sons and daughters will prophesy,
>   your old men will dream dreams,
>   your young men will see visions.
> Even on my servants, both men and women,
>   I will pour out my Spirit in those days. . . .
> And everyone who calls
>   on the name of the LORD will be saved;
>   for on Mount Zion and in Jerusalem
>   there will be deliverance." (Joel 2:28–29, 32)

Of course, the coming of the Messiah was the pivotal event in redefining the relationship between God and his children. We are told that Jesus was literally conceived in Mary's womb by the power of the Holy Spirit. And at Jesus' baptism there was a dramatic imparting of the Holy Spirit:

> At that moment heaven was opened, and he *saw the Spirit of God descending like a dove* and alighting on him. And a voice from heaven said, "This is my Son, whom I love; with him I am well pleased." (Matt. 3:16–17, emphasis mine)

The Spirit of the Lord went with Jesus into the wilderness temptation by Satan, and when Jesus emerged to deliver his first public address at the synagogue in Nazareth, he stood and read the great messianic passage from Isaiah:

"The Spirit of the Lord is on me,

  because he has anointed me

  to proclaim good news to the poor.

He has sent me to proclaim freedom for the prisoners

  and recovery of sight for the blind,

to set the oppressed free,

  to proclaim the year of the Lord's favor."* (Luke 4:18–19, emphasis mine)

Then, just so they wouldn't miss the point, he went on to say, "Today this scripture is fulfilled in your hearing" (v. 21).

In the three years that followed, Jesus referred to the promise of the Holy Spirit on many occasions. Perhaps most significantly, Jesus told Nicodemus, "No one can enter the kingdom of God unless they are born of water and the Spirit" (John 3:5). In other words, entry into God's kingdom requires a baptism of the Holy Spirit. At the Last Supper and during his final long discourse with the disciples just before his arrest, he referred over and over to the coming of the Spirit—the Counselor, the Helper, the Advocate who would literally serve to replace Jesus himself in the lives of the disciples:

"And I will ask the Father, and he will give you another advocate to help you and be with you forever—the Spirit of truth. The world cannot accept him, because it neither sees him nor knows him. But you know him, for he lives with you and will be in you. *I will not leave you as orphans.*" (John 14:16–18, emphasis mine)

Once Jesus had risen and the curtain in the temple had been torn in two, access to God's presence was no longer limited to or controlled by the priesthood. God's presence no longer dwells within the temple but within every follower of Christ. "Do you not know that your bodies are temples of the Holy Spirit, who is in you, whom you have received from God? You are not your own; you were bought at a price" (1 Cor. 6:19–20).

We are now, as Peter said, "a chosen people, a royal priesthood, a holy nation, God's special possession, that [we] may declare the praises of him who called [us] out of darkness into his wonderful light" (1 Pet. 2:9). Heaven has been torn open, and God has come to dwell within us; the kingdom of heaven is near.

So what is the practical benefit of all the theology of the Holy Spirit? It is nothing less than the single enabling power that now makes it possible for ordinary human beings to be transformed and live differently than was ever before possible. Jesus' call to repent and change our lives, to replace our agendas

GOD'S PRESENCE NO LONGER DWELLS WITHIN THE TEMPLE BUT WITHIN EVERY FOLLOWER OF CHRIST.

with his agenda, to literally become a new creation, is only made possible when the Holy Spirit comes into our hearts with power. It is only possible when God dwells in us. When that happens, we have access to abilities and insights previously unavailable. Again, it would take an entire book to unpack this idea fully, but let me list just a few of the gifts made available to us by the Spirit:

- WISDOM: the ability to perceive things from God's perspective
- COMFORT: the ability to have confidence in God and put our minds and hearts at ease
- DISCERNMENT: the ability to discriminate between truth and falsehood, right and wrong
- INTERCESSION: access to the Spirit praying with us and through us before God
- DIRECTION: the ability to sense what God wants us to do and where God wants us to go
- POWER: the ability to do things we could not do before, speak things we could not speak before
- BOLDNESS: the ability to have the courage to take a stand and to face trials
- ENDURANCE: the ability to continue under stress, in suffering, with patience
- CONVICTION: a keen sense of conscience about our sins and our behavior

- STRENGTH: the ability to overcome our weaknesses
- PROTECTION: the ability to remain safe from evil, from the principalities and powers in this world
- UNITY: the ability to bind together with other followers of Jesus within the church
- FRUIT: the ability to demonstrate in our lives the fruit of the Spirit—love, joy, peace, patience, kindness, goodness, faithfulness, gentleness, and self-control

Lastly, the Holy Spirit was characterized by Paul as a *deposit* or down payment guaranteeing that Christ will return to redeem us. The Holy Spirit is a game changer. The Spirit infuses us with God's power, God's wisdom, and God's truth to enable us to live differently. And the Spirit unites the community of believers in the church as well, coordinating and orchestrating the different parts of the body of Christ.

I sometimes speculate on what the world might have been like before the Holy Spirit had been poured out. Do you sometimes wonder why the Old Testament Jews, despite seeing and experiencing miracle after miracle, so often failed to do the right thing or make the right choices? Might it have been because their minds were so clouded and darkened by sin that they were lost without the benefit of God's revealing Spirit? Might the cluelessness of the first disciples, who had the benefit of Jesus' physical presence, his teaching, and his miracles, be attributed to the fact that they did not yet have the illumination of the Spirit to guide them? The transformation that occurred in them between Acts 1 and Acts 2 is profound. And the only variable was Pentecost: the coming of the Spirit in power.

Even looking beyond God's people into secular human history, how much of what we cherish today in terms of human rights, freedom, compassion for others, justice systems, and moral codes was derived from followers of Christ, filled with the Holy Spirit, who shaped cultures, government, art, music, commerce, moral codes, and justice over the two millennia since Pentecost? And what would the world be like had the Holy Spirit not been given? Would it be darker, meaner, and more brutish? I have no doubt that it would. But because you and I have never lived in a world devoid of God's Spirit, we don't see the shocking contrast as the first disciples must have. No wonder they were on fire; they had seen and experienced the before and the after. They had seen heaven torn open and felt the Spirit come upon them like a "violent wind" (Acts 2:2). Both *reality* and *possibility* had changed before their very eyes.

I want you to return now with me to the metaphor of the GPS device because I think it can help us better understand just how the mystery of the Holy Spirit actually works in our lives. In one sense a person without the Holy Spirit is very much like a traveler lost in a foreign country, wandering about without a map. Even if her destination was well defined, she would have almost no possibility of reaching it on her own. There would simply be far too many confusing twists, turns, and intersections along the way. To take this traveler's sense of lostness a bit further, let's add the complication that while there are numerous road signs in place, they are all annoyingly incorrect. If the Holy Spirit had not been given, essentially, this would be our plight as followers of Christ, trying to follow him, trying to live according to his commands, but simply not having the ability to do so. We would be lost and wandering in a foreign and difficult place. The road signs posted in our world, which seem to offer us hope, inevitably point us in the wrong direction. The result would be a life of futility and frustration. We would want to follow Christ, would want to serve him and build his kingdom, but we would not be able to do so.

IF THE HOLY SPIRIT HAD NOT BEEN GIVEN, ESSENTIALLY, THIS WOULD BE OUR PLIGHT AS FOLLOWERS OF CHRIST, TRYING TO FOLLOW HIM, TRYING TO LIVE ACCORDING TO HIS COMMANDS, BUT SIMPLY NOT HAVING THE ABILITY TO DO SO.

Enter the GPS. With a GPS installed in your car, suddenly everything becomes clear. First, because the GPS is connected to a satellite, it knows exactly where you are in relation to everything else. You can see only the part of the road right where you are sitting, but the GPS sees the bigger picture. The satellite the GPS is connected to is, in a manner of speaking, omniscient because it can see the entire map at once and can even assess the traffic jams that lie along your route and suggest detours. Second, because of its greater perspective, the GPS can calculate the best possible route for you to take and can break it down into simple steps—driving directions. Third, the GPS gives you real-time instructions. "In one mile, turn right." "Exit on the left." And if it detects that you have taken a wrong turn, it can redirect you. Even though you may be traveling over foreign roads with faulty road signs, you can relax because you have a helper, a guide, an advisor that has an infinitely wider perspective than your own, one that you can rely on to give you simple, precise, and accurate advice as you travel. You have gone from confusion to clarity; from darkness to light; from radio silence to free, broadband WiFi.

Though the Holy Spirit is much more than some electronic device, the analogy to a GPS is quite helpful here. God has given us an inner voice, an inner compass that will provide the information we need to navigate successfully through our lives. But there are a few essential things we need to do in order to get the full benefit of this spiritual GPS. First, as we learned earlier, we have to set the right destination, the one that involves replacing our agendas with God's agenda—serving him and building his kingdom. Second, just as my own GPS sometimes requires, we need to allow time to acquire the satellite; we need to invest the time to connect to God through his Spirit by spending time in prayer, reading Scripture, practicing spiritual disciplines, worshipping, and spending time with other believers. The stronger our satellite connection, the stronger the signal. Third, we need to listen and pay attention to the driving directions that are given. The thing about a GPS is that you can choose to ignore it, or you can just turn it off. We can choose to ignore the Holy Spirit in our lives as well. We can become so enamored with the sights along life's roadways that we turn off the Spirit, turn off the road, and wander away from God's plan for our lives. The Holy Spirit doesn't coerce us. We need the Holy Spirit only if we want to obey God's will and follow God's path. If we want to follow our own way, we might as well turn it off. We aren't forced to listen or obey just as we aren't forced to heed a GPS. The choice is still ours.

Invariably, when I have used a GPS in a place I am not familiar with, I still make wrong turns. Despite the map, the words on the screen, and the voice in my ear, I still get off at the wrong exit or do something stupid that gets me off track. That's when I hear the little voice (I call mine Hugh because he has an Australian accent) chirping, "Recalculating." I love that feature more than any other offered by my GPS because it always gives me a second chance to get it right, to pay attention and listen and get back on the right course. God offers us those same second chances. We will always make mistakes, take the wrong turn, or get off at a wrong exit. If we make just one or two wrong turns, we won't be too far from the right path and the correction won't take long. But if we've had the GPS turned off for the last fifty turns, we will find ourselves miles and miles from God's chosen route, and the rerouting will be more painful. But he will lead us back if we are willing to stop, listen, and obey.

The presence of the Holy Spirit in our lives is a remarkable gift. As Christians baptized in the Holy Spirit, God now literally dwells within us. We can speak directly to God in prayer as the Holy Spirit intercedes for us. We can take our hurts, our needs, and our uncertainties directly to the Lord as a child might come to a father. And through the Spirit within us, we can gain access to the Father's comfort, reassurance, and advice. We now have new access to God's truth, new access to God's wisdom, and new access to God's power. The Spirit is a lamp unto our feet, and we no longer have to wander in the darkness. We are a holy nation, a royal priesthood, and we have now been sent into the world as Christ's ambassadors, as heralds of his kingdom, to invite other children into a restored relationship with their Father through the forgiveness offered in Jesus Christ, his Son; and the power of his Spirit, offered to us as a deposit "guaranteeing our inheritance until the redemption of those who are God's possession" (Eph. 1:14).

WHAT SHALL WE DO?

I have been crucified with Christ and I no longer live, but Christ lives in me. (Gal. 2:20)

In Acts 2 we read the dramatic account of the giving of the Holy Spirit, God coming to dwell within the hearts of men and women. This was an event perhaps even as significant as the incarnation of Christ as a babe in the manger of Bethlehem. It was another unprecedented spiritual turning point in the big story of God. Here is Luke's account:

> Suddenly a sound like the blowing of a violent wind came from heaven and filled the whole house where they were sitting. They saw what seemed to be tongues of fire that separated and came to rest on each of them. All of them were filled with the Holy Spirit and began to speak in other tongues as the Spirit enabled them. (Acts 2:2–4)

After this remarkable and public event, Peter, the leader of the disciples, stood up to preach. He spoke of the life, ministry, and death of Jesus, using the Old Testament prophecies of the Messiah to declare Jesus' true identity and quoting the prophecy that, one day, God's Spirit would be poured out:

> "'In the last days, God says,
> I will pour out my Spirit on all people.'" (Acts 2:17)

The people could plainly see not only the truth of Peter's claims about Jesus but also that God had indeed poured out his Spirit as Joel had prophesied. And they responded with passion and urgency:

> When the people heard this, they were cut to the heart and said to Peter and the other apostles, "Brothers, what shall we do?"
>
> Peter replied, "Repent and be baptized, every one of you, in the name of Jesus Christ for the forgiveness of your sins. And you will receive the gift of the Holy Spirit. The promise is for you and your children and for all who are far off—for all whom the Lord our God will call." (Acts 2:37–39)

Repent; change your life; replace your agenda with God's agenda; be filled with the Holy Spirit, and go; bring this same truth to "all who are far off." The Spirit still blows like a violent wind with fire in the hearts of those who believe. The gospel revolution is now in our hands. It is our time to lead. And God is now calling us to the front lines of service. Brothers and sisters, what shall we do?

REPENT; CHANGE YOUR LIFE; REPLACE YOUR AGENDA WITH GOD'S AGENDA; BE FILLED WITH THE HOLY SPIRIT, AND GO; BRING THIS SAME TRUTH TO "ALL WHO ARE FAR OFF."

II

. . .

CALLED FOR A PURPOSE

However, I consider my life worth nothing to
me, if only I may finish the race and complete
the task the Lord Jesus has given me—the task
of testifying to the gospel of God's grace.

—ACTS 20:24

I am only one, but I am one;
I cannot do everything,
But I can do something.
What I can do I ought to do,
And what I ought to do
By God's grace I will do.[1]

—EDWARD EVERETT HALE

Christians tend to throw around the word *calling* quite liberally. Some might use it only to describe a call into full-time ministry, as in "he was called to be a pastor" or "she was called onto the mission field in Cambodia." The assumption here is that most other people haven't been called at all. And since *I* haven't been *called*, I am now free to do whatever I want.

On the other extreme are those who claim that whatever they are doing is God's call on their lives. These people might say, "I was called to become an insurance actuary" or "God called me to live in California." This second way of defining *calling* sometimes serves to legitimize whatever we decide we might want to do. Either one of these approaches can lead to distortions. So then how should we understand God's call on our lives?

As I stated in the introduction, the main thesis of this book is that God has invited you to join him in changing the world.

- God has a dream for this world that Jesus called the kingdom of God.
- God created you to play an important role in his kingdom vision.
- You will never find your deepest purpose in life until you find your place in building God's kingdom.

My belief is that every follower of Christ, regardless of who they are and what they might be doing currently, was meant to participate in this kingdom work; in other words, we have all been *called* into this mission of Christ. The Great Commission had no footnotes stating that "the following people are excluded from this assignment . . ." The statements above describe the general calling of all Christians into mission, but they still don't describe the specific calling that God has for you as an individual. Therein lies the conundrum with which each of us must struggle. Think of it this way: If we all worked for Boeing, our general calling would be to engage in the building of airplanes. But our specific calling might be to assemble the landing gear, wire and install the instrumentation, assemble the wings, or design the roomy and comfortable coach seats. And which of those specific tasks we were called to would be determined by the boss's best judgment, taking into consideration our unique skills and abilities. We might be called to a specific role working directly on the airplane, or we might be assigned a role that provides support to those who are working on the plane—like accounting, human resources, parts procurement, or warehouse management. But the thing we would all have in common would be our shared calling to build airplanes.

The same is true in building the kingdom of God. We all have the same general assignment but our specific roles within it will be unique to us as individuals and will take into account our gifts and talents but also our experience, our assets, our physical location, and our connections and associations. You might be a missionary stationed in Cambodia, or you might be a barista at Starbucks who serves coffee every day with a smile and volunteers at the Ronald McDonald House in your community each week, ministering to families with gravely ill children. Remember the lesson of the past few chapters—our careers and our life circumstances are not ends unto themselves; they are means to the end of serving Christ and building his kingdom. For the follower of Christ there is no such thing as an ordinary teacher, fashion designer, homemaker, retail clerk, or barista; there are only kingdom-focused teachers, fashion designers, homemakers, retail clerks, and baristas. So then the great question we all must struggle with is what our specific calling to kingdom building looks like. What part of airplane building are we called to support?

As I have traveled around the world telling my own story of calling, I can't tell you how many people have come up to me to ask how they can find God's calling on their lives. This is a very serious and personal matter for each of us as followers of Christ, and I certainly don't have the corner on how someone else can discern God's calling on his or her life. But I do think that there are some helpful and logical steps, derived from Scripture, that can bring greater clarity to this universal longing to know God's will for our lives. Let me suggest six of them:

- Commit
- Pray
- Prepare
- Obey
- Act
- Trust

1. Commit

As I have suggested, before we begin the journey we must first commit to the destination. We need to be willing to replace our agendas with God's agenda, put God's will above our wills, and replace our priorities with God's priorities. This first step toward discerning God's calling on our lives is the most difficult because it involves dying to self. It means putting everything else aside in order to put God first. This gets to the heart of who is in control of our lives. It should come as no surprise that we like to be in control. The very first sin in the garden of Eden was over control. God had placed a limitation on Adam and Eve, and they didn't like it. Their way seemed more desirable than God's way.

IT DOESN'T TAKE MUCH TO GET PULLED OFF COURSE BY A SEEMINGLY BENIGN AND ATTRACTIVE DESIRE. AND IF ANY OF THESE THINGS BEGIN TO GAIN TRACTION IN YOUR LIFE IN A WAY THAT CAUSES YOU TO LOSE YOUR WAY, YOU CAN EASILY FIND THAT YOU ARE NO LONGER FOLLOWING THE CALLING AND PURPOSE GOD INTENDED FOR YOU.

If you live in the Magic Kingdom kind of world I described in chapter 4, there are countless temptations that can lure you away from God's plan: money, comfort, prestige, security, pleasure, success. It doesn't take much to get pulled off course by a seemingly benign and attractive desire. And if any of these things begin to gain traction in your life in a way that causes you to lose your way, you can easily find that you are no longer following the calling and purpose God intended for you. After we commit our lives to Christ, we are not called to just "be happy" and live the good life, killing time until we die and go to heaven. We have enlisted, and our lives are no longer our own; we have laid them down and made them available in service of the King.

In ancient Greek mythology the epic ten-year journey of Odysseus, as he returned from the Trojan War, required that he sail through treacherous straits guarded by the beautiful and tempting Sirens. These seductive creatures sang so beautifully that sailors listening to them would be lured off of their courses and into the destruction of the rocks. To avoid the same fate, Odysseus ordered his men to plug their ears with wax so they could not hear the beguiling music. Then he ordered them to tie him to the mast and to ignore all his commands until they were safely out of the Sirens' reach. Like Odysseus, we need to heed the danger and take it seriously. As we navigate through a world filled with sirens beckoning us off course, we must set our course for Christ's kingdom mission and tie ourselves to the mast of Christ's truth as we navigate through life.

I got a new perspective on this concept recently from a remarkable Indian man named Benny Prasad. Benny was a sickly teenager with serious health problems. Failing at school and sliding into self-pity and depression, Benny attempted suicide when he was just sixteen. Fortunately he did not succeed. Shortly after, at a youth retreat his mother urged him to attend, Benny had an encounter with God. Benny believes that he heard God speak to him, saying, "Benny, even though you have been useless all your life, I can make you a new creation." In Benny's own words, "God gave me new dreams, new goals, and a positive desire to serve him." Benny felt called to become a musician and to join Christ in bringing the gospel of the kingdom to all the nations. Despite lacking money or connections, he trusted that God would somehow enable him to travel the world and share the gospel. And between 2004 and 2010, Benny's spiritual GPS took him to all of the world's 224 sovereign and dependent nations plus Antarctica, setting the world record for visiting them in the shortest amount of time ever achieved. He lived each day in faith that God would open the doors and provide the resources to do something he could never arrange on his own. He gave up comfort, career ambitions, and even family as he left his parents for months at a time and never married. In many cases Benny even risked his life by sharing his faith in closed and repressive countries. Here is what he said to me: "Once you have decided you are willing to lose your life for Christ, the rest—money, pleasure, possessions, comfort—is easy to give up."

> "If anyone would come after me, he must deny himself and take up his
> cross daily and follow me. For whoever wants to save his life will lose it,

but whoever loses his life for me will save it. What good is it for a man to gain the whole world, and yet lose or forfeit his very self?" (Luke 9:23–25)

The paradox we find in this difficult passage is that we will find the fulfillment of our deepest yearnings and purpose only when we let go of our lives altogether and give them to God. Whatever our "Isaac" is, God asks us to take it to the altar and sacrifice it to him. As was the case with Abraham and Isaac, God may not take away what we offer, but that is his decision, not ours. Remember the question posed a few chapters back? "What is the most valuable thing you possess, and are you willing to offer it to the Lord?" The rich young ruler said no and walked away from Jesus in sadness. But Stu and Robin Phillips offered Moriah Ranch and found that their hearts had crossed over as they began to put God's agenda above their own. Benny Prasad found that once he was willing to lose his life, the rest was easy. But both had to first commit to God's purposes and his destination before they could see God's plan for their lives.

2. Pray

If the Holy Spirit is within us, acting as a kind of spiritual GPS device, then we need to listen to the driving directions we are being given. As I have already suggested, even once we are committed to the right destination, we can easily go astray if we stop listening to the GPS or, worse still, turn it off. So we must pray. Prayer is as much about listening to God as it is about talking to him. On our journey we must constantly take everything to him in prayer: our questions and concerns, our fears and our hopes, and our repentance for sometimes drifting off course. This is one of the methods God uses to steer and direct us.

"But when he, the Spirit of truth, comes, he will guide you into all truth. He will not speak on his own; he will speak only what he hears, and he will tell you what is yet to come. . . . All that belongs to the Father is mine. That is why I said the Spirit will receive from me what he will make known to you." (John 16:13, 15)

If we look analytically at the Lord's Prayer, the principal example of how we should pray given to us by Jesus, we can get another glimpse of the role played by prayer in discerning his will for our lives. We find these three main elements:

1. ACKNOWLEDGING WHO HE IS: *Our Father who art in heaven . . .* In other words, he is God, and we are not. We acknowledge his power and authority in our lives. In my GPS metaphor this is where we seek to acquire the satellite by appealing to the almighty and all-knowing God.

2. AFFIRMING HIS AGENDA: *Thy kingdom come, thy will be done, on earth as it is in heaven.* Here we are formally affirming that we are committed to his kingdom agenda and submitted to his will for our lives; thy will, not my will. This is our pledge to embrace his agenda and not our own. His destination becomes our destination.

3. ASKING FOR HIS HELP: *Give us this day our daily bread and forgive our debts as we forgive our debtors. Lead us not into temptation but deliver us from evil.* We are asking him to provide what we will need for the journey. Since we have forsaken our own pursuit of money, power, and success, we will need to depend on him to provide those things. He must now put the gas in our tank. We also ask him to forgive our sins and our bad driving and to give us the grace to do the same for others. And, finally, we ask him to lead us; give us the driving directions that will help us avoid temptations and protect us from evil. Tie us to the mast, Lord. Help us avoid these pitfalls as we seek to embrace your will for our lives.

PRAYER IS THE METHOD AND THE HOLY SPIRIT IS THE MECHANISM WHEREBY GOD HAS GIVEN US THE ABILITY TO DISCERN HIS DIRECTION IN OUR LIVES.

Prayer is the method, and the Holy Spirit is the mechanism whereby God has given us the ability to discern his direction in our lives. If you are confused about what God expects of you, pray.

3. Prepare

As we seek to discover and follow God's plan for our lives, we also have the entirety of Scripture at our disposal and the wise counsel of fellow believers in the church who are also filled with the Holy Spirit. Scripture provides for us the bigger blueprint for what God is doing in the world, and it gives us all the principles we need in order to live our lives in his service. I find that even when I am driving using my GPS, it is still very helpful to look at the bigger map in order to get a broader perspective on my journey. Scripture provides us with that larger map, the blueprint we can follow. The moral law, the stories and examples, the exhortations of the prophets, the books of Psalms and Proverbs, the life and teachings of Jesus, the history of the early church, and the instructions of Paul and the other New Testament writers all provide tremendous insight for our lives. Of course, blueprints have to be read to be of any use. Have you ever opened up some new item that comes with a couple hundred parts (some assembly required) and then tried to assemble it without reading the instructions? It might work for something simple, but it can be disastrous for something complex. And life is quite complex, so if you think you can handle whatever comes your way without reading, studying, and meditating upon Scripture regularly, you are sorely mistaken.

And just as it is a mistake not to prepare ourselves by studying God's Word, it is also a mistake to try and go it alone. God brought us together in community to strengthen and encourage one another. Wise disciples who have traveled the same road before you can offer crucial advice for the journey. Fellow Christians can offer guidance, insight, correction, practical tools, and great encouragement to us as we seek to discern God's will for our lives. There is an African proverb I love that goes like this: "If you want to run fast, run alone. If you want to run far, run together." Good advice for all of us on the journey.

4. Obey

Being a citizen of and an ambassador for God's expanding kingdom requires an entirely different way of living, one defined by radically different values and characterized by a revolutionary way of acting in the world.

If we are to be successful at following Christ, we must first understand that he cares not only about where our lives are going but also about how our lives are lived. The Great Commission itself called us to first go and make disciples. Then it defined what making disciples entailed: "teaching them to *obey* everything I have commanded" (Matt. 28:20, emphasis mine). Disciples are known by their obedience. "Do not merely listen to the word, and so deceive yourselves. Do what it says" (James 1:22). John is even clearer about obedience, if not as succinct as James:

> We know that we have come to know him if we obey his commands. The man who says, "I know him," but does not do what he commands is a liar, and the truth is not in him. But if anyone obeys his word, God's love is truly made complete in him. This is how we know we are in him: *Whoever claims to live in him must walk as Jesus did.* (1 John 2:3–6, emphasis mine)

Disciples are not expected to just "talk the talk" of obedience; they are to "walk the walk." Studying the blueprint in Scripture means that we follow its instructions. It requires that we obey what Scripture teaches.

Anyone seeking to truly know God's calling on his or her life must be serious about obedience. Do we really think that God is going to give a critical kingdom assignment to someone who hasn't been faithful in day-to-day obedience to his commands? Would a coach put a player into the big game if that player had missed all the practices, skipped all the training, and blown off all the drills? Would a boss promote someone and give her greater responsibility if she had failed to do well the job she had already been given?

DO WE REALLY THINK THAT GOD IS GOING TO GIVE A CRITICAL KINGDOM ASSIGNMENT TO SOMEONE WHO HASN'T BEEN FAITHFUL IN DAY-TO-DAY OBEDIENCE TO HIS COMMANDS?

Our lives are comprised of thousands of small daily decisions and actions: how we treat others, how we use our money, what we do with our abilities, where we invest our time, and what example we set for others to see. Before God will call you to something greater, he first wants to see what you have done in the small things. Only if we seek to live our lives as his disciples, seeking his kingdom in every sphere—work, family, money, relationships, community, and church—will we fully discover that unique thing God has called us to do and become the people he created us to be. If we live for ourselves we will likely miss it. I am always surprised when people are disappointed that they can't seem to discover "God's calling on their lives" when they haven't obeyed even his most basic commands. A life lived for Christ will always bear fruit.

> "A good tree cannot bear bad fruit, and a bad tree cannot bear good fruit. Every tree that does not bear good fruit is cut down and thrown into the fire. Thus, by their fruit you will recognize them." (Matt. 7:18–20)

Have you adopted kingdom values and principles, worked to change your bad habits, forgiven those who have wronged you, been loving to others, been generous with your money, become part of a local church, volunteered at church for the more humble jobs, put others ahead of yourself, and tithed your income? If you have, you are more likely to hear these words from the master, the same words he pronounced to the faithful steward in the parable of the talents:

> "'Well done, good and faithful servant! You have been faithful with a few things; I will put you in charge of many things. Come and share your master's happiness!'" (Matt. 25:23)

5. Act

If you have committed to God's agenda, prayed fervently for his direction in your life, prepared diligently by studying the teachings of Scripture and seeking counsel, and obeyed faithfully his commands, then it is time to act. My former pastor Earl Palmer observed that "God can't steer a parked car." It does little good to get in the car, fill the tank with gas, and power up the GPS if your car never gets out of the garage and onto the road. Just as a practiced athlete gets into the game and a trained soldier engages in the battle, so, too, must the disciple of Christ pursue the kingdom's mission.

My friend Lynne Hybels likes to ask the question, "What is mine to do?" There is much to do in God's kingdom, but you must first ask what part of it is yours to do. God has uniquely created you with gifts and talents, abilities and proclivities, passions and insights, assets and opportunities, hopes and dreams. Os Guinness has said of God's calling, "The truth is not that God is finding us a place for our gifts but that God has created us and our gifts for a place of his choosing—and we will only be ourselves when we are finally there."[2] Just as a plumber knows what is "his to do" in the building of a house and a goalie knows what is "hers to do" in a soccer game, you, too, can assume that God equipped you in specific ways to build his kingdom. The key is first to look around you. As you look through the lens of God's kingdom rescue mission and in the context of your own gifts and abilities, what is it that needs doing that you can do? It might be something at church, in your community, or at your workplace; it might even be something halfway around the world. You must seize opportunities. If God opens a door, walk through it. My wife, Reneé, almost always says yes when she is asked to teach a class, give a talk, develop a curriculum, or host an event. She believes that God can't steer a parked car and that if she is asked to serve in some way, it might just be God who is knocking at her door, so she'd better open it and walk through.

AS YOU LOOK THROUGH THE LENS OF GOD'S KINGDOM RESCUE MISSION AND IN THE CONTEXT OF YOUR OWN GIFTS AND ABILITIES, WHAT IS IT THAT NEEDS DOING THAT YOU CAN DO?

I talk to many people who feel that God has given them a burning passion for something quite specific. It might be to go to a particular country, be involved with handicapped children, do something about homelessness, or reach out to new immigrants. It could be a passion to pursue a particular career direction, such as financial services, teaching, or producing movies. These same people become incredibly frustrated when their passion does not result in the outcome they hoped for. So what should you do if God has given you such a passion? Again, God can't steer a parked car. Act. If you want to work for the International Justice Mission, look at their website for job openings, send them your résumé, call to arrange an interview, find someone who works there to speak to. Be persistent. I spoke recently to a young woman who felt called to work for the newly established Tim Tebow Foundation. She had just graduated as a Rotary Fellow from the London School of Economics with an astonishingly strong academic résumé. Though she might have had many job offers, she felt called to pursue a position with Tim Tebow's foundation, believing it offered a great opportunity to make a difference through a new kind of sports philanthropy. She tried writing and calling multiple times and got no response. Finally, she had the idea to send them one of her Irish clogging shoes (she is a talented folk dancer) in a gift box with a note saying that she had tried everything else and just wanted to "get her foot in the door." They were so intrigued they invited her for an interview and then, seeing her passion and vision, hired her.

In 1987, I was unemployed with three kids and a mortgage to pay. I heard that Lenox had an open position and was looking for a president for their smallest division. I found out that the head of human resources was a man named Wayne, so I called him. No reply. I called again. Still no reply. Some twenty calls later I was on a first-name basis with his administrative assistant, and she began to conspire with me to see just how we might get him to return my phone call. Finally, he did and then promptly blew me off, thanking me for my interest in Lenox and explaining that Lenox had hired a search firm and was conducting a national search. In other words, we are not going to hire some crackpot on the phone who claims he should be our next division president. I sent in my résumé anyway. Thirty days later I was hired, and the search was called off. A few years after that I became the CEO of all of Lenox, and Wayne, whom I had learned was also a follower of Christ, became one of my closest friends. Twenty-five years later he now works with me at World Vision. It all began with persistent action.

I cannot guarantee that God will grant you the desire of your heart, but I can guarantee that he will steer you once you put yourself in motion. Commit to serving him without conditions and move in the direction of your gifts and your passions, trusting that God will steer and lead. But accept that he may open some doors and possibly close others. "No" is also an answer. Listen to this remarkable passage from Acts 16:

> Their plan was to turn west into Asia province, *but the Holy Spirit blocked that route.* So they went to Mysia and tried to go north to Bithynia, *but the Spirit of Jesus wouldn't let them go there either.* . . . That night Paul had a dream: A Macedonian stood on the far shore and called across the sea, "Come over to Macedonia and help us!" The dream gave Paul his map. We went to work at once getting things ready to cross over to Macedonia. All the pieces had come together. We knew now for sure that God had called us to preach the good news to the Europeans. (Acts 16:6–10 MSG, emphasis mine)

Paul wanted to go to Asia but the Spirit blocked him—twice. Then he received the call to go to Macedonia. God closed one door and opened another. But note that Paul's "car" was on the road and very much in motion. God was steering.

6. Trust

Finally, you must trust in the assurance that God is in control. If you have faithfully taken each of the first five steps and still feel frustrated that you haven't felt God's calling on your life in a specific way, you need to relax. You may be waiting for some glamorous and dramatic way to serve and missing the fact that there is always a way to further God's kingdom right where you are. You cannot say that the place where you are stationed, the task that is before you, or the seemingly small opportunity that you have is insignificant to the larger mission. The Boeing worker assigned to design the latch on the cargo door might long for the glory of working on the majestic wings

WE ARE TO LIVE WITH THIS QUESTION ON OUR LIPS AT ALL TIMES: "HOW CAN I SERVE THE LORD TODAY, HERE IN THIS PLACE?"

or perhaps the jet engines because they seem so much more significant . . . until the cargo door latch fails, and a plane crashes, killing everyone aboard.

We are to live with this question on our lips at all times: "How can I serve the Lord today, here in this place?" And we are to trust that only God knows the full significance of the role he has called us to play in his greater mission. Remember that God asks us to be faithful in a little before he will entrust us with a lot. Sometimes an enlisted soldier, itching to go to the front lines, is held back on a military base in his or her home country thousands of miles from the front, awaiting orders. In the meantime, he must remain ready by practicing his drills and sharpening his skills, being faithful in a little. There may come a time when the commanding general calls him to the front; it's just not now.

I was forty-seven before I was called to lead World Vision. After my first year, when I realized how fulfilling my job was and how suited it was to my gifts and talents, I asked Reneé why I hadn't done something like this before. "Because you weren't ready," she said. "God had a lot of work to do in your life to prepare you to serve at World Vision." She was right again. God had been patient with me, testing, disciplining, shaping, and preparing me. He had asked me to be faithful with what was right in front of me, and when the time was right, he called me away to something different. And I had to be willing and available to go.

Abraham was one hundred years old when his promised son, Isaac, was born. Joseph was sold as a slave and spent years in prison before rising to become pharaoh's right-hand man who would save Egypt and his family from famine. Moses was eighty years old before he was given his great calling to rescue Israel from their Egyptian captivity. The key to discovering your specific calling in the end is patience and faithfulness. Make yourself available, serve where you stand, be faithful with what's in front of you, and trust God for the outcome.

A "NOT SO WONDERFUL" LIFE

In the perennially popular Christmas classic *It's a Wonderful Life*, the main character, George Bailey, suffers disappointment after disappointment. As a boy he saves his younger brother from drowning but loses his hearing in one ear in the process. Later, on the very day he is set to go off on his honey-moon, a Depression-era banking crisis requires that he stay back to hold the Bailey Bros. Building and Loan Association together to prevent the citizens of Bedford Falls from losing everything. He spends the next two decades of his life standing up to the evil Mr. Potter, who wants to control the whole town to increase his own wealth, thereby driving its inhabitants into poverty. At every step along the way, George Bailey does the right thing, the unselfish thing, putting the welfare of the town ahead of his own. And at every step along the way, George feels like a failure, a nobody whose dreams died long ago. Finally, as the movie climaxes, George is driven to the verge of bankruptcy and maybe even prison because his uncle Billy loses a large sum of depositors' money for which George is responsible. This last straw drives poor George to consider taking his life, believing that he has failed at everything: failed to realize his dreams of college, failed to fend off Mr. Potter's evil schemes, failed the citizens of Bedford Falls, and failed even his own wife and children. George declares that it would have been better if he had never been born.

But this is where the surprise ending occurs. Clarence, a bumbling angel, is sent to earn his wings by ministering to George in his time of need. Clarence takes George on a nightmarish tour of Bedford Falls to show him just how different life would have been had he, in fact, never been born. This alternative Bedford Falls is an appalling slum named Potterville, rife with poverty, gambling, alcoholism, and despair. George gets to see how badly the lives of those people he had helped in simple ways would have turned out had he never lived. In short, George gets to see what none of us ever see this side of eternity, the true impact of our lives on others, for good or for bad. The movie ends happily as George is rescued when the hundreds of people whom he has helped over the years contribute to restore the lost money, and Clarence finally earns his wings.

I want to suggest to you that for the faithful followers of Jesus Christ, ones who have lived in obedience to his Word, made themselves faithfully available in his service, and loved others passionately as his ambassadors, there is no such thing as an ordinary life.

12

· · ·

SPIRITUAL DOMINOES

There are no *ordinary* people.[1]

—C. S. LEWIS

When they saw the courage of Peter and
John and realized that they were unschooled,
ordinary men, they were astonished.

—ACTS 4:13

There are different kinds of gifts, but the same Spirit
distributes them. There are different kinds of service, but
the same Lord. There are different kinds of working, but in
all of them and in everyone it is the same God at work.

—1 CORINTHIANS 12:4–6

One of the embarrassing little pleasures of the Stearns family is watching
the TV program *America's Got Talent* every summer. There is something
about this corny show that intrigues me. It is a bizarre snapshot of the tex-
ture and diversity of American life and the seemingly unquenchable desire

that people have to be "discovered," to show the world that they are special, to catapult from obscurity to fame, to go from rags to riches. With its array of performers—from sword swallowers to opera singers, ventriloquists to trapeze acts—it is almost as if *America's Got Talent* has brought the carnival Midway, with all of its glitz and tawdriness, into our living rooms—minus the funnel cakes and the cotton candy. And I quite enjoy the spectacle.

Last year an unlikely character from Minnesota who called himself the Kinetic King caught America's imagination for a few weeks with his astonishing chain-reaction gadgets. Essentially, the Kinetic King designed and set off chain reactions based on the old falling-dominoes paradigm, but his creations were dominoes on steroids that wowed the audience with collapsing towers, "stick bombs," and flying Ping-Pong balls. As I watched these incredible chain reactions unfold, I discerned an important spiritual truth—yes, a spiritual truth from a reality TV show!—it is that a sweeping and profound series of events can begin with the falling of a single *domino*. Each domino in the contraptions set up by the Kinetic King played just a small part. Its main job was to set off the next link in the chain. Yet when arranged by the Kinetic King, these dominoes together created a spectacular result. I believe that this is exactly how God works in history.

> A SWEEPING AND PROFOUND SERIES OF EVENTS CAN BEGIN WITH THE FALLING OF A SINGLE *DOMINO*.

Most of the stories in the Bible illustrate the incredible impact of ordinary people willing to be used by God, setting off a chain reaction that had profound significance later. When Joshua was preparing to lead God's people into the promised land, he sent spies into Jericho to bring back a report; the spies were hidden and kept safe by a prostitute named Rahab. This seemingly unsavory woman was willing to risk her life for the Israelites because she sensed that God was with them and doing a powerful thing. *One domino fell.* When Joshua conquered Jericho, he saved Rahab and her entire family out of gratitude. They were allowed to live among the Israelites from then on. A lowly prostitute had been used by God to conquer the promised land for the Israelites. Pretty amazing, but that was not the end of the chain reaction that Rahab set off. Read on.

A few decades later a Jewish family living in Moab suffered a terrible loss. Naomi lost both her husband and her two sons, leaving her and her two Moabite (non-Jewish) daughters-in-law, Ruth and Orpah, alone. Widows in those times were extremely poor and vulnerable since they did not have husbands to care for them. Naomi decided she would return to her homeland in Bethlehem where she might find help. She urged Ruth and Orpah to return to their families in Moab and to find new husbands. Orpah did, but Ruth, out of concern for Naomi, insisted on following her home to Bethlehem. *The chain reaction continued.*

Arriving in Bethlehem, Ruth had a "chance" encounter with a wealthy landowner named Boaz as she was gleaning for food in his fields. Over time Ruth and Boaz grew closer together, and she ultimately became Boaz's wife and bore him a son named Obed. So what does any of this have to do with a courageous prostitute named Rahab? We are told that Rahab was Boaz's mother.[2] And just why is that so significant? Because Obed, the son of Ruth and Boaz, was the father of Jesse who was the father of King David, Israel's greatest king. *More dominoes fell.* One thousand years later the line of David—the line of Rahab and Ruth and Boaz—produced a man named Joseph, "the husband of Mary, of whom was born Jesus, who is called Christ" (Matt. 1:16). Wow!

The spiritual truth here is significant. I doubt that Rahab considered herself to be a very significant or successful person. She was likely driven to prostitution because she was poor and had no other means of support. In the eyes of most, maybe even herself, she was a nobody. But God saw her differently. God chose to use her in the unfolding of his great story of rescue and redemption. The Author of the big story had written Rahab into the plot, and she had been willing to play the role set out for her.

Most of us today are a lot like Rahab. We are ordinary people struggling to live what may feel to us like ordinary lives. It is hard for us to see how our lives can make any difference at all in God's great kingdom vision to restore and redeem his creation and rescue his children. And because we doubt that anything we might do could be significant, we can easily miss our appointments with destiny in the story of God.

HOW NEW JERSEY CHANGED KOREA

"From one man he made every nation of men, that they should inhabit the whole earth; and he determined the times set for them and the exact places where they should live." (Acts 17:26)

Another property of a domino chain reaction is how a very small domino can topple an even bigger domino. In fact, each domino in a chain can knock down another one half bigger than itself. But here is the amazing part: the impact of a domino just half an inch tall can multiply so much that in a chain of twenty-nine increasingly larger dominoes, the last one to fall would be as large as the Empire State Building![3] That's how a student in Princeton, New Jersey, started a chain reaction that launched the Christian church in Korea.

In the 1880s, Robert Wilder was among the first generation of American missionary kids. From his childhood in India as the son of missionaries, he had an abiding passion to go onto the mission field despite being chronically ill, physically weak, and fearful of public speaking. But Robert is not known today for being one of history's great missionaries; he is known instead for launching the Student Volunteer Movement for Missions (SVM). During college at Princeton, he and four other students signed a pledge to become missionaries. *Five dominoes fell.* His enthusiasm was contagious. During the 1886–1887 school year, Robert spoke at 167 different college and university campuses, challenging students to commit their lives to the Great Commission.

While preaching in Chicago, he spoke to an audience at McCormick Theological Seminary that included Samuel Moffett. Samuel was moved to sign Robert's Princeton Pledge, and within two years he traveled to Korea. *Another domino fell.* A few years later, Samuel then influenced and shared the gospel with a young Korean named Kiel Sun-chu, who had become disillusioned with his practice of Taoism. Kiel Sun-chu trusted Christ, and quickly *another domino fell.* After becoming a Christian, Kiel became active in the Central Presbyterian Church founded by Moffett. He was appointed a lay leader and eventually became one of the first seven graduates of Pyongyang Presbyterian Seminary.

Kiel was one of the instigators of the Pyongyang revival, a movement that began in January 1907, when spontaneous prayer and confession broke out during regular church meetings. *Thousands of dominos fell.* Those days of fervent prayer are now considered the birth of an independent, self-sustaining Korean church. When Kiel died in 1935, five thousand people attended his Pyongyang funeral. He had preached the gospel throughout the country and had done more than any other person to make Christianity a Korean faith through his social work and efforts toward Korean independence.

But God's chains of spiritual dominoes aren't linear; they crisscross with other chains as they are woven into incredibly intricate patterns. A separate and equally amazing series of events crisscrossed Robert Wilder's chain reaction. In *The Hole in Our Gospel*, I tell the story of an incredible series of events that began with a Sunday school teacher named Edward Kimball, who led a wayward seventeen-year-old boy to Christ in 1855. His name was Dwight L. Moody, and he became the foremost evangelist of the nineteenth century, leading hundreds of thousands of people to Christ. There was a direct chain as each person influenced the next, from Moody to F. B. Meyer to J. W. Chapman to Billy Sunday to Mordecai Ham and, finally, to the eventual conversion, more than seventy-five years later, of a seventeen-year-old boy in Charlotte, North Carolina, named Billy Graham at a Mordecai Ham revival. Another wow!

Here's the connection between Moody and Wilder: In the summer of 1886, Robert Wilder attended a monthlong Bible conference organized by D. L. Moody. Moody agreed to let Wilder lead an evening dedicated to international missions. It was at this Moody conference that Wilder's student movement was born, initiating Wilder's 167-campus tour just a few weeks later. So Moody, and Sunday school teacher Ed Kimball, who led Moody to Christ as a teenager, were critical dominoes in Robert Wilder's chain reaction. Can you catch just a small glimpse of the incredibly intricate purposes that God orchestrates with his precious dominoes?

And here is yet another outcome of the Kimball–Moody–Wilder–Moffett chain reaction: In 2001, at the fiftieth-anniversary celebration of the founding of World Vision in Seoul, South Korea, I had the privilege of meeting Pastor Kyung-Chik Han. He was ninety-eight years old at the time and confined to a wheelchair. Pastor Han, I learned, had grown up and come to faith in the church established by Samuel Moffett. As a young man he had an opportunity to attend Princeton Seminary just as Robert Wilder had decades earlier. Pastor Han not only became another great Korean church leader but is also credited with something else. Pastor Han was instrumental in encouraging a young American named Robert Pierce, a war correspondent stationed in Korea in 1950, to form a charity in the United States in order to address the appalling poverty of the Korean widows and orphans resulting from the conflict. In September of 1950, Bob Pierce filed papers in Portland, Oregon, to register a new charity he named World Vision.

The church in Korea now numbers 23 million, and it sends more foreign missionaries than any other country outside the United States. World Vision, now with forty-five thousand staff members in almost one hundred countries, provides assistance to tens of millions of children living in poverty each year—all because a Sunday school teacher named Ed Kimball showed up every week to teach, and a sickly kid named Robert Wilder made a commitment to promote foreign missions. Speaking of the student movement Wilder began, one writer said, "The SVM became the greatest single force for missions that the world has ever seen. At least twenty thousand young people went overseas as a result of its ministry."[4]

Do the math. Because of Kimball, God gave us Moody and Billy Graham. Because of Moody, Wilder. Because of Wilder, Moffett. Because of Moffett, Kiel Sun-chu, Kyung-Chik Han, explosion of Christianity in Korea, and World Vision. That is the profound nature of spiritual dominoes.

THE GREATEST HUMANITARIAN OF OUR TIME

Drudgery is the touchstone of character. The great hindrance in spiritual life is that we will look for big things to do. "Jesus took a towel . . . and began to wash the disciples' feet."[5]—Oswald Chambers

Let me tell you something you probably don't know. The person who has perhaps had the single greatest impact on addressing global poverty, the AIDS pandemic, and economic justice on the planet in the past twenty-five years is . . . wait for it . . . Steve Reynolds. Steve who? That's right, not Bill Gates, not Bill Clinton or George Bush, not Mother Teresa or Jimmy Carter—Steve Reynolds. Let me explain.

In 1985, a young Steve Reynolds was working as World Vision's communications officer in Ethiopia, during what was the worst famine of a generation. If you were around back in 1985, you know that the great Ethiopian famine was probably the top news story of the year as the entire world rallied to come to Ethiopia's assistance. Steve's job was primarily to get stories from the front line back to the US media, and he spent a lot of dreary and difficult days in the relief camps as an eyewitness to the horrors of massive starvation and death, gathering information that he hoped would provoke more people to help back home. Steve was just one domino in the midst of the enormous humanitarian response inside of Ethiopia.

One day he got a call from headquarters asking if he would host a young European couple, Ali and Paul Hewson, who wanted to visit the famine zone to learn firsthand what was happening. They wanted to help but felt they first needed to see with their own eyes. Steve was willing to help. *Two more dominoes fell.* Knowing how rough the conditions were for guests and the shocking grimness of the human suffering, Steve doubted whether this couple would last even a few days, but he agreed to be their host. To his surprise, they lasted. They stayed almost a month, rolling up their sleeves to help, offering encouragement, making the children laugh again, and showing tireless compassion. Paul was a musician, and he entertained the kids by writing little songs about eating healthy vegetables and washing hands before you eat. Paul and Ali finally went home but not before they had committed to do whatever they could to help. You may know Paul better by his nickname, Bono.

Since that trip in 1985, Bono, the lead singer of the phenomenal Irish rock group U2, has indeed *helped.* Countless dominoes have fallen. He has traveled the globe as an advocate for the poorest of the poor and as a crusader for justice. He has met with kings and queens, presidents, prime ministers, and the pope. He has lobbied members of parliaments and congresses. His support of the Jubilee 2000 debt relief movement resulted in billions of dollars of debt relief for poor nations, allowing them to invest in building schools and clinics instead of paying interest on their debts. He has persuaded governments to appropriate billions of dollars of aid to the poor, perhaps culminating in America's greatest foreign assistance program since the Marshall Plan, President Bush's PEPFAR program, which declared war on one of the greatest humanitarian pandemics of our time, AIDS. He launched the One Campaign and helped start Product Red. He was nominated for the Nobel Peace Prize in 2003 and named *Time*'s Person of the Year in 2005 along with Bill and Melinda Gates. Since 1985, his list of accomplishments on behalf of the world's poor could literally fill an entire book.

In an interview a few years back with *Christianity Today* magazine, Bono had this to say about the impact of Steve Reynolds and his 1985 trip to Ethiopia with Ali:

> "All of this started for me in Ethiopia in the mid-'80s, when my darling wife and I went out there as children, really, to see and to work in Africa," he told the congregation at Louisville's Northeast Christian Church.
>
> World Vision marketer Steve Reynolds played a key role, Bono says. "Honestly there is no chance that I would be here if [World Vision] hadn't called me up and asked me to make that journey. It's a journey that changed my life forever."[6]

Twenty-seven years later Steve still works for World Vision. He has served in numerous jobs and in numerous ways, working behind the scenes on behalf of the world's poorest people. Steve has been faithful in the little things. He has been obedient to God and taken seriously his command to "love our neighbors as ourselves." Steve has been willing and available to be used however God wanted to use him. And God has used him indeed . . . as part of one of the great domino chain reactions let loose in our lifetime on behalf of God's beloved poor.

FOOLISH THINGS

The apostle Paul understood that the Christian movement in the first century had to be carried by ordinary people. From a worldly perspective early Christianity was hanging by a thread, led by a rough band of men described in the book of Acts as unschooled and ordinary. There were no members of Caesar's family involved, no Roman senators or governors, no great Roman citizens of wealth or military leaders—just a collection of unlikely revolutionaries: fishermen, tradesmen, tax collectors, and zealots. The Vegas odds for this whole Christianity thing making it past AD 50 would have been exceedingly slim—but for God. When Paul wrote the following words to the young Corinthian church, he understood that God had chosen a different way, a new way, to change the world. He had chosen the weak over the powerful, the humble over the noble, the poor over the rich, the servant over the master; he had chosen a baby in a manger over a king in a palace:

> GOD HAD CHOSEN A DIFFERENT WAY, A NEW WAY, TO CHANGE THE WORLD. HE HAD CHOSEN THE WEAK OVER THE POWERFUL, THE HUMBLE OVER THE NOBLE, THE POOR OVER THE RICH, THE SERVANT OVER THE MASTER; HE HAD CHOSEN A BABY IN A MANGER OVER A KING IN A PALACE.

> For the foolishness of God is wiser than man's wisdom, and the weakness of God is stronger than man's strength. Brothers, think of what you were when you were called. Not many of you were wise by human standards; not many were influential; not many were of noble birth. But God chose the foolish things of the world to shame the wise; God chose the weak things of the world to shame the strong. He chose the lowly things of this world and the despised things—and the things that are not—to nullify the things that are, so that no one may boast before him. (1 Cor. 1:25–29)

Paul understood. And because he understood the significance of what God wanted to do with and through his church, Paul laid out the principles by which a coalition of the ordinary could accomplish the extraordinary. In 1 Corinthians 12, he lays out the powerful metaphor of the church as a body:

> Now the body is not made up of one part but of many. If the foot should say, "Because I am not a hand, I do not belong to the body," it would not for that reason cease to be part of the body. And if the ear should say, "Because I am not an eye, I do not belong to the body," it would not for that reason cease to be part of the body. If the whole body were an eye, where would the sense of hearing be? If the whole body were an ear, where would the sense of smell be? But in fact *God has arranged the parts in the body, every one of them, just as he wanted them to be.* If they were all one part, where would the body be? As it is, *there are many parts, but one body.*
>
> The eye cannot say to the hand, "I don't need you!" And the head cannot say to the feet, "I don't need you!" On the contrary, *those parts of the body that seem to be weaker are indispensable,* and the parts that we think are less honorable we treat with special honor. And the parts that are unpresentable are treated with special modesty, while our presentable parts need no special treatment. *But God has combined the members of the body and has given greater honor to the parts that lacked it,* so that there should be no division in the body, but that its parts should have equal concern for each other. If one part suffers, every part suffers with it; if one part is honored, every part rejoices with it.
>
> Now you are the body of Christ, and each one of you is a part of it.
> (vv. 14–27, emphasis mine)

Paul used this amazing metaphor to reveal just how God intended to work through his church to accomplish his kingdom mission to rescue his children and to begin the process of restoring his creation. God's strategy was to organize his disciples into a "body," which he called the church. This body would have capabilities far beyond those of any single disciple, just as fifty thousand dominoes can be organized to do something no single domino can do. From this passage we can draw out five *domino principles,* which are crucial for Christ's disciples to understand.

1. *The whole is stronger than the sum of the parts.*

One domino is of little use without the support of other dominoes. Paul paints a humorous picture of a body that is just a giant ear or eye. Of course, such a body would not be able to function at all because it would lack all of the other critical functions. This is one reason that all disciples are called to become part of a local church and join with other believers in worship, training, prayer, and outwardly focused mission.

2. *We each have a different role to play.*

What is obvious of a body—that ears, eyes, kidneys, and feet all have different but complementary roles—is also true of the church. God has created each one of us with a unique array of gifts and abilities, and he has also given us different life experiences and placed us individually in different places. We don't all live in Hoboken, New Jersey, nor are we all connected to the same people, opportunities, and resources. This diversity of capabilities and connections is the great strength of the church.

3. *Every role is critical.*

In a chain reaction of fifty thousand dominoes, which domino is the most important? All of them. Paul took pains to emphasize that "those parts of the body that seem to be weaker are indispensable" and that "the parts that we think are less honorable we treat with special honor" (1 Cor. 12:22, 23). I believe that he went out of the way to say this in order to quell any sense of hierarchy, status, or false prestige within the church. Again, Paul understood that God intended to powerfully use the "weak" things, the "lowly" things, and the "things that are not" to accomplish his great purposes, and so it was absolutely critical that every one of Christ's followers understood that they had a crucial role to play in God's kingdom, and that no role was insignificant.

4. *We are interdependent.*

How many dominoes need to fail in order for the entire chain reaction to fail? Just one. What if Robert Wilder didn't start the SVM or Samuel Moffett didn't go to Korea; Bono never went to Africa or Steve Reynolds failed to be his host; Ed Kimball quit teaching Sunday school or D. L. Moody never committed his life to Christ? Everything changes. If one link in the chain fails to play its designated role, the entire chain of events is altered. Now, God is still sovereign, and his purposes will ultimately be accomplished, but when any one of us fails to do that which God created us to do, it somehow changes the course of events for the worse; there are consequences. There were always consequences for the Jewish nation in the Old Testament for their failure to obey God: plagues, captivity, and even the delay of God's promises. In the book of Esther, when Mordecai, Esther's cousin, speaks to her about the critical role she is called to play in saving the Jewish people from King Xerxes, he says this: "For if you remain silent at this time, relief and deliverance for the Jews will arise from another place, but you and your father's family will perish. And who knows but that you have come to your royal position for such a time as this?" (Est. 4:14). Mordecai recognized just where Esther's domino was situated and the role she was uniquely positioned by God to play. But he also recognized that God would provide a different way to save his people should Esther fail to act. He stated that there would be consequences for Esther's failure: "You and your father's family will perish." If Esther failed, the chain reaction would fail, too, but God would still find a way to accomplish his purposes, and there would be consequences to Esther and possibly those further ahead in the chain of events. Might "failure to obey" also explain why two thousand years after the Great Commission was given, the mission Christ gave to his church remains unfinished?

> WHOEVER YOU ARE AND WHEREVER YOU ARE PLACED, KNOW THAT YOU WERE PLACED THERE BY THE KING TO ACCOMPLISH HIS GOOD PURPOSE.

5. God brings the body to life.

Not only does God arrange the dominoes; he created each one: "God arranged the members in the body" (1 Cor. 12:18 ESV). He is the true Kinetic King. A dead body has all of the same parts as a living one. God brings life and purpose to the church through his Holy Spirit just as the Kinetic King of domino fame takes a lifeless box of dominoes, sticks, cups, and gadgets to create spectacular chain reactions. If you think about the complexity of human beings and the infinite ways to place them and arrange them in our world, you quickly realize the importance of the One who weaves them all together to accomplish his will. Whoever you are and wherever you are placed, know that you were placed there by the King to accomplish his good purpose, "for it is God who works in you to will and to act in order to fulfill his good purpose" (Phil. 2:13).

THE CARDS YOU WERE DEALT

My great concern is not whether you have failed, but whether you are content with your failure.[7]—Abraham Lincoln

Before I close this chapter, I need to deal with perhaps the single greatest obstacle that prevents followers of Christ from becoming the people he intends them to be; I call it the loser syndrome, the belief that you don't have what it takes to do anything significant for God. Sometimes it masquerades as humility in the church. You're not smart enough, rich enough, talented enough, courageous enough, or spiritual enough to make much difference in God's great kingdom work. It's something for other people to do—not you. Your pastor has the training to do it; your neighbor has more skills. Someone else is a better leader or has a better education. Once you have allowed yourself to believe these lies, they will become self-fulfilling . . . and guess what? You won't be very useful to God.

There is a related issue that will also render you fairly useless—the attitude that if only you had been dealt a better hand of cards, you could have done so much more. You had a rough childhood; it left some emotional scars, and you weren't able to go to college. You made some bad choices when you were younger and never quite recovered. Maybe you're divorced and a single parent or suffering from a chronic illness, on the verge of bankruptcy or unemployed. You've been passed over at work and passed over in life. It's too late for you to turn it all around. Let's face it; you're just a loser who has been dealt a bad hand of cards.

But hear this: God doesn't make any losers. Jesus came to turn losers into winners. You are a child of the King, a unique one-of-a-kind miracle, and you were created to play a critical role in the big story of God. And God really intends to use you to change the world. A couple of years ago I spoke to a group of teenagers in World Vision's Youth Empowerment Program in Washington, DC. These kids were from some of America's roughest urban and rural neighborhoods. They had been abused and neglected, dragged through the foster parenting system, pressured to join gangs, threatened with violence, and just generally had been dealt a bad hand of cards. They might have justifiably thought of themselves as losers. So I told them a story of another kid who had been dealt a pretty bad hand of cards as well.

This kid got off to a bad start. At age seven he and his parents had been forced out of their home. Then his mother died when he was nine. As a result, he never finished grade school, let alone high school or college. At twenty-three he tried to start a business, but it failed. He then tried politics, running for an office in his state and lost. Then he lost his job. He wanted to go to law school but couldn't get in. At twenty-four he borrowed money to start another business, but it failed, too, and he spent the next seventeen years trying to pay off the debt. At twenty-six he got engaged, but his fiancée died before the wedding. At twenty-seven he had a total nervous breakdown and spent six months in bed. Talk about a loser! This guy should have quit right there.

At twenty-nine he tried politics again, running for his state legislature; he lost again. Two years later he tried again and lost. Three years later he ran for Congress. You've got it: he lost again because that's what losers do. At age thirty-seven he ran for Congress again and actually won, but two years later when he ran for reelection he was, of course, defeated. Giving up on national politics for the time being, he sought a more humble job as a land officer in his home state, but he was rejected. He then had the bad judgment to run for the US Senate twice (he lost both times) and then sought to be his party's nominee for vice president and failed again. This was a guy who clearly just didn't know when to give up. He had been dealt more bad cards than any person deserves to be dealt. He may have been a loser, but he wasn't a quitter. Instead of folding his hand as most people would have, he was determined to keep playing.

So what is the point of this whole story? Have you given up? Have you concluded that the cards you've been dealt are not a winning hand? Have you convinced yourself that God can't use someone like you—that you are a loser? Are you, maybe, even angry with God for dealing you those cards in the first place? Are you tired of picking yourself up after every failure and setback?

The remarkable thing about our "loser" friend is that he never gave in to that inner voice telling him he was a nobody. Because you see, he was a man of faith, and he knew that God doesn't make any losers. He knew that his job was to play the cards he was dealt to the best of his ability and leave the winning and losing to God. When he was fifty-one, after a lifetime of failure and loss, he had the audacity to run for president of the United States. Maybe he is better known to you as Abraham Lincoln, the sixteenth and perhaps the greatest US president ever to serve our country. Throughout his life, Abraham Lincoln was dealt some of the worst cards imaginable. He suffered failure after failure, hardship after hardship. But each time he picked himself up, dusted himself off, and made a conscious choice not to let his circumstances define him. Lincoln ended slavery, led the nation through the Civil War, and preserved the union of the United States. And he paid the ultimate price for his service when he was shot and killed on April 14, 1865. Changing the world for Christ isn't easy, and there is always a price to pay. Abraham Lincoln was a follower of Jesus Christ, a child of the King, and he believed against all odds that there was a role for him to play in God's big story because God doesn't make any losers.

A STAFF, A SLING, A NET, AND A PEN

You may have heard it said that "God does not call the equipped, but rather he equips those whom he calls." If we look at the sweep of history and specifically to those men and women God has used to change the world, we can take comfort in knowing that God does use the foolish things—and often the most unlikely people—to shame the wise. Moses, a simple shepherd, challenged the most powerful man on earth, Pharaoh, with nothing but a staff in his hand. That same staff later parted the Red Sea and led a nation to the promised land. God used Moses.

David was the youngest of Jesse's ten sons, the runt of the litter, but he stood before Goliath with only a sling in his hand and shouted with confidence: "You come against me with sword and spear and javelin, but I come against you in the name of the LORD Almighty, the God of the armies of Israel, whom you have defied. This day the LORD will deliver you into my hands, and I'll strike you down and cut off your head" (1 Sam. 17:45–46). God used David.

> WHEN WE FACE OUR GOLIATHS, ARE CONFINED BY SOME PRISON, OR FEEL INADEQUATE TO THE TASK, WE CAN TAKE COMFORT KNOWING THAT THE GOD WHO FASHIONED US IN OUR MOTHERS' WOMBS HAS ALSO PLACED US IN THE WORLD FOR "SUCH A TIME AS THIS" (EST. 4:14).

Peter, a rough-hewn fisherman working his nets, was Jesus' choice to become a fisher of men and to lead his church. And God used Peter.

Paul, a well-educated Pharisee, challenged the Roman Empire from a prison cell with nothing more than words and a pen. God used Paul too.

The one characteristic these men all had in common was that they were willing to take what they had in their hands and lay it down in service to God, willing to be used by God to accomplish his will regardless of the cost. And use them he did. It should be of great comfort that God's plan does not rely on our greatness but rather on his. We must simply be willing to be used. God has called each one of us to follow him and to join him in his kingdom mission, to play a role in the great story he is writing. When we face our Goliaths, are confined by some prison, or feel inadequate to the task, we can take comfort knowing that the God who fashioned us in our mothers' wombs has also placed us in the world for "such a time as this" (Est. 4:14). And he will not abandon us. No Goliath we face is mightier than the God we serve. We need only to lay down our lives in his service.

13

• • •

OUTPOSTS OF THE KINGDOM

Go to the people of all nations and make them my disciples.
Baptize them in the name of the Father, the Son, and the Holy
Spirit, and teach them to do everything I have told you.

—MATTHEW 28:19–20 CEV

I do not know of a denomination or local
church in existence that has as its goal to teach
its people to do everything Jesus said.[1]

—DALLAS WILLARD

The first twelve chapters of this book have focused primarily on us as individual followers of Christ. We started with the very meaning of our individual lives and the mystery story into which each of us was born. Then we tackled some of life's other big questions:

- What is the big story that God is writing?
- How did it culminate in the life, death, and resurrection of Jesus?
- Why was Jesus obsessed with the coming of the kingdom of God?

- Why did Jesus leave after his death and resurrection?
- How do we understand the kingdom mission Jesus gave us before he left?
- Where do our lives today intersect with that mission?
- What response does God require from us?
- How do we discern our calling, our unique role, in the mission of God?
- Does God really use ordinary people to do extraordinary things?

All of this so far has been mostly focused on how God wants us individually to participate in his great work. But God has wisely chosen to organize his individual followers into communities called churches. None of us was meant to go on this journey alone. So now we must turn to the question of just why churches exist in the first place and how God intends his church to carry out his purposes in the world.

To get very logical about all of this, we might say that the only reason we need to organize ourselves at all is because Jesus left us behind. As we saw in chapter 3, he might have instead brought all of history to its conclusion right then—the final judgment, the defeat of sin and evil, the resurrection of the faithful departed, the restoration of God's creation, and the ultimate establishment of his eternal kingdom. This could have been a much shorter movie. But, as we know, he didn't tie it all up with one big conclusive bow.

THE ONLY REASON WE NEED TO ORGANIZE OURSELVES AT ALL IS BECAUSE JESUS LEFT US BEHIND.

Instead, he began a new chapter intended to extend the good news of his kingdom to as many people as possible. The doors to the kingdom of God were open to everyone as a result of Jesus' atoning death and resurrection, and we were given the assignment to invite everyone to come in. The lead character in this new chapter is the church; in fact, this period of time after the Ascension and before the second coming of Christ is commonly called the Church Age. The mission of these newly incorporated communities of disciples, aka the church, was now to go into all the world to invite God's children to enter, to be reconciled to the Father, and to become disciples of and ambassadors for a new way of living. And Jesus said once this inviting, reconciling, and discipling was widely, deeply, and sufficiently accomplished, he would return.

Bottom line: the church was established for a purpose.

The implication of this, therefore, is profound: the chief purpose of the church is to bring glory to God by accomplishing the Great Commission pronounced by Jesus. Everything else—worship, preaching, teaching, discipling, congregational care, the sacraments, feeding the hungry, caring for the poor, and so on—while valuable for us and pleasing to God in and of themselves, are ultimately means to the end of faithfully completing the assignment given to the church by Jesus just before he left.

THE CHIEF PURPOSE OF THE CHURCH IS TO BRING GLORY TO GOD BY ACCOMPLISHING THE GREAT COMMISSION PRONOUNCED BY JESUS.

If we compare the mission of the church to the mission of a military at war, the same is true: everything that happens in boot camp is a means to the end of preparing the soldiers to accomplish their mission and win the war. Our churches are the boot camps of the kingdom revolution. I don't want to minimize the importance of the many other roles the church plays in our lives as followers of Jesus. Churches are indeed communities of believers united by shared belief and mission. When properly aligned with Christ, they can enrich every dimension of our lives and provide great help and comfort to us, both in times of need and times of plenty. But all of this, I want to suggest, carries with it the overarching objective to deepen and strengthen God's people to do God's work and to do it in God's way. Make no mistake; God's people have been called to a task, and the church's responsibility is to equip them to do it. This is why Paul powerfully states that Christ has given us (his church) a *ministry of reconciliation* and has now commissioned us as his *ambassadors*; that his appeal to the world is literally being made through us:

> Therefore, if anyone is in Christ, the new creation has come: The old has gone, the new is here! All this is from God, who reconciled us to

himself through Christ and gave us the ministry of reconciliation: that God was reconciling the world to himself in Christ, not counting people's sins against them. And he has committed to us the message of reconciliation. *We are therefore Christ's ambassadors, as though God were making his appeal through us.* (2 Cor. 5:17–20, emphasis mine)

The notion that God has decided to make his appeal to the world through you and me literally sends a chill up my spine every time I read it. His mission: to reconcile the world to himself. His strategy: the church. His soldiers: you and me. Can there be anywhere else a higher calling, a more urgent mission or a more important priority? The big story of God is not yet finished. The next chapter is being written by the church.

VIVA LA REVOLUTION

I have used the metaphor of a revolution to describe the coming of the kingdom of God through the work of the church. The dictionary definition of revolution is "an overthrow or repudiation and the thorough replacement of an established government or political system by the people governed," or "a radical and pervasive change in society and the social structure."[2]

Revolutions challenge the prevailing values of a culture, a nation, or a society. Revolutions are fueled by a sense of outrage against the way things are: the falsehood, the corruption, the injustice, the hypocrisy, and the oppression. They seek to replace the principalities and powers that are in control with a form of rule that stands in stark contrast, and they gain momentum as more and more people join the revolution and bring it to a tipping point.

As I look at the Great Commission given to us by Christ, I see just that kind of revolutionary principle:

"I have been given all authority in heaven and on earth! Go to the people of all nations and make them my disciples. Baptize them in the name of the Father, the Son, and the Holy Spirit, and teach them to do everything I have told you." (Matt. 28:18–20 CEV)

To paraphrase: My "government in exile" has returned to overthrow the established regime. Go as my ambassadors to the people of all the nations and enlist them to become citizens of my kingdom, calling them away from the corruption of the status quo. Teach them the new ways of thinking and living under my authority, and then send them out, too, to join the revolution.

Since a revolution seeks to change a society from within, it establishes outposts, places where the revolutionaries gather to plan and organize, train their soldiers, mobilize resources, and then launch outwardly as they seek to expand their territory. The roiling change in the Middle East that began with the Arab Spring in 2011 has given the world a fresh glimpse of how revolutions work, starting small and gathering steam as more and more people embrace the revolutionary goals and principles and join the cause. The result has been that entire governments have been toppled, new constitutions are being adopted, and new leaders are being installed. Revolutions shake up the status quo.

While I am in no way suggesting that the church should mount a violent revolution, I am suggesting that the church must adopt a revolutionary mind-set. We are indeed trying to topple the prevailing regimes that have oppressed the human race since the fall, those based on power, money, oppression, corruption, and falsehood. And we are seeking to replace them with the good news of God's rule, based on truth, love, forgiveness, compassion, and justice. We're trying to shake things up.

I have written in my earlier book that the manifesto of this kingdom revolution can be found in the great messianic passage of Isaiah 61, read by Jesus in the synagogue in Nazareth at the very beginning of his public ministry. This event, recounted in Luke 4, was a declaration of Jesus' identity and mission:

> The Spirit of the Sovereign LORD is on me,
>> because the LORD has anointed me
>> to proclaim good news to the poor.
> He has sent me to bind up the brokenhearted,
>> to proclaim freedom for the captives

and release from darkness for the prisoners,
to proclaim the year of the LORD's favor. (Isa. 61:1–2)

From this we can glean the principal strategies of the revolution Jesus came to ignite:

- PROCLAMATION: telling the good news that the Messiah has come, sins can be forgiven, and the kingdom of God is now available to all who repent and believe
- COMPASSION: the Messiah's kingdom characterized by love and by a concern for the physical, emotional, relational, and spiritual needs of people
- JUSTICE: God's justice and jubilee, now established, freeing us from every kind of oppression and exploitation at the hands of men

And this is, in fact, just what Jesus modeled over the next three years. He boldly proclaimed the good news but always accompanied his preaching with action: healing, feeding, forgiving, and caring. One of the primary reasons people listened to Jesus at all was that his actions spoke as loudly as his words. Help people, feed people, heal people, and love people and they will be, not surprisingly, willing to listen to what you have to say. Jesus also took on the injustice and hypocrisy of the Pharisees, chiding them for neglecting justice, mercy, and faithfulness.

"Woe to you, teachers of the law and Pharisees, you hypocrites! You give a tenth of your spices—mint, dill and cumin. But you have neglected the more important matters of the law—justice, mercy and faithfulness. You should have practiced the latter, without neglecting the former." (Matt. 23:23)

Jesus' words and actions represented a kind of symbolic "turning back of the curse." He forgave sins, healed diseases, cast out demons. He was offering a cure for the evils brought upon us by the fall. He was dealing with the consequences of sin by first addressing its symptoms and then offering a permanent cure. Jesus was providing us with a foretaste of his ultimate kingdom when every tear would be wiped away; sin, suffering, disease, injustice, and death would be no more, and he would reign forever. And when the church imitates the words and deeds of Jesus, when it embraces the redemptive mission of Jesus, it also echoes the kingdom yet to come and holds out hope to a hurting world. Just as John the

> JESUS' WORDS AND ACTIONS REPRESENTED A KIND OF SYMBOLIC "TURNING BACK OF THE CURSE."

Baptist prepared the way for the Lord, and made straight the paths for Jesus at his first coming, so are churches to be the revolutionary outposts of the kingdom preparing the way for his Second Coming.

What then are the hallmarks of these new kingdom outposts, and how do they best carry out the assignment given to them by Jesus? Let me suggest five dimensions that should define us as communities of believers:

1. Worship

We start by acknowledging the majesty of God, the power of God, and the authority of God in our individual and communal lives. He is the King, and we seek to live in his kingdom under his perfect rule. He is the all in all. We ask to be filled with his Spirit, and we pray without ceasing in the knowledge that he must empower us if we are to accomplish anything in his name.

2. Model

We seek to demonstrate a new way of postrevolution living, modeling the new truths, the new values, and the new practices that characterize God's plan for human flourishing. We are compassionate, loving, and generous with our resources. We take care of each other by showing what it means to love our neighbor as ourselves. We walk the walk of our values and demonstrate a level of caring not found in other communities. We become the change we want to see in our world, and in doing so, we demonstrate a foretaste of God's future kingdom: living examples and attractive beacons that stand in stark contrast to the failed human systems by which others live.

3. Disciple

We invest our time and effort to become conformed more closely to his will. Or, as John Stott put it: "to become like Christ, for Christlikeness is the will of God for the people of God."[3] The church becomes our lifelong academy for discipleship, our boot camp as we seek to train our minds and bodies to become effective ambassadors for Christ in the world. We recognize that without discipline we cannot model Christ's new way of living to the world any more than an athlete can win a race without training:

> Run in such a way as to get the prize. Everyone who competes in the games goes into strict training. They do it to get a crown that will not last, but we do it to get a crown that will last forever. (1 Cor. 9:24–25)

4. Mobilize

Because we have a mission, we organize, strategize, and mobilize to accomplish that which we have been given to do. We appoint leaders and organize our people according to their giftedness and callings. We assess opportunities, assemble resources, and identify the strategies that will enable us to challenge the established values in our world and allow us to begin the process of restoration and reconciliation that God desires. We become leaders of the revolution.

5. Go

We do not stay within the four walls of our homes and churches but we go out, equipped to expand the revolution: "We demolish arguments and every pretension that sets itself up against the knowledge of God, and we take captive every thought to make it obedient to Christ" (2 Cor. 10:5). We deploy our "soldiers" to the front lines. We go into our world, neighborhoods, schools, workplaces, cities, and towns displaying this new way of thinking and living. We speak of the good news that through Christ sins can be forgiven and that the kingdom of God is now available to all. We comfort the sick, feed the hungry, care for the poor, and stand up for justice. We lead with love in our hearts and truth on our lips, earning respect and trust, winning friends and inspiring hope. We become *the pleasing aroma of Christ* to all we encounter as we invite them to the wedding banquet of the King.

So just what might this look like in practice? Jesus envisioned these communities of believers would transform the world in which we live, much as springtime melts the cold and snow of winter and releases the exuberance of new life bursting forth. We would be drawn to the cold places, the broken places, the ragged edges of our world. We would be drawn to the open sores upon our societies: poverty, disease, hunger, injustice, and exploitation, becoming a healing balm to those who feel marginalized, excluded, and discarded. We would be voices for fairness, inclusion, and transparency in our governments and town halls, standing as lighthouses of integrity, compassion, and reason in our workplaces. We would come alongside the struggling single mother; take up the cause of the poor, the alien, and the stranger; fight on behalf of the mistreated; and bring real hope to the hopeless. Our generosity would astound, our determination amaze, and our love be irresistible. Spring would burst forth from the church with new life as the Lord's ambassadors of the kingdom go out announcing and demonstrating this new way of living: believing what we pray, that "his kingdom come, his will be done, on earth as it is in heaven" (Matt. 6:10, author's paraphrase).

While delivering a sermon, one of the pastors at my church, Ken Kierstead, lamented that somehow the church in America was becoming less and less relevant in our society; that people increasingly showed little interest in what Christians had to say or contribute; that Christianity was no longer viewed as offering intriguing ideas or approaches relevant to the issues of our day. In an attempt to explain this inability to penetrate our culture, he said this: "It is as if we have been vaccinated by a weaker strain of Jesus that makes us resistant to the real thing. I pray for a strain for which there is no vaccine."[4]

Like a vaccine, a little bit of Christianity injected into a society causes it to form an immunity to the virus itself. If the church, in its responsibility to multiply the kingdom of God, is to spread like a virus as it did in its first few centuries, then the virus must be spread at full strength, not in some weakened and anemic form. We need to relaunch and reboot the revolution.

A FIVE-POINT CHECKUP

If one observes the churches in the global North[5] through the lens of "leading the revolution" that Jesus began, one can find the full-spectrum outcomes: the good (even the great!), the bad, and the ugly. It is dangerous to generalize because out of the hundreds of thousands of individual communities of faith, there are many who have gotten it right. At least they have come as close to getting it right as we can hope to come. There are clearly many who have gotten it wrong. Even at the end of the first century, in the letters to the seven churches found in Revelation, we see a similar distribution of outcomes: good, bad, and yes, ugly. I am no church scholar, nor am I in a position, thankfully, to judge at all, but I do want to offer encouragement to those pastors and congregations who truly want to be faithful and effective in the task with which they have been entrusted. As I have had opportunity to speak to groups of pastors over these past few years, I have identified five different traps I believe churches often fall into, five traps that prevent our churches from realizing their full potential to change the world for Christ. I offer them here, too, hoping they might be helpful to any congregation wanting to go through the diagnostic exercise of a five-point checkup. Most churches will find they have slid into one or two of these traps, to one degree or another. Some will have avoided them all. Either way, just being aware of a trap helps keep one from falling prey to it in the first place.

> IT IS DANGEROUS TO GENERALIZE BECAUSE OUT OF THE HUNDREDS OF THOUSANDS OF INDIVIDUAL COMMUNITIES OF FAITH, THERE ARE MANY WHO HAVE GOTTEN IT RIGHT.

1. We have valued belief above behavior.

So many of our churches have hung their hats on right belief. We will stand on solid ground only as long as we believe the right things: about salvation, the Trinity, free will and predestination, heaven and hell, the rapture, and fill in the blank—marriage, divorce, Israel, sexuality, evolution, abortion, big government, and so on. Over the centuries cherished beliefs not only have caused a great deal of strife and division within the church but also have been used often as judgmental clubs to alienate those outside the church. But loving our enemies, living with integrity, caring for the sick, feeding the hungry, and being generous with our possessions don't ever seem to divide or make enemies. Sometimes we believe so passionately that we are right that we end up being *dead right*, chasing away the very people Christ wants us to reach with his love.

Right belief is important, but without right behavior it is little more than hypocrisy. James challenges us most directly with this: "Show me your faith without deeds, and I will show you my faith by what I do. You believe that there is one God. Good! Even the demons believe that—and shudder" (James 2:18–19). I would argue that it is not what we believe that counts most to God but, rather, what we do with those beliefs. We will all undoubtedly discover on the Day of the Lord how woefully wrong many of our cherished beliefs turned out to be. Jesus said time and again that it was our fruit that would define us and mark us as his. John sets a high bar when he speaks to this very issue: "Whoever claims to live in him must live as Jesus did" (1 John 2:6).

The mark of the one who "knows him" is her obedience, not her doctrine. The essence of becoming disciples is to turn our right beliefs into right behaviors. For people who want to compete in the Olympics, it is not enough to know thoroughly the rules and techniques of their sports. They must spend thousands of hours practicing so that their actions align with their knowledge. Their goal is to make right behavior so second nature that when the moment of their testing comes, their bodies automatically know what to do. No gold medals are awarded to those with just the greatest knowledge. Our churches must be training camps for right behaviors, challenging disciples to put their beliefs into action in every sphere of their lives. Believing is only the beginning.

2. We have replaced exhortation with explanation.

Far too many Sunday sermons bat around theological ideas like badminton birdies for half an hour. They quote a few verses of Scripture, tell a few stories, throw in a line or two from C. S. Lewis or Dietrich Bonhoeffer, but never challenge the congregation to change anything in their lives. The sermon is offered like a piece of gum for congregants to chew on for half an hour, but as soon as they get to the parking lot, most will spit it out. The job of the church is not merely to explain the truth but, rather, to use the truth to bring about life change. It is instructive to again look back at the very first words of Jesus as recorded in Mark 1, just after his baptism and his forty days of temptation in the wilderness: "Time's up! God's kingdom is here. Change your life and believe the Message" (Mark 1:15 MSG). Here, in what might be the world's shortest sermon, Jesus got straight to the point and didn't mince words. "This is urgent—God's kingdom is here so you need to change your lives right now. Copy?" Jesus' words fit the dictionary definition of *exhortation* pretty well: "an utterance, discourse, or address conveying urgent advice or recommendations."[6]

Some pastors seem afraid to confront or offend their congregations by challenging them with the considerable demands the Lord makes upon those who choose to follow him. They rarely talk about the dangers of affluence, the importance of sexual integrity, the suffering of the poor around the world, the sin of apathy, or the demands that Scripture makes upon our behavior and lifestyle. They speak to the privileges of faith but not often the price. Perhaps the least preached sermon in America is the one that instructs us to tithe our incomes and be generous with our resources. As evidence of this, in the wealthiest nation of Christians in history, our churchgoers give just 2.4 percent of their incomes to the work of the kingdom—76 percent less than the biblical tithe. Yet pastors seem reluctant to challenge people directly about this, even though Jesus spoke more about money than about prayer and faith combined. The great commandments of Scripture have now become just great suggestions, offered like fortune cookies, to take with us or leave behind in the pews. Jesus said, "If anyone would come after me, he must deny himself and take up his cross daily and follow me" (Luke 9:23). If churches are going to lead a revolution to change the world, then our pastors need to act and speak less like spiritual cheerleaders and more like drill sergeants.

3. We have turned inward instead of outward.

Rather than providing bases from which we can effectively launch into the world in mission, too many of our churches have become comfortable bubbles, where we can escape from the world. When our churches become attractive social clubs, our church programs end up focusing too much on our needs and too little on the needs of those outside the church. I have been invited to churches whose worship services are like Vegas shows—state-of-the-art sound and graphics, video on four different screens, huge worship bands, strobe lights, and even smoke machines. They have restaurants and latte bars, bookstores and gift shops—even bowling alleys—all within the church. Then I get up and preach for thirty minutes about God's concern for the poor. Sometimes it feels surreal. It is not mine to judge whether any of these things are right or wrong in and of themselves, but every church has to draw a line between how much they focus on themselves versus how much they focus on the mission of the church outside of their four walls. Every element of our church programs, from the strobe lights and smoke machines to the buildings and discipleship training programs, should be evaluated with one simple criterion: Will these things enhance our ability to complete the mission given to us by Jesus or not? If the answer is no, we ought to refocus our efforts on the things that will. We have bought into a church-growth consumer mentality that compels us to make our churches as appealing as possible to "consumers." One pastor lamented, given the expectations of the consumerist community where his church was located, he needed all of these shiny attractions to get people to come at all. It was all about marketing and competing for his share of the consumer's time.

As you can tell, I'm not a real proponent of marketing gimmicks just to get more people in the door. Better the church should shrink than risk losing its God-given purpose and identity. A community of true disciples, authentically living out the teachings of Scripture, is far more attractive than a latte bar or a Vegas-style musical performance. Jesus called the church to be salt and light in our world—salt to literally prevent decay (as in rotting meat) and light to counter the darkness of our culture. Jesus also recognized that when salt loses its unique properties it is no longer good for the purpose it was intended: "But if the salt loses its saltiness, how can it be made salty again? It is no longer good for anything, except to be thrown out and trampled underfoot" (Matt. 5:13). I believe that churches are in the very serious business of preparing serious people for a serious mission: going into the world to win the hearts and minds of men and women. If I have appropriately described churches as boot camps, from which we are to launch into the world to conquer it for Christ, then the goal for Christ's church should not be to build nicer and nicer boot camps so that we never have to leave them at all. The revolution is being fought outside the walls of our churches. Better to have no walls at all than to stay hidden within them.

4. We have allowed apathy to replace outrage.

World Vision's founder, Bob Pierce, was known for his famous prayer—"Let my heart be broken by the things that break the heart of God."[7] The profound truth that he captured in this simple prayer was that we should always try to see the world as Christ sees it, to value what Jesus values, treasure what he treasures, love what Jesus loves, and feel outrage at that which outrages him. Does that sound too strong? Have we so domesticated God in the twenty-first century that we have forgotten the wrath of God toward sin and evil? Whatever happened to good, old-fashioned outrage? If we get outraged at all anymore, we tend to get outraged over frivolous things. The Seattle Mariners make a terrible trade, and fans are outraged. Our property taxes go up 2 percent, and we are outraged. But where is our sense of grief and moral anger over the fact that one in five American children live below the poverty line?[8] Where is our outrage over the plight of the homeless in our cities? Can we not find even a bit of outrage that nineteen thousand children die *every day* of mainly preventable causes?[9] More than 40 percent of the people on the planet have never heard the good news of Jesus Christ, and we shrug our shoulders—no big deal.[10] One of the sure signs that we have been co-opted by our culture is that, like frogs in the proverbial kettle, we have grown comfortable with things that should shock us and mobilize us to action. We no longer feel the heat of outrage against things that anger God. We have so embraced the American dream that we can no longer see or feel the world's nightmare of poverty, suffering, and hopelessness. We are Magic Kingdom Christians, too busy pursuing our careers, planning our vacations, and sitting in the pews on Sunday, staring at our PowerPoint screens and singing songs. In the meantime, the urgent mission of God, the vital work of his kingdom, lies unfinished.

5. We have prioritized the institution over the revolution.

Trap number five is perhaps just the summary of the first four. When we invest all our energies into building and sustaining an institution, it is deceptively easy to lose sight of the reason the institution exists in the first place. The tyranny of the urgent draws our pastors and leaders away from the crucial things and bogs them down into the minutiae of church life. Like a guy juggling eight dinner plates in the air, trying to prevent any from falling, a pastor can forget that his original mission was to use those plates to feed the hungry. It was broadcaster Paul Harvey who once reportedly said of the church, "We have gone from being fishers of men to becoming keepers of the aquarium."[11] We can get distracted and diverted in a thousand ways. The evil one wants nothing more than for the church to lose sight of its critical mission to assault the very gates of hell and bring the good news of the kingdom to all of God's children. Insulated social clubs with fabulous facilities and Broadway-caliber Sunday worship services bring delight to the devil—"no harm, no foul!" The church that causes the demons to shudder is the church hell-bent on finishing the job that Christ commanded the church to do. Just as Odysseus tied himself to the mast so that he would not be lured off course, so, too, must our churches focus unwaveringly on completing the unfinished mission of the kingdom. Jesus did not call us to build an institution; he called us to lead a revolution.

As I read back through my descriptions of these five traps, I acknowledge I did not mince any words. I ask you to forgive me for my boldness, where I may have overstepped, while understanding that my passion comes out of a conviction that Christ commissioned his church to literally storm the gates of hell in a life-or-death struggle for the hearts and souls of men and women. There is just so much at stake when churches lose their vision and passion for the great mission of Christ in our world. And again, I want to reaffirm that there are so very many churches doing heroic things. If you are a member of one of them, I may be preaching to the choir. But then again, sometimes even the choir needs a kick in the pants to sing a little louder. The church is God's plan to change the world and win it for Christ. That's why it is so very important that we get it right.

Church, the Verb

When the church is most effective in building the kingdom, it plays a role similar to that of a general contractor engaged in building a house. Based on the overall blueprint, a contractor stages the various phases of construction by identifying the skills needed, organizing the various workers, and then coordinating the phasing of each group's contribution at just the right time. Each team of workers plays a key role: first the ones who lay the foundation, then the framers, plumbers, electricians, roofers, painters, and so on. A good general contractor builds a house by directing a variety of skills, bringing every player into the job, and using their unique talents in just the right place and at just the right time. That's how First Presbyterian Church, in Bellevue, Washington, reached out to build the kingdom in their community.

BelPres is the church where our daughter Sarah, her husband, Irving, and our darling little grandson, David, attend. If you visit there some Sunday, you might not at first think that it is an "outpost of the revolution," but you would be wrong. As churches go, it is fairly affluent, with about two to three thousand members and regular attenders. The facilities are beautiful, and there are some pretty nice cars in the parking lot.

It is not terribly ethnically diverse and probably skews a bit older in the age demographic.

Bellevue, Washington, is an interesting community. On the one hand, it has neighborhoods of tremendous wealth; Bill Gates lives less than two miles from BelPres. On the other hand, Bellevue has serious social problems—gangs, drugs, crime, poverty, homelessness. More than eighty languages are spoken in the Bellevue school district; it is 49 percent white and 51 percent minority. For one-third of the students, English is their second language, and about one in five students is on the subsidized lunch program.[12]

In 2005, on the occasion of the church's fiftieth anniversary, Pastor Scott Dudley was encouraged by the elders to launch a multimillion-dollar building campaign to upgrade the church facilities. Scott, a pastor with a strong outward-looking focus, strongly pushed back, telling the elders that they would have to launch the campaign over his dead body. "Church isn't supposed to build church; it's supposed to build the kingdom," he said. But they finally did manage to persuade him that parts of the church's building structures were failing and even dangerous. And through prayer God revealed a bigger plan. The church would launch a fund-raising campaign if $3 million of the total was designated for local and international ministry to children and youth. BelPres already ran the Eastside Academy, a Christian high school for at-risk youth. Scott liked to say that he wanted to see the blue-haired ladies in the church interacting with the pink-haired teenagers from the school. That was his vision of how the church should be, so the campaign moved forward, and more money was raised than they had thought possible.

> HE WANTED TO SEE THE BLUE-HAIRED LADIES IN THE CHURCH INTERACTING WITH THE PINK-HAIRED TEENAGERS FROM THE SCHOOL.

The church earmarked $1 million for building a residential-educational center for street kids in Rwanda, but there wasn't a lot of clarity about just what they would do in the local community. But (since God can't steer a parked car) they started moving anyway. A few of the leaders met with a group of public school principals to just listen and learn, and they got an earful. The challenges were daunting—drugs, gangs, teenage pregnancies, broken homes, alcoholism, domestic abuse, poverty. And all of these things were affecting the kids and spilling into the classrooms. The principals were open to any kind of help that BelPres might offer. Ultimately, with tremendous leadership from the laypeople of the congregation, the church's intent to invest in community outreach first found its expression in funding a new nonprofit, Jubilee REACH, to acquire a deteriorating building—littered with needles, bottles, condoms, and trash—in the heart of one of Bellevue's most challenging areas. The first vision was to create a safe place for kids to come before and after school while their parents were at work. On the first day, before 7:00 a.m., thirty-two kids and eleven volunteers showed up, and they served the kids breakfast. Brent Christie, a former top executive in the hospitality industry, left his career to become the full-time director of Jubilee REACH. Brent told me that his number-one goal with the kids was to just "love, listen, and learn," and learn they did. Over the next few years amazing things began to happen as they followed their hearts. Today Jubilee REACH ("JR") has about five thousand people a month coming through its doors. Believing that JR was not just about BelPres, Scott invited other churches to join. JR now has more than two thousand volunteers from more than thirty churches. Local businesses have gotten involved, too, and each morning a different business sends its volunteers to cook breakfast for the kids and to "love, listen, and learn." Every morning in that part of Bellevue, the fragrance of hope smells a lot like bacon.

As the volunteers got to know the kids, they sometimes met their parents and learned of other ways they could help. Some families were too poor to own furniture, so Home 2 Home was started, a program that solicits donated furniture and provides it to families in need. More than one hundred families a year are helped through Home 2 Home. Then Auto Angels got started for people who desperately needed cars. Volunteers fix up old donated cars so single moms have something to drive. Doctors, lawyers, dentists, and accountants from the various churches found a ministry outlet for their skills as they continued to add programs that address the medical, dental, legal, and financial management issues of the kids and families they serve. These things started having an impact, and the school principals noticed a change in the kids. Something was different. The Bellevue School District was so impressed by what was happening that they actually invited Jubilee REACH into the schools to run the entire middle school recreational and sports program—for seven middle schools and four thousand students. JR staff have offices inside the schools. That's right; the church was invited into the public schools! Brent Christie told me that Bellevue's city manager refers to Jubilee REACH as "the soul of the community" and "a trusted partner." The school principals now report that academic performance has increased significantly among the kids involved with JR.

Brent likes to talk about "church, the verb"—the church in action. He believes that as much as Jubilee REACH has changed the community, it has also changed BelPres, as hundreds of volunteers have found their calling, to a place on the front lines of what God is doing in Bellevue. One volunteer, a financial planner, asked himself, "How much money do I need to make?" Then he actually reduced his work hours and his family's income so he could spend more time with the kids. And when an unmarried couple with eight children got evicted from their apartment and couldn't find a place to live, another volunteer, a doctor from one of the partner churches, invited the family to live in his home . . . and then he moved out of his own home and rented an apartment! A year later the couple, who had become Christians, decided to get married in his church. Now the whole family is there every Sunday.

Pastor Dudley told me that Jubilee REACH has "changed the church's DNA. We're closer to getting our hearts broken, and it's made us more of a kingdom church." At BelPres the blue-haired ladies (and a lot of other volunteers) have actually gotten to know those pink-haired kids, to the benefit and blessing of both. Brent said, "Churches like to hold on to their m&m's—their money and their members; they let them melt in their hands instead of turning them out into the world." I think Jesus would agree with Brent. "The harvest is plentiful," Jesus said, "but the workers are few. Ask the Lord of the harvest, therefore, to send out workers into his harvest field. [Go!] I am sending you out like sheep among wolves" (Matt. 9:37–38; 10:16).

Jubilee REACH is an outpost of the kingdom; it is laboring outside the four walls of the church and on the ragged edge of the revolution. It is storming the gates of hell.

14

. . .

The Gates of Hell

"The White Witch? Who is she?" [asked Lucy.]
"Why, it is she who has got all Narnia under her
thumb. It's she who makes it always winter. Always
winter and never Christmas; think of that!"
"How awful!" said Lucy.[1]

—C. S. LEWIS

But woe to the earth and the sea,
    because the devil has gone down to you!
He is filled with fury,
    because he knows that his time is short.

—REVELATION 12:12

There are two equal and opposite errors into which
our race can fall about the devils. One is to disbelieve
in their existence. The other is to believe, and to feel
an excessive and unhealthy interest in them.[2]

—C. S. LEWIS

There is an enemy.

And he will oppose every act of obedience to Christ, every decision to serve, every act of kindness, every proclamation of truth, every cry for justice, and every advance of Christ's kingdom. He is perhaps the chief reason that the great mission of Christ remains unfinished. He is the one who stands in the way. He will exact a price from those who choose to serve the King, and we commit a grave error if we ignore him.

It is not popular today to talk about the devil, the evil one. A personal being who personifies evil just seems, well, so medieval and so not twenty-first century. But this being is the adversary in God's great story and is found in Scripture from Genesis to Revelation. Though murky about the details, Scripture is clear that there is a spiritual realm or reality apart from our own. We are told that before God created mankind, he created spiritual beings called angels; and that some of those angels, led by Satan, not only rebelled against God's authority but continue to oppose the working out of God's will on earth among men and women. It was likely Satan who took the form of a serpent in the garden of Eden and who tempted Adam and Eve to disobey God. Jesus confronted Satan in the wilderness where he triumphed over Satan's efforts to tempt him to disobey God, the Father. The New Testament authors warn over and over that Satan is the adversary of the church. Paul, in Ephesians, acknowledged that we are locked in a spiritual battle and warns us:

> Put on the full armor of God, so that you can take your stand against the devil's schemes. For our struggle is not against flesh and blood, but against the rulers, against the authorities, against the powers of this dark world and against the spiritual forces of evil in the heavenly realms. (Eph. 6:11–12)

Peter soberly warns us: "Your enemy the devil prowls around like a roaring lion looking for someone to devour" (1 Peter 5:8).

Jesus, in the parable of the sower, blames the devil for thwarting the message of the gospel:

"Those [hearers of the Word] along the path are the ones who hear, and then the devil comes and takes away the word from their hearts, so that they may not believe and be saved." (Luke 8:12)

The devil—Satan—is described in Scripture in various ways . . . all of which are bad:

- adversary
- accuser
- enemy
- opponent
- wicked one
- antichrist
- murderer
- tempter
- thief
- father of lies
- man of lawlessness
- power of darkness
- son of perdition

He is also called

- prince of this world
- angel of light
- god of this world
- ruler of the kingdom of the air
- spirit who is now at work in those who are disobedient
- ruler, authority, and power of this dark world

In Revelation 12, we are told that this same Satan was cast down to our world: "The great dragon was hurled down—that ancient serpent called the devil, or Satan, who leads the whole world astray. He was hurled to the earth, and his angels with him" (Rev. 12:9).

All of this suggests that somehow Satan has been allowed by God to have temporary dominion over our world. He is determined to lead men and women away from God's purposes and toward sin. He may even be instrumental in bringing about some of the devastating manifestations of the fall—disease, natural disasters, tragic accidents, and death. I often say to people that if they don't believe Satan exists, they should just come with me on a trip. When you see eight-year-old girls who have been sold for sex; infants whose arms have been hacked off by rebel machetes; and the mass graves in Cambodia, Rwanda, and Bosnia, the reality of the living, personified presence of evil in our world is the only explanation that comes close.

It is critical for the church to understand that it is, in fact, caught in the midst of a great cosmic struggle between God and Satan, between good and evil. For reasons we don't fully understand, God, for a time, has relinquished some authority to Satan; he has allowed Satan to invade and infect our world and hold it captive. Since God is all powerful and Satan is not, this had to be done of God's own will and only with his consent. But why he chose this course and not another is not fully revealed.

The book of Job gives us a unique peek behind the curtains and into the spiritual realm. In Job 1, we find Satan appearing before God with a challenge. Satan contends that Job, a man faithfully devoted to God, is only faithful because God has blessed him in many ways. Satan, the accuser, suggests that Job would curse God if he were to remove his hedge of protection from Job. And what unfolds is a kind of wager. God allows Satan to take his best shot at Job, knowing that Job will remain faithful and true. Satan believes he can demonstrate that human beings will defect from their faithfulness to God when hardships come their way. Ultimately, the testing of Job revealed that despite his circumstances, he was able to remain faithful in trusting God, not based on his circumstances but because he trusted in God's power, goodness, and wisdom.

Somehow in the midst of this wager, we catch a glimpse of a larger truth. In the working out of God's ultimate purposes for mankind, he has for a season allowed Satan to tempt and afflict us; he has allowed a struggle between good and evil to play itself out; and somehow the choices we make in the midst of this struggle allow God to demonstrate that his way is the only way of truth, justice, and righteousness. It is almost as if God is saying to Satan, "Go ahead and try to corrupt my creation with your schemes. Challenge my children; tempt them and afflict them if you choose. In the end it will serve only to demonstrate the triumph of righteousness over evil. It is already certain how this contest will end, but let's go ahead and let it run its course so that all will see my wisdom and truth. Then I will restore my creation and my reign, be reconciled with my children, and deal with you and your evil ways once and for all."

We might think of this as a kind of spiritual chess game in the heavenly realms. God, the Grand Master, can see twenty moves ahead to the ultimate checkmate of Satan and of evil. The outcome is a foregone conclusion, but the process of resolving the conflict is somehow important as God methodically unfolds his plan for the redemption of all things one move at a time. In the book of Ephesians we are provided another brief behind-the-scenes glimpse into the power of the gospel and the wisdom of God's plan as Paul reveals the intent of God:

His intent was that now, through the church, the manifold wisdom of God should be made known to the rulers and authorities in the heavenly realms, according to his eternal purpose that he accomplished in Christ Jesus our Lord. (Eph. 3:10–11)

This suggests that through the church, through you and me, God is demonstrating his profound wisdom to "rulers and authorities in the heavenly realms, according to his eternal purpose."

We, like Job, are somehow in the middle of it all. We live in the midst of the chess game. And in God's design our decisions, our choices, matter. We get to play for the winning side. Even though Job could not comprehend the reasons behind his suffering, his faithful response to his circumstances not only strengthened his own faith but also gave glory and testimony to God. But we have something that Job could only long for. In Job 9, he cries out, appealing to God and lamenting the fact that he has no real way to make his case before God:

> "He is not a mere mortal like me that I might answer him,
>> that we might confront each other in court.
> If only there were someone to mediate between us,
>> someone to bring us together,
> someone to remove God's rod from me,
>> so that his terror would frighten me no more.
> Then I would speak up without fear of him,
>> but as it now stands with me, I cannot." (vv. 32–35)

That *Someone* Job imagined has now come, and he stands in the gap to make our case and to remove both our sins and our fears. Job longed for but could not see the checkmate that would finally end the contest, the Messiah.

In the *incarnation* of God in Christ, God's government in exile returned in dramatic fashion; it returned to liberate God's children and directly challenge the dominion of Satan and sin. And in the *death and resurrection* of Christ, Satan was decisively defeated as Jesus removed the barrier of sin and alienation by paying its full price, thereby flinging wide open the doors to God's kingdom under God's reign. The analogy I have used throughout the book, comparing the gospel and the coming of the kingdom of God to a revolution, now takes on new meaning. The defeat of Satan at the cross represented the decisive battle in the revolution, the overthrow of the ruler of this world. And the authority he once held has been revoked by God in Jesus Christ. But we, like Job, in this time before God's final victory, must still endure the

WE LIVE IN THE MIDST OF THE CHESS GAME. AND IN GOD'S DESIGN OUR DECISIONS, OUR CHOICES, MATTER.

evil and suffering that are consequences, both of the fall and of the spiritual battle that Satan still wages in our world.

GOD IN THE RUBBLE OF HAITI

Our present sufferings are not worth comparing with the glory that will be revealed in us. For the creation waits in eager expectation for the children of God to be revealed. (Rom. 8:18–19)

Nothing challenges our faith or fuels our doubts more than the presence of pain, suffering, and evil in our world. "Why," we ask, "would a loving God allow such horrors?" This nagging question, perhaps more than any other, can undermine our faith and hobble our determination to storm the gates of hell. But the One we follow knows something about pain and grief. He did not sit safely behind the lines as the battle was fought. He led the charge, and he paid a price much higher than he asks of us. He opened the way and beckons us only to follow.

On January 12, 2010, the world was confronted with human suffering on a massive scale after an earthquake in Haiti killed more than two hundred thousand and left more than a million homeless.[3] Trying to make sense of it all in the days after the quake, I wrote these words:

January 2010

Last week I stood in the streets of Port-au-Prince, Haiti, weeping at the scope and scale of human suffering. Tens of thousands died—men, women, and children, mothers and fathers, pastors and priests—no one was exempt. Hundreds of thousands wandered stunned, hungry, and homeless in the streets, who, though still alive, had had their lives taken from them. Who of us in these past days has not asked the question, "Where was God?" or "Why, God?" The sudden deaths of so many innocent people and the staggering human suffering that persists seem to mock the very notion of a loving God. Just where is God in Haiti?

There was another time that God was mocked in the face of suffering and evil. It happened on Calvary as our Lord and Savior Jesus Christ, God's own Son, was spat upon, beaten, and hanged on a cross. And people asked where God was then:

"Come down from the cross and save yourself! . . ." [They] mocked him among themselves. "He saved others," they said, "but he can't save himself!" (Mark 15:30–31).

If he was God, why didn't he save himself? Why not prevent this suffering from happening? Why not save the Jewish people from their bondage to Rome? Why not face this evil and turn it back? But God chose another way. On that cross we are told that Jesus faced all the evil that ever was or ever would be. He took upon himself the sins of mankind, the evils of injustice, the pain of suffering and loss, the brokenness of the world. He felt every agony and took every punishment for every person who would ever live. Seven hundred years earlier, the prophet Isaiah had seen this Son of God hanging on a distant cross:

> He was despised and rejected by men,
>> a man of sorrows, and familiar with suffering.
> Like one from whom men hide their faces
>> he was despised, and we esteemed him not.
> Surely he took up our infirmities
>> and carried our sorrows,
> yet we considered him stricken by God,
>> smitten by him, and afflicted.
> But he was pierced for our transgressions,
>> he was crushed for our iniquities;
> the punishment that brought us peace was upon him,
>> and by his wounds we are healed. (Isa. 53:3–5)

Where is God in Haiti? Christ is not distant from us in our times of suffering. He is not indifferent or detached. He does not look upon us from far away. He, too, lies crushed under the weight of concrete walls. He, too, lies wounded in the street with his legs broken and walks homeless through the camps, hungry and unfed. He hobbles beside us on crutches with a missing leg and weeps uncontrollably over the child that he has lost.

Where is God in Haiti? He hangs bloody on a cross . . . "a man of sorrows, and familiar with our suffering."

But where is hope, we might ask? Where is justice for the dead, the broken, and the grieving? Where is redemption and restoration? Here, alas, we need to see something not easily seen. We, not God, are trapped in time. We, not God, see only in part and cannot yet see the whole. We, not God, must wait for that day when "he will wipe every tear from their eyes. There will be no more death or mourning or crying or pain, for the old order of things has passed away" (Rev. 21:4).

We live in the *not yet*, but God sees the *already*. We see today and yesterday but not tomorrow. God sees all three at once. In him, those crushed in Haiti are alive already. In him, those orphaned in Haiti are reunited with family already. In him, those broken in Haiti are healed already. In him, those grieving in Haiti rejoice already.

He is no distant God who turns his back on us, no callous God who sheds no tears. He is the God who "so loved the world that he gave his one and only Son, that whoever believes in him shall not perish but have eternal life" (John 3:16). He is God, who shed his own blood for us.

> WE LIVE IN THE TIME BETWEEN THE *ALREADY* AND *NOT YET* AND WE MUST WAIT *UNTIL THEN*.

How then should we think? How then should we live? What then, must we do? Unlike God, we live in the time between the *already* and *not yet* and we must wait *until then*. Until then, we are commanded to love our neighbors as ourselves. Until then, we are called to comfort the afflicted, give food to the hungry and water to the thirsty. Until then, we are to shelter the homeless, clothe the naked, and grieve with the grieving. Until then, we are to care for the widow, the orphan, the alien, and the stranger. We are to "let [our] light so shine before men, that they may see [our] good works and glorify [our] Father in heaven"

(Matt. 5:16 NKJV). Until then we are Christ's heart and hands and feet—the ambassadors of his love in a hurting world. Until then *we* are called to show forth God's deep love for Haiti.

D-DAY

It is mind-boggling today to consider just how completely Adolf Hitler dominated Europe by 1944. France, Poland, Austria, the Netherlands, Czechoslovakia, Norway, Denmark, Belgium, Luxembourg, Yugoslavia, Greece, Finland, Romania, Hungary, Latvia, Estonia, Belarus, Italy, and Bulgaria were either under German control or were allies of Hitler. The evil Nazi empire was within reach of its goal to conquer all of Europe and perhaps a good part of the world. The Allied Forces knew that Hitler's defeat could be accomplished by only a full-scale invasion of Europe. Hitler was already battling Russia on the Eastern front; if the Allies could open up a western front, Hitler could be defeated, as he would be forced to divide his resources across two battlefronts. But an Allied invasion of Europe would be costly. On June 6, 1944, under the command of General Eisenhower, more than 160,000 Allied troops stormed the beaches at Normandy to gain a foothold in Europe. Another 195,000 naval troops and 5,000 ships supported the invasion. On that day alone some 3,000 Allied troops were killed and 9,000 wounded or missing. By the time they crossed the Seine and liberated Paris in late June, perhaps 200,000 men had been killed, wounded, or reported missing. But the D-Day invasion, though costly, was successful, and the trajectory of the war shifted dramatically.

Historians today tell us that once the invasion at Normandy succeeded, Hitler had, for all practical purposes, lost the war. It was checkmate; his defeat was inevitable. But if you looked at the world just a few days after D-Day, there was little sign that the war was over. Europe was still occupied. Hitler still commanded the German forces from Berlin. The concentration camps at Auschwitz, Buchenwald, and Treblinka were still grimly killing tens of thousands, and some of the fiercest battles of the war still lay ahead. Hundreds of thousands would yet die, and the grief of the world would deepen still before Europe was liberated, the captives were freed, and Hitler lay dead in a bunker in Berlin.

In the months after D-Day individual soldiers were deployed to fight key battles across Europe, and even though the final outcome was assured, they still had to fight bravely, many giving their lives in the effort. Most did not know the full outline of General Eisenhower's final strategy. They couldn't see the big picture of how each offensive thrust, each defensive maneuver, would ultimately bring the Third Reich to its knees. They knew only the specific job that they had been called to do. Some managed the critical supply lines; others ensured communications or managed field hospitals. Back home many worked in factories to produce the tanks, planes, and ammunition. Others invested by buying war bonds, all to support the ultimate goal of defeating Hitler and liberating Europe.

The cross was D-Day in God's plan to rescue his children. It was the decisive battle in a great struggle and represented the defeat of Satan. And it, too, was costly. Yet while the ultimate victory had been won, some of the fiercest battles still lay ahead. There would still be strife, hardship, and casualties as the followers of Jesus joined the revolution and pressed the battle to liberate God's children and establish his kingdom in every nation of the world. Each one would be called by the General to a specific place at a specific time. Each one would be equipped with the right gifts and abilities and empowered by the Spirit of Christ. Each one would play a critical role in the great mission of God.

I sometimes wonder what might have happened if those soldiers in 1944 and 1945 had made different choices. What if, on their way to liberate Paris, they had stopped in the beautiful French countryside? The good life might have beckoned to them—beautiful women, good food, and fine wines. What if, tempted by these things, they had taken off their uniforms, laid down their weapons, and settled down in the appealing French farmhouses and villages? What if they had lost sight of the mission and the urgency of their cause? What consequences might have been suffered? Would Hitler have remained in power and the end of the war been postponed? I wonder, too, what consequences will be felt when followers of Christ desert the front lines of his revolution to settle down in comfortable lives far from the battle. Today the "occupation" is still with us. The lost hunger for the good news of the gospel, and the poor cry out in their suffering. The battle still rages, and the rescue mission of God remains unfinished as all "creation waits in eager expectation for the children of God to be revealed" (Rom. 8:19). The gates of hell have not yet fallen.

STORMING THE GATES

In 2011, Reneé and I traveled to the Holy Land and visited the area called Caesarea Philippi, a region in which Jesus spent some considerable time. At the foot of Mount Hermon, there is a place (once called Panium) where you can dip your feet into the headwaters of the Jordan River. It is also the place where it is believed that Jesus pronounced to Peter that "on this rock" Jesus would build his church. But we learned something new and quite astonishing that day about the significance of this place—something that brings a much deeper meaning to Jesus' words. Let's first read the passage:

> When Jesus came into the region of Caesarea Philippi, He asked His disciples, saying, "Who do men say that I, the Son of Man, am?"
>
> So they said, "Some say John the Baptist, some Elijah, and others Jeremiah or one of the prophets."
>
> He said to them, "But who do you say that I am?"
>
> Simon Peter answered and said, "You are the Christ, the Son of the living God."
>
> Jesus answered and said to him, "Blessed are you, Simon Bar-Jonah, for flesh and blood has not revealed this to you, but My Father who is in heaven. And I also say to you that you are Peter, and on this rock I will build My church, and the gates of Hades shall not prevail against it. And I will give you the keys of the kingdom of heaven, and whatever you bind on earth will be bound in heaven, and whatever you loose on earth will be loosed in heaven." (Matt. 16:13–19 NKJV)

We stood on that same spot, at the foot of a high cliff beneath the mountain where Jesus had stood that day with his disciples. But here is the remarkable thing you wouldn't know from reading the New Testament: at the base of the cliff, there is an enormous gaping cave that tunnels deeply into the cliff wall and then downward and out of sight. Josephus, a first-century historian, wrote this about the cave:

> The place is called Panium, where is a top of a mountain that is raised
> to an immense height, and at its side, beneath, or at its bottom, a dark
> cave opens itself; within which there is a horrible precipice, that descends
> abruptly to a vast depth; it contains a mighty quantity of water, which is
> immovable; and when anybody lets down anything to measure the depth
> of the earth beneath the water, no length of cord is sufficient to reach it.[4]

In the classical world this cave was thought to have supernatural significance. It was believed to be the entrance to the underworld, the Gates of Hades, where the mythological Demeter had been carried off by Hades, the god of the underworld. It was the place where the gods came out of the underworld to roam the earth and to prey upon men and women. At the time of Jesus the Temple of Pan, a massive pagan temple built by Herod the Great, stood imposingly over the entrance to this cave. At the front of this columned temple was an open altar perched at the very brink of the deep abyss. The pagan worshipers would offer animal (and perhaps human) sacrifices on that altar and then cast their offerings into the abyss with the hope that the gods would accept them and respond by granting greater fertility and better harvests. It was at this unholy place, the very spot people believed the pagan gods to dwell, that Jesus chose to announce that he, "the Christ, the Son of the living God," would build his church, "and the gates of Hades shall not prevail against it." So why did Jesus choose this specific location to make his announcement? Because it was his declaration of war on the principalities and powers of this dark world.

On September 11, 2001, when Al Qaeda launched an assault on the United States, they chose to attack three powerful symbols of United States power: the Pentagon, a symbol of American military power; the World Trade Center, a symbol of US economic power; and the Capitol, the seat of the United States government.[5] They did this to challenge and undermine US authority and to declare war on America in the most shocking way possible. They chose those locations to make a statement. Fortunately Al Qaeda's declaration of war ultimately failed. I believe that Jesus symbolically chose the Temple of Pan to challenge the authority of Satan and to serve notice that his kingdom was now certain to fall. Jesus knocked on the front door of hades to make an in-your-face declaration of war upon the evil powers of this world. He put them on notice. And unlike Al Qaeda's declaration, this one would not fail.

But there is a second highly significant meaning to the words Jesus chose in his declaration. Jesus used an offensive, not defensive, metaphor; his

THE CHURCH WAS THE ONE ON THE ATTACK, THE GATES OF HELL WOULD SUFFER THE ASSAULT, THE REVOLUTION WOULD ADVANCE, AND THE PREVAILING POWERS WOULD FALL.

church would go on the offense to storm the gates of hell, and those gates would not stand. The church was the one on the attack, the gates of hell would suffer the assault, the revolution would advance, and the prevailing powers would fall.

Before we leave this place, we need to look at one other incredible symbolic event that may have taken place on this same spot, the Transfiguration. We are told in Scripture that six days later "Jesus took with him Peter, James and John the brother of James, and led them up a high mountain by themselves. There he was transfigured before them"

(Matt. 17:1–2). Some scholars believe that shortly after the gates-of-hades declaration, the transfiguration of Christ took place near this same location on Mount Hermon, directly above the Temple of Pan. It was again on this spot, the symbolic stronghold of the underworld, that the full divinity of Christ was first revealed. Jesus was transfigured in brilliant white light. God the Father spoke audibly and pronounced Jesus' true identity and authority: "This is my Son, whom I love; with him I am well pleased. Listen to him!" (Matt. 17:5). The God of the universe knocked on the front door of the god of the underworld and revealed his true identity. Not long after, this same Jesus marched resolutely to Jerusalem and went to the cross—to storm the gates of hell. It was D-Day.

THEREFORE GO . . .

Soldiers, Sailors and Airmen of the Allied Expeditionary Force! You are about to embark upon a great crusade, toward which we have striven these many months. The eyes of the world are upon you. The hopes and prayers of liberty loving people everywhere march with you. In company with our brave Allies and brothers in arms on other fronts, you will bring about the destruction of the German war machine, the elimination of Nazi tyranny over the oppressed peoples of Europe, and security for ourselves in a free world.

Your task will not be an easy one. Your enemy is well trained, well equipped and battle hardened, he will fight savagely.[6]—General Eisenhower's D-Day message to the Allied troops: June 6, 1944

Then Jesus came to them and said, "All authority in heaven and on earth has been given to me. Therefore go and make disciples of all nations, baptizing them in the name of the Father and of the Son and of the Holy Spirit, and teaching them to obey everything I have commanded you. And surely I am with you always, to the very end of the age." (Matt. 28:18–20)

The victory is secured. The powers and authorities have been disarmed. The kingdom of God is at hand. Therefore go! In light of the victory at the cross, we need to take one final look at the Great Commission but in a new light. Jesus begins by stating that now—because of the cross—all authority in heaven and on earth has been given to him. We are told here, in no uncertain terms, that Christ decisively defeated and disarmed Satan and his authority. The outcome is now assured because the decisive victory has been won. Paul reassures us of this very thing in two key passages:

God made you alive with Christ. He forgave us all our sins, having canceled the charge of our legal indebtedness, which stood against us and
condemned us; he has taken it away, nailing it to the cross. And *having
disarmed the powers and authorities, he made a public spectacle of them,
triumphing over them by the cross.* (Col. 2:13–15, emphasis mine)

And God placed all things under his feet and appointed him to be head
over everything for *the church, which is his body,* the fullness of him who
fills everything in every way. (Eph. 1:22–23, emphasis mine)

The significance of these two passages is, first, the reign of Satan as the
ruler, authority, and power of this dark world is coming to an end; and second, the reign of Christ is now here, all authority and power has been given
to Jesus, and Jesus is the head of the church. The church of Jesus Christ will
go into the world to establish his reign and his kingdom, thereby defeating his
enemies, taking its stand against the rulers, against the authorities, against
the powers of this dark world, and against the spiritual forces of evil in the
heavenly realms. Paul reveals to us that before the return of Christ, these
enemies of Christ must first be defeated and put under his feet:

Then the end will come, when he hands over the kingdom to God the
Father after he has destroyed all dominion, authority and power. For he
must reign until he has put all his enemies under his feet. (1 Cor. 15:24–25)

This then is the dark side of the Great Commission. Going into the
world with the good news of the gospel and inviting God's children to
accept his great grace and become disciples would come with a cost. It
would require us to wage war against the forces of evil in our world by challenging injustice, righting wrongs, proclaiming truth, and demonstrating a
different way to live, with God as our King and Lord. With Satan defeated
at the cross and Christ now the head of his church, we can see the Great
Commission as the battle orders given by the Supreme Commander to the
forces under his command, the church, to go and finish the fight:

"The victory is now assured. I have not only defeated and disarmed Satan, but I have broken through enemy lines to give you access to my kingdom, my power, and my Spirit. Now go—finish the job, establish my rule in all the nations, preach the good news that sins are forgiven and death has been defeated, and announce boldly that my kingdom is now open to everyone. And take heart because I will be with you to the very end. Viva la revolution!" (Matt. 28:18–20, author's paraphrase)

We have not been promised rescue from this world; we have been commanded to go and take back this world. The Great Commission is Jesus' call to storm the gates of hell and to liberate his children, establishing his kingdom. It is the military mop-up operation intended to finish the job, rescue the rest of God's children, and prepare for the final and comprehensive reign of Christ when he will return to us, and his church will claim the glorious promise of Revelation 21:

"Look! God's dwelling place is now among the people, and he will dwell with them. They will be his people, and God himself will be with them and be their God. 'He will wipe every tear from their eyes. There will be no more death' or mourning or crying or pain, for the old order of things has passed away." (vv. 3–4)

GENTLE WEAPONS OF THE KINGDOM

But when this priest [Jesus] had offered for all time one sacrifice for sins, he sat down at the right hand of God, and since that time he waits for his enemies to be made his footstool. (Heb. 10:12–13)

I have used the metaphors of war because that is exactly how the Bible describes the conflict between God and Satan. But our struggle is a very different kind of war. The revolution of the kingdom is not a revolution of violence to be won by force. It does not advance on the basis of earthly power or principles of warfare. It has no tanks or guns or bombs.

Its weapons are paradoxical: love, joy, peace, forbearance, kindness, goodness, faithfulness, gentleness, and self-control. We go out into the world assaulting the gates of hell by loving our neighbors—even our enemies. We go to the broken and ragged places to comfort the afflicted and bind up the brokenhearted. We carry the message of a new hope into our workplaces, schools, and town halls. We bind up the wounds of abuse, exploitation, addiction, and alienation with acts of forgiveness and healing. We are called to care for the widow, the orphan, the alien, and the stranger—to lift up justice and fight economic disparity, to speak up for the voiceless and hold our governments accountable, to challenge racism and bigotry, to be generous with our money, and to live lives of integrity. We see value in the worthless, find strength in the weak, and anoint the downtrodden with significance. We seek to right every wrong and take every thought captive to obedience to Jesus Christ. Our opponents are disarmed by the sword of the Spirit; they take flight when they see our breastplate of righteousness, the belt of truth buckled around our waist, and the helmet of our salvation. We march on feet fitted with the readiness that comes from the gospel of peace. Every act of kindness, each moment spent in prayer, and every expression of love in the name of Christ pierces the heart of the enemy and sends him into retreat. These are the gentle weapons of the kingdom. There is still evil in the world, but evil is on the run.

> EVERY ACT OF KINDNESS, EACH MOMENT SPENT IN PRAYER, AND EVERY EXPRESSION OF LOVE IN THE NAME OF CHRIST PIERCES THE HEART OF THE ENEMY AND SENDS HIM INTO RETREAT.

15

. . .

God's Great Adventure
for Your Life

It's never too late to be who you might have been.
—ATTRIBUTED TO GEORGE ELIOT

Though no one can go back and make a brand new start,
anyone can start from now and make a brand new ending.
—ATTRIBUTED TO CARL BARD

The story continues. The great Author's pen is working mightily; ink flows, and pages fly forth. The final chapters are being written; new characters step into the drama, and new adventures await them. As his great story unfolds, there is danger and intrigue, love and joy, disappointment and hope. There are victories to be won and setbacks to be suffered, and much is at stake. The Father's great rescue mission is gaining momentum, and the hearts and souls of his children hang in the balance. His great pen has written you into this newest chapter; your name now appears on his pages. There is something important to be done, and he calls you to do it; a key part to play, and he has chosen you for the role. He has written you into the story, located you carefully in time and place, equipped you with unique gifts and talents, empowered you with his mighty Spirit, and bid you to join his great kingdom revolution. He has invited you. It's time to RSVP.

I love the great and epic story of Tolkien's The Lord of the Rings trilogy. Middle Earth is in the midst of a titanic struggle between good and evil. The evil wizard Sauron has amassed great power and colossal armies. Civilizations and armies are clashing and colliding. The fate of all things hangs on the outcome. And in the middle of it all are two small hobbits, Frodo and Sam. They stand at the center of the stage, and in the end it is somehow up to them to save the day, to defeat the forces of evil, and to rescue Middle Earth. They have no obvious strengths or dazzling powers. But there is something about their characters, something about their self-lessness, that makes them the key players in the drama—not Gandalf, not Boromir or Strider or Legolas. Though each of them also would play their roles, the outcome turned on the obedience and actions of these two hobbits. I really believe that Tolkien structured his story in that way to illustrate the same great truth about the kingdom of God. The key battles, the dramatic turning points, the crucial roles hinge on the decisions of the little people. "God chose the foolish things of the world to shame the wise; God chose the weak things of the world to shame the strong. God chose the lowly things of this world and the despised things—and the things that are not—to nullify the things that are" (1 Cor. 1:27–28). As C. S. Lewis said, "There are no ordinary people."[1] What amazing news, what an incredible privilege and opportunity God has given us. Like Frodo and Sam, we find ourselves facing the greatest adventure of our lives. Even more than that, God created us specifically for this adventure. But also like Frodo and Sam, in order to realize our adventure, we must leave the comfort and safety of the Shire behind. We must let go of all of those things that hinder us. We must say yes to the King and yes to his kingdom mission.

This doesn't mean that we will have no joy in our lives. It doesn't mean that we must now live spare and stoic lives cut off from the people and things we love. It is actually just the opposite. While God does ask us to lay down all that we are and all that we have in his service, he promises something more precious in their place, something richer, deeper, and fuller. We trade our black-and-white lives for lives lived in full color. He calls us to become the people we were created to be, to live the lives we were meant to live.

Some of us will serve right where we are. He wants to use our vocations, resources, networks, and skills. He can use whatever we possess—money, assets, time. He will even use our weaknesses and flaws, our struggles and our pain as well. If they are yielded to him, he will use them. Some of us, though, he will call away to different places, new vocations, and even different cultures. We need to travel light and be willing to pull up stakes and go, trusting that he goes before us. Our life's greatest adventure is found in serving him. "I have come that they may have life," Jesus said, "and have it to the full" (John 10:10).

Our Christian faith is more than a way to find forgiveness for our sins in order to enter eternal life, yet it is that. It is more than a system of right beliefs about ultimate truth and the order of things, though it is that. And it is more than just a way to find God's comfort in times of trouble or a helpful code of conduct for how to live a good and productive life, though it is those things too. No, it is a call to leave everything else behind, follow our Lord and Savior Jesus Christ, and join in the great mission of Christ in our world. It is a call to live as Jesus lived, to love what Jesus loves and treasure what Jesus treasures. It is a call to forsake all else and follow him. Only then can we become completed people—people living according to God's deepest purpose for our lives. Only then will we find our life's great adventure.

> IT IS A CALL TO LIVE AS JESUS LIVED, TO LOVE WHAT JESUS LOVES AND TREASURE WHAT JESUS TREASURES.

Listen now to the stories of just a few of the Finishers, those who have found their own completion in the unfinished work of the kingdom of God.

BLOOM WHERE YOU ARE PLANTED

And for some reason I got this wild dream that I would someday have an apple orchard and would one day be able to give some of the profits to kids in India somehow.—Ralph Broetje

"I will not sacrifice to the LORD my God burnt offerings that cost me nothing." So David bought the threshing floor and the oxen and paid fifty shekels of silver for them. (2 Sam. 24:24)

Ralph Broetje was in junior high school when he got that idea. God gave him a dream and a passion, and years later Ralph and his wife, Cheryl, bought a small orchard and began farming. Broetje Orchards in the state of Washington is one of today's most remarkable kingdom outposts you are likely to find anywhere. On the surface it looks like they are in the business of growing apples and cherries to sell to people, but in reality they are in the people-growing business; apples and cherries are just the means to that end. Ralph and Cheryl have lived out the gospel in ways that few of us do. They give away 50 percent of their profits, always investing to make their community and the larger world a better place for all people, especially the poor. Because they employ hundreds of people, most of them migrant workers, they found a mission field at their front door. Ralph and Cheryl treat their workers like family. With their farm at the center, they have built a unique community for those who work in the business. Seeing that most of these families had never owned their own homes, the Broetjes had the idea to build real homes for them; they created a community they called Vista Hermosa and built 120 houses. They made these homes available to the families who worked in their orchards, offering them at half the price of other homes in the area. Then, recognizing that the women needed day care so they could work, they built a preschool for the toddlers and later added an elementary school and a small church. They also helped many of the mothers get their high school equivalency degrees.

After their cherry orchard had failed several years in a row, Ralph decided to cut it down rather than risk another crop failure, but just before the chain saws were sent in, he had the idea of giving the trees to ministry. The next year the crop came in, and Ralph and Cheryl pledged to give all the cherry profits away. The Broetjes ask the pickers and workers to participate. They meet each year and vote on which worthy causes they will fund with the money. Those cherries have yielded millions of dollars for charities over the past twenty-five years. Some of that money has been given locally and some around the world—including India. Ralph's junior high school dream had come true.

Ralph and Cheryl's love for India would also lead them to adopt not one but six orphaned Indian children over the years, in addition to their three biological daughters. Later on Ralph had a vision to create a school on their property, specifically designed to help at-risk kids, and Jubilee Ranch was born. Today the ranch is home to sixty at-risk boys—boys who had run out of other options in their lives. At Jubilee Ranch they earn their high school diplomas, learn skills such as woodworking, and study God's Word. "They come away with changed hearts," said the director of the school. Cheryl has also started a nonprofit called the Center for Sharing, with a vision to use the principles of servant leadership found in Scripture to create more loving and just communities, both in Washington State and internationally. These are just a few of the ways in which Ralph and Cheryl have been able to use what God has given them to be a blessing to others. Their Vista Hermosa foundation, created to fund needs in their local community, rural and agricultural development, education and leadership training, and poverty reduction programs around the world, has donated more than $50 million over the past few decades to support these causes.

Broetje Orchards is a remarkable outpost of the kingdom, shining brightly in Eastern Washington. It became a reality only because two people made the decision to put God first in everything they did. They aren't just farmers; they are kingdom farmers, and that has made all the difference. But don't think it all has been easy. More than once the Broetjes came to the brink of losing everything due to weather, market forces, and the volatility of the farming business. And they've had to face all of the human and social problems that tend to come along with families living in close community.

Ralph is characteristically modest about all he and Cheryl have done. "It's still something I love to do, grow apples, plant trees. I've been blessed to do what I've loved to do. God has really blessed us. I look at it, and everything else I've tried to do I've been a failure at. I think God's put me in this place at this time, and he's really blessed us." You see, Ralph and Cheryl didn't sell everything they had and go onto the mission field; instead, they saw the mission field in everything they had. God used their passions, gifts, and skills right where they were planted, but they first had to make those gifts and skills available to him.

Playing the Cards You Are Dealt

> I consider that our present sufferings are not worth comparing with the glory that will be revealed in us. For the creation waits in eager expectation for the children of God to be revealed. (Rom. 8:18–19)

> Praise be to the God and Father of our Lord Jesus Christ, the Father of compassion and the God of all comfort, who comforts us in all our troubles, so that we can comfort those in any trouble with the comfort we ourselves receive from God. (2 Cor. 1:3–4)

Surely not everyone is called to serve. Aren't some people dealt such bad cards that they can't really be expected to play out their hands? Shouldn't they be excused?

Aurea was dealt a hand few of us could bear. In 1994, Aurea was a young wife living with her husband and her entire extended family of fifty-four men, women, and children in southern Rwanda. That was the year when the gates of hell broke loose, and the great Rwandan genocide ravaged the entire nation. Eight hundred thousand people were killed in just one hundred days. Aurea watched in horror as the other fifty-three members of her family— men, women, and children—were killed before her very eyes. They were shot or hacked to death with machetes. But Aurea, because she was beautiful, was first gang-raped and then mutilated and left to die. But she lived. In addition to her scars, she took two other things with her from that day—the HIV virus and a son named Eric, the result of her rape. Eric, too, is HIV positive.

My good friend and World Vision board member Dr. Steve Hayner, traveling with his daughter, met Aurea a few years back and told me her story. She and Eric have a small three-room mud-brick home now, about ten by twenty feet. She has found work digging and hoeing a neighbor's fields in exchange for a little food. Steve's daughter dared to ask Aurea just how she could survive such a devastating loss. She reflected that she doesn't know how long the two of them will live with the disease they share. But still she said, "Life is good because we are in God's hands." She has forgiven the men who raped her and killed her family because "that was what Jesus had done for [her] on the cross." Aurea has no safety net, no contingency plans, and no retirement accounts—just faith in God. The truth Steve learned from her that day was this: when God is all you have, you discover that God is all you need.

You would think that surely Aurea cannot be expected to join the ranks of God's great kingdom revolution. And, besides, what would she have to offer anyway? But you would be mistaken. Aurea has taken in another child to care for, a girl who lost her parents to AIDS. And she has become a caregiver in her community, visiting and ministering to those sick with full-blown AIDS. World Vision has trained her, given her a medical kit, and provided a bicycle so she can make her biweekly visits—caring, loving, encouraging, comforting, and praying with those God has put into her care. Yes, Aurea is much more than a soldier; she's one of the officers in the kingdom revolution, serving at the pleasure of the King. Like Luke Skywalker from *Star Wars*, the force is strong with her.

SURRENDERED

The most important thing to remember is this: to be ready at any moment to give up what you are for what you might become. —attributed to W. E. B. DuBois

Again, the kingdom of heaven is like a merchant looking for fine pearls. When he found one of great value, he went away and sold everything he had and bought it. (Matt. 13:45–46)

Joey Lankford and his wife, Courtney, had it all. He was in his early thirties, served as the COO of his family's thriving hospital equipment company, earned a nice six-figure salary, and had a strong family. They have four kids, three of them biological and one adopted from Ethiopia. They went to church at Brentwood Baptist in Tennessee and had a wonderful circle of faith and friends. "I had three houses," Joey said, "and all of the toys a thirty-one-year-old would have on his bucket list: cars, trucks, four-wheelers, horses." Joey talks about how he defined success in terms of owning "the golden pony," all the goodies that come with success and wealth. But a decision to accept his younger brother's invitation to take a short-term mission trip to Nicaragua in 2008 really messed with Joey's head. It was the beginning of a spiritual restlessness in his life. He had everything he wanted, but something was missing.

> HE HAD EVERYTHING HE WANTED, BUT SOMETHING WAS MISSING.

Joey had a barn that he called his man cave, and one weekend he went out there with his Bible in his hand. He stayed there the whole weekend, reading and praying. *There's got to be something deeper,* Joey thought. *Why am I here? What's going on?* "God met me in the barn that day." He felt God saying, "You can keep going your way, but you're not going to be happy outside of the plans I have for you. You have to make a choice on this." Joey said he wrote the word *surrender* that weekend all over the barn walls. When he finally emerged, Courtney said, "I hope you've had some revelation." Joey's answer was that he now knew who was in charge of his life.

"I began selling everything I owned, including my stock in the family business. This looked like suicide," Joey recalls. Joey applied to the International Mission Board of the Southern Baptist Convention to become a full-time missionary, but because of funding challenges he was rejected. Joey and his family went anyway. In 2009, he relinquished his role in the company, and in 2010, he and his whole family moved to South Africa to serve at Living Hope Ministries—the group working with the poor and the sick that I profile in *The Hole in Our Gospel.*

Today Joey is using his business skills to develop new approaches to farming and food production. "I'm a tomato and cucumber salesman," he said. "I've got less than I've ever had, and I'm happier than I've ever been.

I'm just a country boy from Tennessee. I was not qualified. God was not calling me because of my qualifications. He called me because he wanted me to love him more." And so Joey surrendered to the King.

A DIVIDED LIFE

A ship in harbor is safe, but that's not what ships are for. —attributed to John A. Shedd

We have seen how God was able to use a farmer and a genocide survivor, but what about an investment manager on Wall Street? Is the kingdom of heaven at work even there? Bob Doll was the chief equity strategist for BlackRock, Inc., the world's largest asset management firm, which has more than $3.5 trillion under management. Yes, that's right, trillion, as in one thousand billion! Bob Doll appeared on all of the financial TV programs and was regularly quoted by investment columns and magazines. He was one of the elite gurus of Wall Street. He is also a follower of Jesus who plays the organ at his church and directs the choir. Bob admits that for years he had a divided life because he worked in New York and lived in Princeton, New Jersey. He had his Monday-through-Friday life, and he had his weekend life, and they were separated by both distance and content . . . until one day Bob's place of work moved ten minutes from his home, and his two worlds came together. He saw people he worked with at his kids' school and at their soccer games. And he came to see that there was really no separation between the sacred and the secular; his work was part of his sacred calling, his "sweet spot" in the kingdom. "I realized I had a ministry field right there," he said. So Bob began to be more intentional about his faith, bringing it into his work relationships where appropriate, taking the time to plant a seed or encourage someone who needed it. "Too many of us [Christians in the workplace] are quiet for too long," he said. "It takes courage; not many are willing to speak out." Bob realized that his business success could also be his platform for wider ministry, and he became a popular speaker at Christian conferences, sharing with and mentoring younger Christian leaders who had their own questions about how to live out their faith in the workplace. In fact, I met Bob when he spoke at the annual retreat of the New Canaan Society I mentioned in chapter 9.

Bob told me that Romans 12:2 has had a strong influence in how he views his faith in the context of his work: "Do not conform to the pattern of this world, but be transformed by the renewing of your mind. Then you will be able to test and approve what God's will is—his good, pleasing, and perfect will." His encouragement to Christians in the workplace is to take the risk to live out their faith in front of others. The easiest thing to do in the workplace is to conform to the pattern of this world—to seek what the world seeks, value what the world values, and behave as the world behaves—but that is not the call of Christ in our work. Instead, we are to be transformed by the renewing of our minds so that we might be agents of transformation in our workplaces. The call to build the kingdom of God is a call to go into the world as Christ's ambassadors, to lift up kingdom values, model Christ's values, take captive every thought, and establish beachheads for his kingdom. When we bring Christ with us into the workplace, our work becomes sacred. In 2012, Bob changed direction and left BlackRock. The King is redeploying this soldier of the kingdom, and I can't wait to see what assignment God has chosen for him next.

SOMETHING OLD, SOMETHING NEW

She did what she could. (Mark 14:8)

Reneé and I ran into a new friend at church who was brimming with excitement. Carl Harris had been accepted by the Peace Corps and was leaving for the Philippines later that week to begin a two-year adventure teaching English as a second language. We were inspired, not just because Carl was joining the Peace Corps but because Carl was just four months away from celebrating his eightieth birthday. Carl's entire life has been an adventure with God. As a young man he was an Episcopal priest. His passion for the world later led him to Cambodia, where he served from 1973 to 1975, as World Vision's national director. He was forced to evacuate in

1975, as the country disintegrated into mayhem and genocide when Pol Pot's evil forces swept across the land. Carl then spent many years working for USAID, always with a passion to help the poorest of the poor. Carl believes that God isn't done with him yet. He still has time and energy left, and there are still people who need God's love. Even though Carl is eighty years of age, his adventure just began a fresh new chapter.

Raven Thuman is not eighty; she is eight. She is in the second grade at Niagara Street Elementary School. Raven's mom and dad are kingdom parents who have raised their little girl with a strong faith. Raven's dad, Dennis, runs a restaurant and offers a weekly Bible study for restaurant patrons who want to learn more about issues of faith. And Raven's mom, Joanne, runs a club four days a week, where local kids come to play, sing, and learn about Jesus. They adopted Raven and learned later that she had cerebral palsy. Though Raven uses a wheelchair, her mom said, "Raven never complains about her disability."

Raven has an infectiously sweet and generous spirit. A few years ago at Christmas, her grandfather sent her a World Vision Gift Catalog along with a check. He asked her to spend half the money on a gift for someone in the developing world, and the other half on herself. Raven combed through the catalog and knew right away what she had to buy—a wheelchair for another child. At her next birthday party she asked her friends for money so she could give another gift to poor children; this time she gave musical instruments to kids who had none. "I love music," Raven said, "because it makes me happy." When asked what she wants to do when she grows up, Raven said, "I want to tell people about Jesus." This little eight-year-old girl in a wheelchair, stationed in Niagara Falls, New York, is a winsome ambassador for the kingdom. "Raven spreads her faith like a sweet aroma wherever she goes," her mom said. "She is Jesus at Niagara Street Elementary."

DELIVERING GOD'S MAIL

You show that you are a letter from Christ . . . written not with ink but with the Spirit of the living God, not on tablets of stone but on tablets of human hearts. (2 Cor. 3:3)

Jim Plantenberg works in the mail room at World Vision. Every day he swings by my office, pushing his cart and delivering the mail. Jim's wife, Cheryl, also works at World Vision, serving me faithfully in the president's office. Jim has always felt pestered by his desire to be a pastor, but life's path took him in different directions. He worked at Sea-Tac Airport for twenty-five years in logistics and later worked for a landscaping firm, driving a truck and doing procurement. Desiring to be part of a Christian ministry, seven years ago he came to work in World Vision's mail room. Last year when Cheryl's dad became ill and moved into a hospice facility to live out his last days, Jim and Cheryl went to visit often with him and to pray. At one point Jim felt so compelled just to be with Cheryl's dad, he took a week off from work so he could be with him every day. During that time, Jim began to meet some of the nurses and other patients. Perceiving that Jim was a man of faith, the nurses began asking Jim if he wanted to become more involved. First they asked if he would lead a regular Sunday worship service for the patients who wished to attend. That bloomed into a ministry of one-on-one meetings as people started to ask for him.

A year later Jim finds himself at the center of a thriving ministry. He leads a service every other Sunday for between twenty and forty souls, and, by popular request, he is also there quite a few nights and weekends to comfort and pray with people as they face the end of their lives. He distributes Bibles and prays with family members who are there to visit their loved ones. One thirteen-year-old girl, after her grandfather died, followed Jim into the hallway. She grabbed his arm and said, "I need to know; where did Grandpa go?" Jim was able to share with her the good news of the gospel. Though a hospice center, with its sights, smells, and ambiance of sickness and death, is not a place most of us want to be, Jim told me, "I feel like I absolutely have to do this. I would rather be here than anywhere else." He never expected to have such a vital ministry at this stage of his life. He just made himself available and listened to the Spirit's voice. "I'm just a tool in God's toolbox," he told me. "I just want people to know the good news of Jesus Christ before they

HE NEVER EXPECTED TO HAVE SUCH A VITAL MINISTRY AT THIS STAGE OF HIS LIFE.

die." You see, he knows that the King is inviting people to his great banquet, and Jim wants to be the one to deliver that mail.

A TALE OF TWO OBITUARIES

Only one life, 'twill soon be past, only what's done for Christ will last.
—attributed to C. T. Studd

It's not the things we do in life that we regret on our deathbed, it is the things we do not.[2]—Randy Pausch

Every adventure has a beginning and an end, and there is nothing that puts our lives in clearer perspective than the unavoidable fact that we all are going to die. So, as I end this book, I want to focus for a few moments on this not-so-cheerful truth: you're going to die. Birth and death may be the only two truly universal human experiences, but it's always what happens in between that distinguishes one person's life from another. Most of us don't like to think much about death for the obvious reasons, but let me ask you for a minute to imagine that today is going to be the last day of your life. I want you to reflect back on all the days of your life so far and ask yourself what you treasure the most. Now imagine reading your own obituary in the local paper. What would you want it to say about you? Better still, if you could write it yourself, what would you write? How would you want to be remembered?

Would you write about the money you've made, the titles you've held, or the real estate you've owned? Would you focus on how much time you spent at the office, the investment gains achieved in your portfolios, or the hobbies you pursued? Or would you instead want to write about the lasting things, the deeper things, and the sacred things in your life: the people you've loved, the lives you've enriched, the things you've done to help others, and the adventures you've had in your walk with the Lord? Wouldn't you want to be remembered as a person whose life was marked by love, compassion, and generosity and who left the world a better place than before? Wouldn't you want to write about a life that "counted" for the kingdom?

I want to look at two stories in Scripture of two different men and what their obituaries might have said. Though both of these stories involve wealthy men, their significance isn't really about wealth at all but, rather, about how they viewed their lives. The first is the story Jesus told in Luke 12 of a "certain rich man":

> Then he said to them, "Watch out! Be on your guard against all kinds of greed; a man's life does not consist in the abundance of his possessions."
>
> And he told them this parable: "The ground of a certain rich man produced a good crop. He thought to himself, 'What shall I do? I have no place to store my crops.'
>
> "Then he said, 'This is what I'll do. I will tear down my barns and build bigger ones, and there I will store all my grain and my goods. And I'll say to myself, "You have plenty of good things laid up for many years. Take life easy; eat, drink, and be merry."'" (Luke 12:15–19)

What do we see when we look at this man's worldview? What would he write in his own obituary? Here was a man who defined himself by his success, his possessions, and his accomplishments. These were the things in which he found both his identity and security. This was a guy who had entered "success and financial security" as his destination in his life's GPS. He had a Magic Kingdom worldview. His fields had produced a large abundant harvest, much more than he could consume. His response was to build bigger barns to store up for himself the excess God had provided. He came from the "eat, drink, and be merry" school of theology. But Jesus finished the story by telling his disciples just how God viewed the man's life:

> "But God said to him, 'You fool! This very night your life will be demanded from you. Then who will get what you have prepared for yourself?'
>
> "This is how it will be with anyone who stores up things for himself but is not rich toward God." (Luke 12:20–21)

You see, this man was asking all the wrong questions. He was asking whether he should build bigger barns for *his* wealth when he should have been asking how he could wisely invest *God's* wealth. He was focused on how to best maximize *his* comfort and security rather than how he might have provided comfort and security to *others*. Before he asked the question, "What shall I do?" he should have answered the question, "Whom shall I follow?" He had lived his life with all the wrong priorities. We can imagine that he might have written for himself quite a glowing obituary, one filled with lists of his accomplishments and assets, his stature, and his status. Jesus wrote for him a much shorter one: "You fool!"

Our second man is Job, the wealthy man we discussed in the last chapter, who lost everything he owned when Satan attacked him. Yet Job remained faithful through all that he suffered. At one point in the story, Job reflects back on his life as he cries out to God. He is essentially recounting the things in his life that mattered most, the things he most wanted God to consider. Job was, in effect, reciting his own obituary:

> "Whoever heard me spoke well of me,
>   and those who saw me commended me,
> because I rescued the poor who cried for help,
>   and the fatherless who had none to assist them.
> The one who was dying blessed me;
>   I made the widow's heart sing.
> I put on righteousness as my clothing;
>   justice was my robe and my turban.
> I was eyes to the blind
>   and feet to the lame.
> I was a father to the needy;
>   I took up the case of the stranger.
> I broke the fangs of the wicked
>   and snatched the victims from their teeth." (Job 29:11–17)

What a remarkable contrast to our first man. Job also had been a wealthy man who owned extensive property and assets and had achieved success in all of his business ventures, but these were not the things he valued most in the life he had lived. Job valued most his obedience to God, his commitment to justice, his compassion toward the poor, and the things he had done to love his neighbors. Here were two different men, two different lives, and two different legacies. It is quite clear to me which one is likely to hear the Master's praises: "Well done, good and faithful servant! You have been faithful with a few things; I will put you in charge of many things. Come and share your master's happiness!" (Matt. 25:21).

You don't get to write your own obituary, but you do get to live the life that will be written about. The question is, what will be written about you? I don't know where you now stand in your journey with God. Perhaps

YOU DON'T GET TO WRITE YOUR OWN OBITUARY, BUT YOU DO GET TO LIVE THE LIFE THAT WILL BE WRITTEN ABOUT.

you are someone who has already forsaken everything else to serve Christ, investing your life in his kingdom mission. If you are, I hope you have been inspired to stay the course and to keep running the good race set before you. Or maybe you are someone who accepted the good news of the gospel with great joy many years back but have never fully laid down your life in his service. You have held back. You have had other priorities. You have been sidetracked by hardships and setbacks. For whatever reasons you have stayed safely on the sidelines, watching, but have never gotten into the game. You have accepted Jesus as your Savior but you have never fully allowed him to be your Lord, and as a result you have never really felt God's calling on your life. You have never found that which you were created to do, never become that amazing person you were meant to be, never lived that kingdom adventure you were meant to live. If that describes you, I have wonderful news for you: there is still time. You can begin today. "It's never too late to be who you might have been."[3] We serve a God of second chances, third chances, fourth chances—as many chances as we need. Our loving Father will always welcome us home.

I began this book stating this bold premise: God has invited you to join him in changing the world.

- God has a dream for this world that Jesus called the kingdom of God.
- God created you to play an important role in his kingdom vision.
- You will never find your deepest purpose in life until you find your place in building God's kingdom.

Two thousand years after Jesus left, the great mission of God in our world remains unfinished. The body of Christ in the twenty-first century has everything required to finish the job: the knowledge, the scale, the gifts and skills, the resources, and the mandate. And you have everything required to play your part. All that's required is the commitment to "throw off everything that hinders" in order to "run with perseverance the race marked out for us, fixing our eyes on Jesus, the pioneer and perfecter of faith" (Heb. 12:1–2). All we lack is the will. For followers of Christ, answering God's invitation to join this kingdom mission is not just one of the things we are supposed to do; it is the very reason we were created. We will never become the people God intends us to become until we embrace the mission we were made to fulfill.

Look around you. What can you see? What is yours to do? Where is your Normandy Beach? In God's expanding kingdom there is no unimportant job and no insignificant person. Every one of his spiritual dominoes is positioned to ignite a sprawling chain reaction that will echo through the years. But that first domino must fall; *your* domino must fall. Is there a single mom who needs your encouragement, a child who needs your love? Do you see the elderly woman, lonely for a friend; a drowning teenager, hungering for a dad? Have you looked into the hearts of those you work with and seen the desperation in their lives? Is there an immigrant family struggling to adjust, needing a friend to guide them in a foreign place? Is there a social problem that you might mobilize people to solve? Do you have in your bank account the money that a floundering ministry needs to survive, that a homeless man needs to get a fresh start? Do you have skills and abilities that others need—in finance, as a doctor or lawyer or handyman who can repair a broken-down car? Is there an issue of justice for which you can advocate, a wrong that you can right? Do you ache for the children who die from hunger, the orphans lacking a home, or the widow with children who just needs a loan? So many people are crying out to God for his help. Might you be the answer to one of their prayers? How many people still wait to see and hear the good news of Jesus Christ? How many invitations from the King have yet to be delivered? "How beautiful are the feet of those who bring good news!" (Rom. 10:15).

There are as many ways to join the great mission of Christ in our world as there are people. You have met in this book just a few of the hundreds of people I've encountered who are living their own kingdom adventures. The one thing they all share is the unwavering belief that God made them for a purpose, to serve him and build his kingdom. They have rearranged their lives to put Christ and his kingdom mission at the center. They have enlisted; they have joined the rescue mission to take the world for Christ, to serve as ambassadors of his love and herald the good news of the gospel. They are the Finishers, and the thing they have in common is that they have all said yes to God's great adventure for their lives. It doesn't matter who you are: rich or poor, young or old, educated or not. You are a child of the King. You are loved beyond measure. You were created for a purpose. And you have been invited to join the great rescue mission of our Father who is in heaven. He asks only that you bring whatever you hold in your hands; then he asks you to let it go, to offer it to him.

That's when the adventure begins.

Afterword

There are things that *only you* can do, and you
are alive to do them. In the great orchestra we call
life, you have an instrument and a song, and you
owe it to God to play them both sublimely.[1]

—MAX LUCADO

Flash Mob

I want to leave you with one final thought—a striking metaphor of sight and song, a beautiful picture of what God is calling us to be and to do in our world. A few days back my friend Leighton Ford sent me a link to a remarkable video on YouTube. Leighton promised me that it would bring me joy . . . and it did. If you can, watch the video now or right after you have finished reading, but please don't miss it. (Please scan the image above to watch the video, or go to the web address in the Notes section.)[2] This flash mob video captured something quite singular and compelling. On May 19, 2012, the Vallès Symphony Orchestra, the Lieder, Amics de l'Òpera, and Coral Belles Arts choirs transformed a city square in Sabadell, Spain.

I believe God is calling us to sing and to play—sing and play his amazing song of love, forgiveness, and transformation in every city square and in all the nations of the world. He has equipped each of us with instruments that only we can play, and he has given us his voice. He bids us to go, to join together and sing and play the good news of his salvation.

The video begins when just one lone tuxedoed man appears in a busy city square and quietly starts to pluck out the notes of Beethoven's Symphony No. 9, better known to many Christians as the majestic hymn "Joyful, Joyful, We Adore Thee." At first no one notices. Then some children step closer to watch the curious sight. A few seconds later a woman playing cello walks up and joins him. And the two of them play the song. Then a bassoonist steps out of a nearby door, followed by two people with violins. The music grows in strength and power. A crowd begins to gather: children, shoppers, business folk, a couple holding hands. A young child climbs a lamppost to get a better look. More musicians join, coming from different buildings and doorways around the square—now twenty, then fifty, each with their own instrument, all playing the same lyrical notes. *Joyful, joyful, we adore thee.* Smiles, laughter, cameras clicking, children hoisted up on shoulders, people pointing and crowding closer; a throng of people have stopped to watch and listen, drawn by the beauty of the music and oddness of the scene.

Then, out of nowhere, the conductor comes into view, lifting his hands and directing his players; all eyes are now on him. Still more appear: clarinets, oboes, flutes, and piccolos—trumpets, trombones, French horns, and drums—seventy, now one hundred. People stop, cafés empty, and offices are abandoned. The audience swells—men and women, old and young, clusters of children, mothers with strollers, loungers, and lovers. There is something magical about all of this. And then, just when it seems that the orchestra is complete, a mighty choir steps out of the crowd, surrounds the musicians, and lifts up the heavenly lyrics with soaring voices:

> Joyful, joyful, we adore Thee,
> God of glory, Lord of love;
> Hearts unfold like flow'rs before Thee,
> Op'ning to the sun above.

Children start to dance. The hundreds of onlookers can no longer resist. They, too, begin to mouth the words, sing the chorus, and lift their hands to the music. The remarkable ensemble of talented musicians plays on, increasing the tempo, filling the city square with their sounds until, finally, the music comes to its magnificent crescendo, and the crowd erupts with praise and applause.

BRING YOUR INSTRUMENTS, LIFT YOUR VOICES, AND JOIN THE KING'S GREAT SYMPHONY OF LOVE.

What beauty! What grace! How extraordinary. What a picture for the church of Jesus Christ. Bring your instruments, lift your voices, and join the King's great symphony of love. The world is watching and listening, longing to hear a new song, a different song, a song of hope.

> Melt the clouds of sin and sadness;
> Drive the dark of doubt away;
> Giver of immortal gladness,
> Fill us with the light of day!

This same song first began long ago in Bethlehem, when just one angel sang:

"Do not be afraid. I bring you good news that will cause great joy for all the people. Today in the town of David a Savior has been born to you; he is the Messiah, the Lord." (Luke 2:10–11)

More angels joined this chorus, then more and still more—"a great company of the heavenly host . . . praising God" (Luke 2:13) and singing the chorus of God's good news:

"Glory to God in the highest heaven,
 and on earth peace to those on whom his favor rests." (Luke 2:14)

Now the King invites you. Come, drop what you're doing, pick up your instruments, and come—into the cities and into the streets. Join the great chorus. The King calls his children, sending them into the world to play and sing. Lift up your voices and join the great mission of the King.

Mortals, join the happy chorus,
Which the morning stars began;
Father love is reigning o'er us,
Brother love binds man to man.
Ever singing, march we onward,
Victors in the midst of strife,
Joyful music leads us Sunward,
In the triumph song of life.[3]

He called you out of darkness
 and called you into light.
He filled you with his Spirit,
 put his song upon your heart.
He asked you to his banquet
 and now . . .
 He bids you sing.

STUDY GUIDE

Unfinished is a challenging book, asking you to reconsider your life and possibly make changes that will enable you to fulfill God's call to build his kingdom. You may be wondering, *What do I do now?* This study guide is designed to help you wrestle with the ideas in *Unfinished* and contemplate its message. It also will help you not only think about the book but also take steps to put its message into action.

You are a character in God's story. In his great plan he has a unique role for you to play. Take the time, in a group or by yourself, to use this study guide to help deepen your commitment to God's call.

CHAPTER 1: THE MEANING OF LIFE AND OTHER IMPORTANT THINGS

1. In this chapter Rich writes that each of us is a character that God has written into his big story. Do you believe this? How does it affect your view of your life?

2. Do you have a worldview that you live by? How do you describe it? Consider your worldview in these dimensions: money, family,

career, morality, politics. How are your attitudes in these areas influenced by God's truth?

GOING DEEPER

Consider some of the prevailing views in our society and reflect on their ramifications. Then go into God's Word and look for the countering truths expressed in the Bible. Jot down your ideas and Scripture references.

Truism	Biblical Truth
You should be able to do whatever you want as long as it does not hurt other people.	
The one who dies with the most toys wins.	
Winning isn't everything; it's the only thing.	
We can all find God in our inner self.	
It's a dog-eat-dog world, and only the strong survive.	
All religions are just different roads to the same truth.	
Everyone should have an equal opportunity to pursue his or her dreams.	

TAKE ACTION

Contemplate what you believe and how you are putting it into practice in your life.

PRAY

Do you struggle to live out the worldview that you espouse on paper? Pray that God would grant you wisdom and courage to build your life on his firm foundation.

CHAPTER 2: GOD'S BIG STORY

1. Rich says the Bible is a love story, and he offers a brief history of God's relationship with humanity as described in the Bible. Have you ever thought of it as a love story? In light of that idea, how do you fit into this story of God's love?
2. Have you had a come-to-Jesus moment, one that transformed the way you saw your life? What was that like, and were you able to sustain that passion longer than those first early days? Is such an experience necessary in order to dramatically change your life to follow Jesus?

GOING DEEPER

Reflect on Rich's suggestion that the Bible is, at its essence, "the story of a Father's love for his children." Study Scripture to make a list of specific stories about fatherly love. Then think about how the love story continues by making another list of the ways God has shown his love for you throughout your life.

TAKE ACTION

How much of the Bible have you read? Make a list of all the books of the Bible you have yet to read and make a plan for reading them in the next twelve months.

PRAY

As the Word of God the Bible is God's direct revelation. Pray that as you read through Scripture, God would reveal himself to you and you would see in his Word the love story Rich described.

CHAPTER 3: WHY DID JESUS LEAVE?

1. Have you ever wondered, *Why did Jesus leave?* Why might it be important to consider this? Do you ever ask God why he doesn't just fix all the brokenness in our world?
2. As you reflect on Rich's description of God's big story in Scripture and the mission Jesus left the church to accomplish, how does that change your worldview? How do you see the world differently? How does or should that change the way you live?

GOING DEEPER

Explore the concept of worldview and how it relates to specific conditions in our world today. First identify your own perspective on these conditions. Then try to step outside yourself to understand the perspective of others in different circumstances.

- Informed by my worldview, here is what I think of . . .
  Poverty: _____
  Success: _____
  Gender: _____
  Capitalism: _____
  Hunger: _____
- If I lived in China, my worldview on poverty might be:

  _____
- If I lived in the West Bank, my worldview about success might be:

  _____

- If I lived in Afghanistan, my worldview about gender might be:

  _____

- If I lived in Russia, my worldview about capitalism might be:

  _____

- If I lived in Ethiopia, my worldview about hunger might be:

  _____

- Discuss with a group whether it is possible for people of diverse nationalities to share the same worldview if it is shaped by faith in Christ rather than culture.

TAKE ACTION

Are you familiar with Ascension Day? It occurs exactly forty days after Easter in the church calendar, and it honors the day Jesus ascended into heaven. Find out more by researching it, and then consider your own ideas about what his departure means for us today.

PRAY

Since "the head thinks where the feet stand," as Frei Betto stated, take time to pray for those living in poverty and ask God for guidance on how you and your church might make a difference in their lives.

CHAPTER 4: MAGIC KINGDOM, TRAGIC KINGDOM, AND THE KINGDOM OF GOD

1. Rich writes about the disparities between his home church and the Haitian church he visited in the refugee camp. Anyone who has witnessed the extreme poverty overseas has experienced the moral discomfort of knowing that some people have so little while others have so much. Do you think it is the responsibility of Christians to alter that disparity? Why or why not?

2. If the kingdom of God provides the solution to the disparity between the Magic Kingdom and the Tragic Kingdom, what can the church as a whole do to be a part of the solution? It may seem overwhelming. What can you do to build the kingdom of God wherever you are?

GOING DEEPER

Rich points out that the kingdom of God is mentioned more than 125 times in the New Testament, often by Jesus himself. Mine the scripture references below for insights about the kingdom values Jesus imparted and what they mean for you and your church today.

Scripture	What values emerge from this?	What does this mean for my church?	What does this mean for me?
Matthew 13:44: "The kingdom of heaven is like treasure hidden in a field. When a man found it, he hid it again, and then in his joy went and sold all he had and bought that field."			
Mark 10:25: "It is easier for a camel to go through the eye of a needle than for a rich man to enter the kingdom of God."			
Luke 9:62: Jesus replied, "No one who puts his hand to the plow and looks back is fit for service in the kingdom of God."			

Scripture	What values emerge from this?	What does this mean for my church?	What does this mean for me?
Luke 13:29–30: "People will come from east and west and north and south, and will take their places at the feast in the kingdom of God. Indeed there are those who are last who will be first, and first who will be last."			
Luke 17:20–21: Once, having been asked by the Pharisees when the kingdom of God would come, Jesus replied, "The kingdom of God does not come with your careful observation, nor will people say, 'Here it is,' or 'There it is,' because the kingdom of God is within you."			

TAKE ACTION

Think of a time in which you have experienced the moral discomfort over the disparity of wealth in the world today. How much of your time and money do you sacrifice specifically to address this disparity?

PRAY

Pray that your heart will be broken by the things that break the heart of God. Ask that God will grant you eyes to see the world's pain and give you the compassion to take action.

CHAPTER 5: THE MISSION OF GOD

1. Rich says that he has never heard a sermon fully explaining "that the central mission of Christ and the purpose he gave to his church was to proclaim, establish, and build God's kingdom on earth." Does your church make the kingdom of God central to its mission and ministry? Describe the hallmarks of God's kingdom coming on earth.

2. Might you be practicing a faith of decisions rather than one of discipleship? Why does Rich link being a disciple of Christ to the "whole gospel" of taking the kingdom of God to the ends of the earth?

GOING DEEPER

Rich writes, "When we say yes to Jesus, we say yes to his forgiveness, but we also say yes to his commands and yes to his kingdom. We merge our stories into his story and join the unfolding plan of God to establish and grow his kingdom."

Look up the verses below and write down their implications for your life.

- Luke 21:2–4 (giving)
- Ezekiel 16:49 (caring for the poor)
- Isaiah 42:3–4 (upholding justice)
- 2 Corinthians 5:20 (being a witness)

Prayerfully explore the changes you can make in your life to more purposefully participate in the mission of God.

TAKE ACTION

Brainstorm—on your own or with friends—what you could do to live out the whole gospel. Be specific as you think of practical ways to take action.

PRAY

When we say yes, we say yes to God's whole and unfolding plan. Pray without ceasing that "thy kingdom come, thy will be done, on earth as it is in heaven."

CHAPTER 6: THE INVITATION OF GOD

1. Many Christians never become full citizens of God's kingdom, as doing so can be a bit like enlisting in an army for Christ. But the truth is, either you're all in or you're not. Which side are you on? Consider 2 Timothy 2:3–4 as you contemplate what being a "good soldier of Christ" means to you.
2. Christians often talk about the gospel only in terms of proclamation. But Rich says being ambassadors for the kingdom also involves compassion, justice, and restoration. What do you think about this broader definition, that the gospel is both words *and* deeds?
3. This chapter says that the church is the organizing principle of God's kingdom. What would it take for the church to really be an "outpost of the kingdom" of God? Do you see your church as a community governed by God's values?

GOING DEEPER

Most Christians know the Sermon on the Mount and can recite some of its famous phrases. But how can Jesus' words cut deeper into our lives and churches as a "blueprint for this new way to live in God's kingdom," as Rich suggests?

Reflect on each of the nine "blessed are" statements (Matt. 5:3–12). Think about and discuss how each was revolutionary in Jesus' time—and how it is revolutionary today. Which cultural truism does each overturn? Also note your own fears or reluctance about being poor in spirit, meek, a peacemaker, persecuted, and so on. Try to articulate what you risk if you live out these new ways of relating to God and others. And what might you gain?

TAKE ACTION

Love requires tangible expression. It needs hands and feet. Read Matthew 22:37–40 several times, listening for God's direction. Commit on paper several tangible actions you can take to be the hands and feet of Christ in the days ahead.

PRAY

We all have withheld a part of ourselves from God's control. Pray that God would shine a light on those parts of you that may not be enlisted fully in God's mission. Ask for the boldness to enlist those areas of your life.

CHAPTERS 7 AND 8: RSVP AND LET'S MAKE A DEAL

1. If Jesus called you to "make you fishers of men," would you hesitate or step right up as Peter and Andrew did? There is a cost to the invitation. Think about the most valuable things you possess and list them. What kind of sacrifice would it involve to lay them unconditionally at Jesus' feet?
2. Reflect awhile on what you may have given up already or placed on the altar for God. How did that sacrifice change your life?
3. Stu and Robin Phillips offered to God what they loved most. What would it mean for you to give to God as sacrificially as Stu and Robin did?

GOING DEEPER

All of us struggle to give up what we most treasure even when God asks us. The sharp edge of sacrifice daunts us, despite God's assurance that the rewards will be great. Explore the counterintuitive depth and power of

Jesus' words in Luke 9:24: "For whoever wants to save his life will lose it, but whoever loses his life for me will save it."

Think about how the following statements can be true in theory—or are true in practice in your life:

- *When I give away my money, I become rich.*
- *I can fast to become full.*
- *Even if I am uprooted, I am at home.*
- *As a slave to God's law, I am most free.*
- *My pain is a route to joy.*
- *My emptiness allows me to be complete.*

What other statements can you think of that are relative to the sacrifice of being "all in" for Jesus?

TAKE ACTION

God may not be asking you to give up anything for him. Still, it can be a good practice *to choose* to give up something for God, as many do for Lent. What symbolic item or habit might you give up for God?

PRAY

We all need to hold the things of this world loosely. Pray that God will release your grip on material things and give you a greater love for him and his.

CHAPTER 9: WE WERE MADE FOR MORE

1. Looking objectively at your life, list two or three things you have entered into your "life's GPS" as destinations. How have those things altered your course?
2. How might your life change if you entered "serve Christ and build his kingdom" into your life's GPS?

GOING DEEPER

Rich suggests a list of new GPS directions for our lives if we allow God's plan to be our destination. Study Scripture to find verses matching each of these:

- Put the needs of others ahead of your own.
- Take detours when someone needs your help.
- Get off the highway to spend time with family and friends, even when it slows you down.
- Pick up hitchhikers.
- Use your money to build up God's kingdom, not yours.
- Don't confuse career success with being a successful person.
- View your work as a means to the end of serving God, not as an end in itself.
- Invest your time, talent, and treasure in being rich toward God rather than becoming rich yourself.
- Stop to help those broken down on the side of the road who need a little help on their journey.
- Pay close attention to your moral compass.
- Keep your relationship with God as your North Star.

TAKE ACTION

There is sacred work to do to be the hands and feet of Christ. Consider the list above, also found on page 110. What would you add to the list for your own journey? Could you begin this week?

PRAY

We all need a more faithful spiritual life. Pray that God will grant you a greater sensitivity to the Holy Spirit. Ask for clarity as the Holy Spirit speaks in your life.

CHAPTER 10: GOD'S SPIRITUAL GPS

1. Rich says that the Holy Spirit is "the single enabling power that now makes it possible for ordinary human beings to be transformed and live differently." From the "cluelessness of the first disciples" to secular human history—the Holy Spirit has made the difference. What other manifestations have you observed of the Holy Spirit informing our lives, culture, society, and churches?

2. The Holy Spirit also provides directions, prompting us to reach out to a neighbor, pray for a family member, or spend time with a hurting friend. How have you experienced the Holy Spirit's direction in your life?

GOING DEEPER

Following the Holy Spirit in our lives requires us to develop ears to hear the promptings of the Spirit. We need to learn to listen to God. When Mother Teresa was asked what she said in her prayers, she responded, "I don't talk. I listen."

She practiced what is known as *apophatic* prayer, which seeks to quiet the mind in order to draw close to and hear God. Take twelve minutes, quiet and alone, and simply listen for God. Don't come with questions and requests, but seek to enter God's presence through quiet listening. Consider how you might pray by listening more.

TAKE ACTION

Reflect on the times when you have felt the prompting of the Holy Spirit. Did you take action? If not, why not do so right now?

PRAY

God is calling you to the front lines of service. Pray that God will pour his Holy Spirit upon you, ignite a holy fire within you, and guide you into his gospel revolution.

CHAPTER 11: CALLED FOR A PURPOSE

1. What do you think of Rich's prescription for discovering God's calling in your life (commit, pray, prepare, obey, act, trust)? How are those steps incorporated into your own life?
2. This chapter explores the idea of *calling*. Do you have the sense that you were called for a purpose? In God's Great Commission, what might God be calling you to do? Are you doing it right where you are today?
3. As you consider the previous questions, you may realize that you are in a season of preparation. What might God be teaching you as you trust him to reveal his calling for your life?

GOING DEEPER

Discerning God's call requires the willingness to obey. Reflect on verses such as Matthew 28:20, James 1:22, 1 John 2:3–6, and others. Choose one verse that is most convicting to you. Isolate the words and phrases that spiritually nudge you and spur you on.

In this chapter Rich writes, "Disciples are not expected just to 'talk the talk' . . . they are to 'walk the walk.'" Check yourself: Are you doing nothing more than waiting for a plum kingdom assignment? Consider Rich's list on page 138 about being obedient in the small things: changing bad habits, sharing your money generously, tithing, putting others ahead of yourself, and so on. Keep a checklist of the small, daily acts of obedience you may need to work on. If you think these things are not important, you may lack trust in God for the right outcome—his, not yours.

TAKE ACTION

God has likely been prompting you about his call on your life, but perhaps you have been too busy to take note. Dedicate some quiet time now for praying, listening, and planning the journey ahead for him.

PRAY

Ask God to strengthen your obedience and to grant you clarity on how you might live an extraordinary life in his service.

CHAPTER 12: SPIRITUAL DOMINOES

1. These stories of "spiritual dominoes"—Rahab, Robert Wilder, Steve Reynolds—are inspiring. Can you think of people you have known or read about, people who, through small acts of faithfulness, have had significant repercussions?
2. How does it change your perspective to realize that God can—and does—turn small acts of faithfulness into extraordinary works?
3. Rich notes how God changed the world through ordinary means: Moses' staff, David's sling, Peter's net, and Paul's pen. What is the staff or pen that you can offer for God to use through you?

GOING DEEPER

Rich describes spiritual dominoes and biblical change agents, such as Moses, David, Peter, and Paul, to show how ordinary people are powerfully used by God. Study some of these examples and take note of the qualities these people brought to the table. How would you rank their qualities against high-profile successful figures in today's society?

Not . . .	But . . .
Ready-made heroes	
In it for themselves	
Craving the glory and the credit	
Needing to know the end from the beginning	
Making it on their own	

Maybe you are ready right now to start a chain reaction. Think about the people in your life whom you can bless and influence. God has put you together for a reason.

TAKE ACTION

Resolve now to encourage one or more of the people you have just identified by telling them about how God uses small things to do great deeds.

PRAY

Mother Teresa said, "Don't look for big things, just do small things with great love. . . . The smaller the thing, the greater must be our love."[1] Pray that God would make you faithful and full of love as you do those small things.

CHAPTER 13: OUTPOSTS OF THE KINGDOM

1. Do you believe the church is the organizational unit of the kingdom of God—God's means for changing the world? Do you think it is important to be connected to a local church?
2. The church may be the instrument God uses, but that does

not mean he needs all the bells and whistles we often have at church—the building, programs, worship teams, and so on. Are there things in your church that may not be contributing to God's kingdom work?

3. What does a church need in order to execute the five dimensions (worship, model, disciple, mobilize, and go) that Rich suggests should define communities of believers?

GOING DEEPER

Rich suggests churches use his five-point checkup to evaluate their potential for changing the world for Christ. Read each point carefully, and then rate your church honestly. Study the Word to discover passages and verses to anchor you in your efforts to turn *church* into a verb.

Checkup Points	Grade	Convicting Scripture
Belief above behavior		
Explanation replacing exhortation		
Inward instead of outward		
Apathy replacing outrage		
Institution instead of revolution		

TAKE ACTION

It is never enough to simply critique. If you feel that your church has failed Rich's five-point checkup, what concrete steps can you take to help achieve the desired outcomes?

PRAY

Ask God to inspire you to be a worker in his "harvest field," a catalyst in your local church to jump-start its transformation into a "kingdom church."

CHAPTER 14: THE GATES OF HELL

1. What do you think about Rich's decision to include a chapter on Satan in this book? As Rich states, talk about the devil can seem so medieval. Do we need to think about spiritual opposition as we pursue God's call for our lives? Why or why not?
2. Rich says, "Every act of kindness, each moment spent in prayer, and every expression of love in the name of Christ pierces the heart of the enemy." This brings the battle between good and evil into our everyday attitudes and actions. Do you see it as spiritual warfare when dealing with coworkers, neighbors, and others with whom you may not be inclined to always act with kindness? Explore your thoughts about this.

GOING DEEPER

Just before Rich accepted his position as president of World Vision, he received an unusually compelling offer from another company for a position that would have been rewarding financially. But it is not unusual for obstacles or distractions to be placed in the path of doing God's will. Consider Job 1.

How might the enemy place obstacles or temptations in your path to prevent you from doing what God is asking of you? Can you list a few? Honestly consider which ones might hinder you from following God's call.

TAKE ACTION

How can you practice greater acts of kindness in the name of Christ? Choose two or three that you can practice every day.

PRAY

We do spiritual battle. Pray for insight regarding spiritual opposition to God's work in your life, and pray for spiritual strength in the battle.

CHAPTER 15: GOD'S GREAT ADVENTURE FOR YOUR LIFE

1. Rich tells a number of stories of people making decisions to more radically follow Christ's call. Which one comes closest to your experience? Is yours a bloom-where-you-are-planted story or one that is more drastic, like Joey Lankford's?
2. Rich says, "The key battles . . . hinge on the decisions of the little people." After reading *Unfinished*, what decisions do you need to make?

GOING DEEPER

Read the "Hall of Faith" in Hebrews 11. What would it look like for you to act in faith like Enoch, Noah, and Abraham? Take some time to create a list of things you hope may someday be included in your obituary. If you died today, which of the things you have listed could not be said truthfully about you? How might that change your priorities and choices going forward?

TAKE ACTION

God has invited you to join him in changing the world. What is the role you are to play in his story? Write down steps you can start taking today that will bring you closer to fulfilling God's call on your life.

PRAY

You already have taken several steps in the direction of God's plan for your life. Pray for endurance as you consider how to join Jesus' mission to change the world. Pray for the perseverance needed to complete the journey and the courage to continue when obstacles or distractions appear in your way.

WHAT ARE YOU GOING TO DO ABOUT IT?

After the release of *The Hole in Our Gospel*, readers began asking me the question, "It's great that you found your calling at World Vision, but what should *I* do?"

I have often advised pastors that any church, no matter the size, can do four things to make a difference: PRAY, ACT, INFLUENCE, and GIVE. The same is true for people who have moved from being a Jesus decider to being a Jesus disciple. The following suggestions are organized under these categories to help you discern what God is calling you to do.

Because I believe that World Vision is one of God's great battalions on the front lines—pushing back poverty and helping to usher in God's kingdom—you will find a number of opportunities here to partner with us. But there is much to do in the kingdom, and there are many great partners. The important thing is to take action. Get moving, and let God guide your steps.

God's great adventure for your life awaits, but God can't steer a parked car. It is time to start knocking on doors and seeing what God is going to do. Here are ways to get started.

—Rich Stearns

Pray

Recommit daily.

In chapter 9, Rich says that he tried to begin every day during his career at Lenox with a simple prayer. He asked "that God would use me in this place to love, serve, and obey him, and that I might be his ambassador, that I might let my light shine in that place." Make a habit of offering to God a similar prayer daily.

Grow your spiritual life.

Building the kingdom of God should be grounded in our relationship with God. Before we try to do great things, we need to be growing in our faith. New Christians may feel they need to firm up their beliefs. The Alpha Course is a great way to get started (www.alpha.org). Very few Christians have actually read the Bible from cover to cover. YouVersion has Bible reading plans that can fit your schedule and your reading habits, even if you read on your phone (www.youversion.com/reading-plans). Begin a personal Bible study by picking a few favorite passages. Visit www.textweek.com and look up those passages. Use the study material there to fashion your own small-group study or family devotion.

Pray for the world.

Operation World is called the definitive prayer guide to every nation. Country by country, the book and website (www.operationworld.org) take Christians on a spiritual tour of the globe, offering the latest information on people groups and how to pray for their needs.

Pray for your community.

Many who feel a passion for their local communities pray for their neighborhoods by establishing a prayer walk. Either by yourself or with others, walk through your neighborhood, and—block by block and building by building—pray for the people, the businesses, and the organizations that make up your town or city. Ask God to lead you as you walk, pray, live, and work in your community. The North American Mission Board also provides prayer walking tips at www.namb.net/prayer-walking-tips.

PRAY FOR YOUR COWORKERS.

In the 1850s, a revival, called the Businessman's Revival, broke out in New York City. For years afterward business was stopped at the lunch hour so people could pray. Learn about the revival (go to CBN.com and search for "Layman's Prayer Revival"); then commit to praying for your coworkers and your company every day during your workday.

PRAY FOR CHILDREN AROUND THE WORLD.

World Vision offers many tools to help you pray with specificity. Sign up for the monthly Hope Prayer Team e-mail (www.worldvision.org /prayerteam) or find compelling stories and information at the *World Vision* magazine website (www.worldvisionmagazine.org). To stay connected on the go, download free iPhone apps: World Vision Now (for news on disasters and humanitarian issues) and World Vision Prayer (which provides specific country requests).

ACT

TAKE A SPIRITUAL GIFTS SURVEY.

LifeWay Christian Resources offers a spiritual gifts survey that takes just thirty minutes (search Google for "Lifeway spiritual gifts survey"). After completing the survey, prayerfully consider what the results tell you about yourself and your God-given gifts. Talk to your pastor or spiritual adviser about what these insights mean for you and how you might use your gifts in your local church.

DEVELOP YOUR WORLDVIEW.

What you believe about the world has implications for how you live in the world. Study a Christian worldview through the Chuck Colson Center for Christian Worldview (www.colsoncenter.org). Learn to explain and defend your faith through the Oxford Centre for Christian Apologetics (http://theocca.org/).

OFFER YOUR TIME AND TALENT.

World Vision can help you match your skills, experiences, and interests with volunteer opportunities that make a real impact on children and families and that demonstrate the gospel around the world. Encourage others to sponsor children, commit to pray for those affected by extreme poverty, join a woman's or advocacy group, volunteer at a World Vision event or program, offer pro bono professional services, or even knit a sweater for a child. However you choose to turn your values into action, you have something meaningful to contribute to those in need. As you do, you'll be joining hands with local World Vision volunteers on every continent, all working together to build a better world for children. For a variety of opportunities to make a difference, visit www.worldvision .org/getinvolved.

SPONSOR A CHILD THROUGH WORLD VISION.

Put yourself on the front lines of the kingdom of God and experience a new country, culture, and context through the eyes of a young boy or girl. Sponsorship helps provide children with access to critical essentials, such as clean water, nutritious food, health care, education, and more. Build a personal relationship with your sponsored child through letters, e-mails, and the wealth of information available about them and their communities at www.myworldvision.org. When you sponsor as a family, you can pray together for your sponsored child and help your own children see the world in a different way. Visit www.worldvision .org/sponsor.

VOLUNTEER WITH A LOCAL MISSION.

Ministries in nearly every city and town in the United States offer assistance to those in need of a helping hand. Homeless shelters, substance abuse recovery programs, and centers offering job training opportunities all demonstrate new ways to bring forth the kingdom of God. Often those who do the "helping" are most changed by the experience. Read *Same Kind of Different as Me* by Ron Hall and Denver Moore for a moving example of how showing up to ladle soup, fold clothes, and spend time getting to know those you serve can change your life.

GET SOMETHING STARTED IN YOUR CHURCH.

Whether you're a pastor or a church member, you can work through and with your church to increase its involvement with the poor. Begin a prayer group focused on local or global needs. Suggest that your congregation or small group take on a service project. Talk to your pastor about hosting a Hope Sunday, encouraging people to sponsor children through World Vision (find out more at www.hopesunday.wvpartner.us). Visit www.worldvision.org/church for resources to help you get started.

ADOPT A SCHOOL.

Churches across the country are discovering that they can have a considerable impact by focusing their outreach on a single school in their area. Consider the story of Jubilee REACH in chapter 13; then think about partnering with the National Church Adopt-a-School Initiative, started by pastor and author Tony Evans (www.churchadoptaschool.org).

JOIN TEAM WORLD VISION.

You might not be a runner, but through Team World Vision you can take on a physical challenge, such as a marathon or half marathon, and use it to raise awareness and funds for communities in need. Team World Vision provides all the resources you need to get to the finish line knowing you are helping bring lasting hope to others. Learn more or find an event near you at www.teamworldvision.org.

BUILD A KIT AND CHANGE A LIFE.

Participating in a World Vision kit build—purchasing essential supplies and rolling up your sleeves to assemble kits for those who lack necessities—is a great opportunity for churches, companies, Bible study gatherings, and other groups to make a tangible difference in the lives of those in need. Our four kit options offer the choice of having an international or local impact: Caregiver Kits for community health workers in rural Africa; Promise Packs for children affected by poverty around the globe; Hygiene Kits for those affected by homelessness, poverty, and natural disasters in the United States; and SchoolTools backpacks for at-risk US elementary students. For more information, call 1-800-478-5481 or visit www.worldvision.org/kits.

HELP RESETTLE A REFUGEE.

Tens of thousands of refugees receive admission into the United States every year. Typically, they come with very few of their own belongings, but they carry years of scars from the trauma of being forced to flee their homes. A number of Christian agencies help to settle refugees, including Church World Service (www.churchworldservice.org), World Relief (www.worldrelief.org), and Exodus World Service (www.e-w-s.org).

GO HUNGRY WITH HIGH SCHOOL STUDENTS.

Every year more than half a million US students raise awareness and funds to fight global hunger through World Vision's 30 Hour Famine, which challenges them to spend thirty hours without food while serving others and learning about poverty in the developing world. This unforgettable experience creates a new kind of hunger and motivation to change lives. Learn more at www.30hourfamine.org.

JOIN A CHRISTIAN BUSINESS PROFESSIONALS' GROUP.

Having a full-time job doesn't mean you can't make a difference for the kingdom of God. Join a group like the National Association of Christian Women Entrepreneurs (nacwe.org) or the New Canaan Society (www .newcanaansociety.org). Many corporate leaders are using their companies to do more than simply provide goods and services. Learn about the Business as Mission movement (www.businessasmissionnetwork .com) to see how you can turn your business into a mission enterprise.

INFLUENCE

START WHERE YOU ARE.

Do you have a passion you want to share with others? You don't need to be a celebrity or a CEO to have influence. Begin with family and friends. Talk to them about how you would like to see the world changed. Discuss with them your vision of the kingdom of God. Find ways to invite others to join you by hosting dinners or launching a discussion group.

SPEAK OUT ONLINE.

In today's digital world it's easier than ever to make your voice a force for change. Join World Vision's *Facebook* community (www.facebook.com/worldvision) and use your own Facebook page to start conversations about poverty alleviation. Follow the World Vision *blog* (http: // blog.worldvision.org) to learn about issues that affect the poor and connect with World Vision staff and others who share your interests; then spread the word using your own blog. *Tweet* messages directly to elected leaders, and retweet comments from other advocates. Join World Vision's online activism network, or sign up for regular news updates (www.worldvision.org/advocacy). Share *YouTube* video links with your social networks that feature your youth group, coworkers, or friends advocating on behalf of the world's poor.

JOIN AN ADVOCACY GROUP OR NETWORK.

You'll receive information and updates about the issues you're passionate about, meet like-minded people, and discover opportunities to get involved. Many advocacy networks exist, focusing on specific issues as well as geographic regions. Start by joining World Vision's Advocate Network (www.worldvision.org/advocacy), or connect with national advocacy organizations, such as Bread for the World (www.bread.org), the ONE Campaign (www.one.org), or Results (www.results.org).

Speak at or invite a speaker to your church or professional or social organizations.

World Vision can provide you with talking points and resources to share with your audience or connect you with a World Vision spokesperson. To invite a speaker or for resources to give your own talk, send a request to our Speakers Bureau at speakers@worldvision.org.

Give women a voice.

World Vision's Women of Vision (www.womenofvision.org) is a movement that seeks to educate and inspire women to action to alleviate the injustice and inequities that exist around the world for women and children. This volunteer program unites women across the country who are passionate about empowering women and girls to rewrite their stories and build a better world for children. As a Women of Vision partner, you'll be equipped to learn about the challenges faced by women and girls, advocate on their behalf, and help make a brighter future possible for the next generation.

Give

Start with your church.

The church is the outpost of the kingdom of God, the organizing principle for building the kingdom. Your local church should be first on your list to invest your gifts and your giving.

Work toward a tithe.

Most Christians give far less than the 10 percent that is the rule of thumb in the Bible. About 2.5 percent is typical. If you are giving 2 percent, try to move up to 4 percent. Giving is a crucial part of committing to the kingdom. If you haven't committed your money, you haven't committed. Discuss with your spouse how you might offer your resources for the kingdom. If you need help arranging your finances to make it possible for you to tithe, get help from Crown Financial Ministry (www.crown.org) or Financial Peace (www.daveramsey.com).

GIVE MEANINGFUL GIFTS.

At Christmas and for other special occasions, opt for a gift that changes lives in place of the latest gadget or unneeded item. Through World Vision Gift Catalog (www.worldvisiongifts.org), you can donate goats, soccer balls, fruit trees, part of a water well, and much more in honor of a loved one. This type of giving can be an educational tool, too; engage your children, students, or Sunday school class in selecting and funding gifts to help them better understand the needs of the poor.

OFFER A HAND UP.

In the world's poorest places multitudes of hardworking entrepreneurs simply lack the opportunity and support to turn their business ideas into a reality. Microloans and training provide the resources they need to create successful enterprises, which enable them to feed their children, send them to school, save for the future, and transform their communities by creating jobs. World Vision Micro (www.worldvisionmicro.org) allows you to invest in and celebrate the success of specific entrepreneurs. When their loan is repaid, your donation is recycled to help even more entrepreneurs.

GET YOUR COMPANY ENGAGED.

Hundreds of companies partner with World Vision through in-kind donations of essential products and supplies that support World Vision's humanitarian efforts. Others engage their employees (and build team morale) through World Vision kit builds or give a percentage of some product sales to World Vision. To learn how your company can connect, call 1-888-511-6443, or for personal giving through your organization, contact employeegiving@worldvision.org.

LEAVE A LEGACY.

Make a difference—even after your lifetime—by designating World Vision as a beneficiary of your will, life insurance policy, or retirement assets. World Vision's Gift Planning team (1-800-426-5753) offers helpful, professional, no-obligation assistance with estate planning to help you ensure a legacy of giving.

ABOUT WORLD VISION

Who we are

World Vision is a Christian humanitarian organization dedicated to working with children, families, and their communities worldwide to reach their full potential by tackling the causes of poverty and injustice.

Who we serve

World Vision provides hope and assistance to communities in almost one hundred countries, joining with local people to find lasting ways to improve the lives of children and families in need. World Vision serves all people, regardless of religion, race, ethnicity, or gender.

Why we serve

Motivated by our faith in Jesus Christ, we serve alongside the poor and oppressed as a demonstration of God's unconditional love for all people.

How we serve

Since 1950, World Vision has helped millions of children and families by providing emergency assistance to those affected by natural disasters and civil conflict, developing long-term solutions within communities to alleviate poverty, and advocating for justice on behalf of the poor.

What you can do

A great way to engage in kingdom work is to show God's love as a child sponsor. Through World Vision Child Sponsorship, you will be connected to one special child in need who will know your name, write to you, and feel your love and prayers. Your monthly sponsorship gift will provide things such as clean water, nutritious food, health care, educational opportunities, and spiritual nurture. Visit www.worldvision.org.

NOTES

Chapter 1: The Meaning of Life and Other Important Things
  1. Ross Douthat, *Bad Religion* (New York: Free Press, 2012), 2.
  2. "Truthiness," Merriam-Webster.com, accessed August 14, 2012, http://www
     .merriam-webster.com/info/06words.htm.
  3. The Word of the Year: "Truthiness," CBS News, February 11, 2009, © 2009 The
     Associated Press. All Rights Reserved. http://www.cbsnews.com/2100-207_162
     -2243870.html (accessed September 24, 2012).
  4. This exchange is found in John 18:37–38.
  5. "Coquette: On greatness and killing your ego," 1840, Jan 01, *The Daily Blog*, accessed
     August 22, 2012, http://blog.thedaily.com/post/15128141204/coquette-on-greatness
     -and-killing-your-ego. Used by permission.
  6. Donald Miller, *Blue Like Jazz* (Nashville, TN: Thomas Nelson, 2003), 180.
  7. "Truthiness," Merriam-Webster.com.
  8. Tony Burton, "Butterflies by the million: the Monarchs of Michoacán,"
     Mexonnect, accessed August 15, 2012, http://www.mexconnect.com/articles
     /1207-butterflies-by-the-million-the-monarchs-of-michoac%C3%A1n.
  9. Vaclav Havel, *Letters to Olga*, trans. Paul Wilson (London: Faber and Faber Limited,
     1990), 237.

Chapter 2: God's Big Story
  1. Stephen Hawking, *A Brief History of Time: From the Big Bang to Black Holes*
     (Toronto, ON: Bantam Books, 1988), 174.
  2. G. K. Chesterton, *Orthodoxy* (Walnut, CA: MSAC Philosophy Group, 2008), 48.

Chapter 3: Why Did Jesus Leave?
  1. Henry Van Dyke, "December Twenty-six," *The Friendly Year* (New York: Scribner,
     1918), 183.

2. The "rapture" refers to the belief held by premillennial theologians that Christ's followers will be literally taken up into heaven during the last days.

3. Charles Spurgeon, *Return O Shulamite! And Other Sermons Preached in 1884* (New York: Robert Carter & Brothers, 1885), 221.

4. George Stevens, *The Greatest Story Ever Told*, written by Fulton Oursler, Henry Denker, James Lee Barrett, and George Stevens, Metro Goldwyn Mayer, originally released April 9, 1965.

5. Quoted in *Book of Jokes & Anecdotes*, Joe Claro, ed., (New York: Random House, 1994), 207.

6. Frei Betto, "Ten Suggestions for the Leftist Millitant," Maltatar.com, accessed August 22, 2012, http://www.maltastar.com/dart/20120404-ten-suggestions-for-the-leftist-militant.

Chapter 4: Magic Kingdom, Tragic Kingdom, and the Kingdom of God

1. Anthony de Mello, *Awareness* (New York: Doubleday, 1992), 88.

2. Ross Douthat, *Bad Religion* (New York: Free Press, 2012), 4.

3. Casey Gane-McCalla, "Haitian Earthquake Death Toll Passes 200,000," February 4, 2010, NewsOne.com, accessed September 24, 2012, http://newsone.com/430192/haitian-earthquake-death-toll-passes-200000.

4. Frei Betto, "Ten Suggestions for the Leftist Militant," Maltatar.com, accessed August 22, 2012, http://www.maltastar.com/dart/20120404-ten-suggestions-for-the-leftist-militant.

5. C. S. Lewis, *The Screwtape Letters* (New York: Harper Collins, 2001), 155.

6. For a fuller analysis of the dimensions and causes of global poverty, see my first book, *The Hole in Our Gospel*.

7. "925 million in chronic hunger worldwide," Food and Agriculture Organization of the United Nations Media Centre, September 14, 2010, accessed September 24, 2012, http://www.fao.org/news/story/en/item/45210/icode.

8. "Children: reducing mortality," World Health Organization Media centre, fact sheet 178, September 2012, accessed September 24, 2012, http://www.who.int/mediacentre/factsheets/fs178/en.

9. "Health through safe drinking water and basic sanitation," World Health Organization, Water Sanitation and Health, accessed September 24, 2012, http://www.who.int/water_sanitation_health/mdg1/en/index.html.

10. Jina Moore, "Congo war leaves legacy of sexual violence against women," *Christian Science Monitor*, June 30, 2010, accessed September 24, 2012, http://www.csmonitor.com/World/Africa/2010/0630/Congo-war-leaves-legacy-of-sexual-violence-against-women; also see Danielle Shapiro, "Congo Rape Crisis: Study Reveals Shocking New Numbers," *Daily Beast*, May 11, 2011, accessed September 24, 2012, http://www.thedailybeast.com/articles/2011/05/11/congo-rape-crisis-study-reveals-shocking-new-numbers.html.

11. "Global Orphan Facts," Christian Alliance for Orphans, accessed August 17, 2012, http://www.christianalliancefororphans.org/resources/orphan-facts/orphan-facts-global-orphan-care.

12. Anup Shah, "Poverty Facts and Stats," Global Issues, accessed August 17, 2012, http://www.globalissues.org/article/26/poverty-facts-and-stats.

13. "How Rich You Are," Giving What You Can, accessed August 17, 2012, http://www
.givingwhatwecan.org/resources/how-rich-you-are.php.
14. Anthony Lake, UNICEF Executive Director, *Committed to Child Survival: A Promise
Renewed* (New York: UNICEF, 2012), from the Foreword, 4; http://www.unicef.org
/publications/files/APR_Progress_Report_2012_11Sept2012.pdf.

Chapter 5: The Mission of God
1. Ed Stetzer, "A Letter to the Church from Billy Graham," The LifeWay Research Blog,
accessed August 17, 2012, http://www.edstetzer.com/2012/06/a-letter-to-the-church
-from-bi.html.
2. Major Religions of the World Ranked by Number of Adherents, Adherents.com,
accessed September 24, 2012, http://www.adherents.com/Religions_By
_Adherents.html.
3. Dallas Willard, *The Divine Conspiracy* (New York: Harper One, 1998), 41.
4. Scot McKnight, *The King Jesus Gospel* (Grand Rapids, MI: Zondervan, 2011), 18.

Chapter 6: The Invitation of God
1. C. S. Lewis, *Mere Christianity* (New York: Harper Collins, 2000), 198–99.
2. John Stott, *The Radical Disciple* (Downers Grove, IL: IVP, 2010), 29.

Chapter 7: RSVP
1. Os Guinness, *The Call* (Nashville, TN: Thomas Nelson, 1998), 46.
2. Personal interview with the author.

Chapter 8: Let's Make a Deal
1. Stu Phillips, speaking at For Every Child conference, Chicago, April 20–21, 2012.
2. Ibid.
3. Ibid.

Chapter 9: We Were Made for More
1. Henry David Thoreau, *Walden; or Life in the Woods* (New York: Dover, 1995), 5.
2. Oliver Wendell Holmes, "The Voiceless," 1858.
3. "Did You Know?" North American Association of State and Provincial Lotteries,
accessed August 22, 2012, http://www.naspl.org/index.cfm?fuseaction=content&me
nuid=14&pageid=1020.
4. "Warhol photo exhibition, Stockholm, 1968," Justin Kaplan, ed., *Bartlett's Familiar
Quotations*, 16th ed. (New York: Little, Brown, 1992), 758:17.
5. Rob Peters, "Man using GPS crashes into train," NowPublic.com, accessed August
22, 2012, http://www.nowpublic.com/life/man-using-gps-crashes-train.

Chapter 11: Called for a Purpose
1. Edward Everett Hale, "Lend a Hand," in *742 Heartwarming Poems*, ed. John R. Rice (Murfreesboro, TN: Sword of the Lord Publishers, 1964), 314.
2. Os Guinness, *The Call* (Nashville, TN: Thomas Nelson, 1998), 46.

Chapter 12: Spiritual Dominoes
1. C. S. Lewis, *The Weight of Glory* (New York: Harper Collins, 1949), 46.
2. Rahab may have simply been an ancestor, not specifically his mother, but the point is unchanged. See Matthew 1:5.
3. Stephen Morris, "Grams to Pounds: A Domino Chain Reaction," YouTube video, accessed December 24, 2012, http://www.howtogeek.com/116890/grams-to-pounds-a-domino-chain-reaction-video.
4. Dan Pierce, "Robert Wilder and the Student Volunteer Movement," accessed December 31, 2012, http://www.ship-ubf.org/leaders/wilder.html.
5. Oswald Chambers, "June 15," *My Utmost for His Highest* (Uhrichesville, OH: Barbour, 2000).
6. Cathleen Falsani, "Mother Africa," in "Bono's American Prayer," *ChristianityToday.com*, posted March 1, 2003, http://www.christianitytoday.com/ct/2003/march/2.38.html?order=&start=7.
7. Mark Shuman, "Back to Lincoln's Springfield," *The Chicago Tribune*, September 2, 2011, http://articles.chicagotribune.com/2011-09-02/travel/ct-trav-0904-springfield-lincoln-20110902_1_abraham-lincoln-presidential-library-lincoln-museum-mary-todd-lincoln.

Chapter 13: Outposts of the Kingdom
1. Dallas Willard, *The Great Omission* (New York: Harper Collins, 2006), 61.
2. "Revolution," Dictionary.com, accessed August 28, 2012, http://dictionary.reference.com/browse/revolution.
3. John Stott, "Becoming Like Christ," Decision.org, originally published July 28, 2010, http://www.billygraham.org/articlepage.asp?articleid=6183, accessed August 27, 2012.
4. Ken Kierstead, "A Cup That Overflows," sermon at University Presbyterian Church, Seattle, Washington, February 13, 2011, http://sermonplayer.com//includes/popup_player.php?c=15482&by=typeP-2875-Sermon_Player&d=http://sermonplayer.com/&rgbval=21369&alpha=100.
5. I do not feel qualified to speak about the churches of the global South.
6. "Exhortation," Dictionary.com, accessed September 24, 2012, http://dictionary.reference.com/browse/exhortation?s=t.
7. Steven Gertz, "Tsunami Catastrophe: 'Let My Heart Be Broken . . . ',"
ChristianHistory.net, *Christianity Today*, accessed August 27, 2012, http://www.christianitytoday.com/ch/news/2005/jan27.html.
8. Sabrina Tavernise, "Soaring Poverty Casts Spotlight on 'Lost Decade,'" *New York Times*, NYTimes.com, September 13, 2011, http://www.nytimes.com/2011/09/14/us/14census.html?pagewanted=all.

9. Anthony Lake, UNICEF Executive Director, *Committed to Child Survival: A Promise Renewed* (New York: UNICEF, 2012), from the Foreword, 4; http://www.unicef.org /publications/files/APR_Progress_Report_2012_11Sept2012.pdf.

10. "Great Commission Statistics," Joshua Project, http://www.joshuaproject.net /greatcommission-statisitcs.php.

11. This quote is commonly attributed to Paul Harvey, but the source is unknown.

12. Bellevue School District, "Diversity," accessed September 24, 2012, http://www .bsd405.org/about-us.aspx.

Chapter 14: The Gates of Hell

1. C. S. Lewis, *The Lion, the Witch and the Wardrobe* (New York: Harper, 1950), 23.

2. C. S. Lewis, *The Screwtape Letters* (New York: Harper, 1942), ix.

3. Casey Gane-McCalla, "Haitian Earthquake Death Toll Passes 200,000," February 4, 2010, NewsOne.com, accessed September 24, 2012, http://newsone .com/430192/haitian-earthquake-death-toll-passes-200000; and Pascal Fletcher, "Haiti quake homeless at risk, shelter crisis drags," Reuters.com, September 29, 2010, http://in.reuters.com/article/2010/09/29/idINIndia-51826720100929.

4. Josephus, *The Complete Works*, ed. William Whiston (Nashville, TN: Thomas Nelson, 1998) 1.21.2.

5. Flight #93 was headed to the Capitol when its courageous passengers stormed the cockpit to take back control. This action saved the Capitol but resulted in the death of all aboard as the plane crashed in a field in Pennsylvania.

6. Gen. Dwight D. Eisenhower, "General Eisenhower's Message Sent Just Prior to the Invasion," Army.mil, accessed August 27, 2012, http://www.army.mil/d-day /message.html.

Chapter 15: God's Great Adventure for Your Life

1. C. S. Lewis, *The Weight of Glory* (New York: Harper Collins, 1949), 46.

2. Randy Pausch, "Carnegie Mellon Commencement Speech," May 2008.

3. Attributed to George Eliot.

Afterword

1. Max Lucado, *The Applause of Heaven* (Nashville, TN: Thomas Nelson, 1990), 154.

2. "Som Sabadell Flashmob," YouTube, accessed September 20, 2012, http://www .youtube.com/watch?v=GBaHPND2QJg.

3. The poem "Joyful, Joyful, We Adore Thee" was written in 1907 by Henry Van Dyke and set to the music of the final movement of Beethoven's Symphony No. 9. Full lyrics available at http://library.timelessthruths.org/music/Joyful_Joyful_We_Adore_Thee.

Study Guide

1. Brian Kolodiejchuk, *Mother Teresa: Come Be My Light* (New York: Image, 2009), 34; http://www.amazon.com/Mother-Teresa-Come-Be-Light/dp/0307589234.

SCRIPTURE INDEX

About the Author

RICH STEARNS is president of World Vision US and author of *The Hole in Our Gospel*, named 2010 Christian Book of the Year by the Evangelical Christian Publishers Association. World Vision is one of the largest humanitarian organizations in the world, working in nearly one hundred countries with more than forty-five thousand staff, committed to serving the world's poorest people in the name of Christ.

Prior to joining World Vision, Rich had a corporate career that spanned a variety of industries, including toys and games, health and beauty aids, video games and software, collectibles and gifts, and fine china and crystal. He served as CEO for both Parker Brothers Games and Lenox. He holds a bachelor's degree in neurobiology from Cornell University and an MBA from the Wharton School at the University of Pennsylvania. Following a sense of God's call on his life, he resigned his position at Lenox in 1998 to become World Vision's US president, where he has had the opportunity to put his faith into action by working every day to improve the lives of the poor.

Driven by his passion to raise awareness and support for poverty and justice issues, Rich has appeared on CNN, Fox, ABC, NBC, and PBS and written pieces for the *Wall Street Journal*, the *Washington Post*, the Huffington Post, and other media outlets. He is a frequent speaker at churches, conferences, and denominational gatherings and has spoken at Harvard University, the Lausanne Congress, and at a variety of international venues.

Rich and his wife, Reneé, live in Bellevue, Washington, and have supported World Vision since 1984. They have five children of their own plus millions more around the world. You can follow Rich on Facebook (facebook.com/RichardStearns.WVUS) and Twitter (@richstearns) or at www.richstearns.org.

OTHER *UNFINISHED*
PRODUCTS AVAILABLE

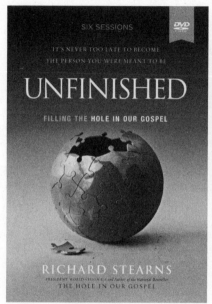

DVD Curriculum

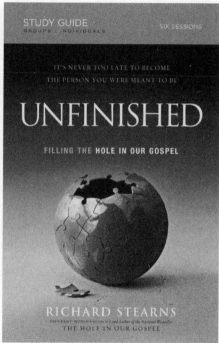

Study Guide

THOMAS NELSON
Since 1798

thomasnelson.com

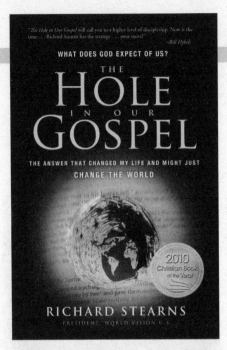

Other Great
Resources from
World Vision
U.S. President
Rich Stearns
and His Wife,
Reneé Stearns

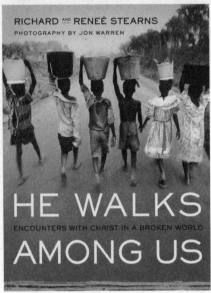

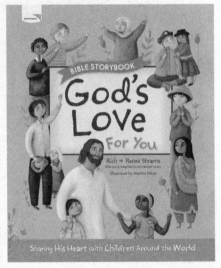